Morgan

The Buccaneer Raid on Maracaibo

———————

by
Rolf Lyon

Order this book online at www.trafford.com
or email orders@trafford.com

Most Trafford titles are also available at major online book retailers.

Note for Librarians: A cataloguing record for this book is available from Library
and Archives Canada at www.collectionscanada.ca/amicus/index-e.html

Printed in Victoria, BC, Canada.

ISBN: 978-1-4269-1795-0

*Our mission is to efficiently provide the world's finest, most comprehensive book publishing
service, enabling every author to experience success. To find out how to publish your book, your
way, and have it available worldwide, visit us online at www.trafford.com*

Trafford rev. 12/18/09

North America & international
toll-free: 1 888 232 4444 (USA & Canada)
phone: 250 383 6864 ♦ fax: 812 355 4082

Acknowledgement

This book would not have been possible with out the creative abilities of the following people:

Stephanie Adames, John Eichinger, Jamie Gyde, Scott Fisher, Valerie Houck, Dustin Housenecht, Eric Lyon, Doug Rush, Jeffrey Patterson

Introduction

The year 1669 sounds like ancient history, but in the Caribbean basin back then, life was very similar to our own present-day world. Jamaica in particular had some of the most fertile soil on the planet, which insured a steady supply of food, coffee, sugar and rum. All of these goods were in high demand in Europe and that resulted in a very lucrative trade arrangement. Ships arrived from European ports on a regular basis loaded with wine, linen, guns, cheeses and virtually anything else that was not perishable.

Port Royal was the Buccaneer capital and it was considered by many to be the wickedest city on the planet, because there were more brothels than churches. The primary Buccaneer rule was, *"No victim, no crime."* It never would have occurred to them lock a person up for smoking hemp or opium. They would have been equally baffled by laws against prostitution. Where is the victim ?

Port Royal's water supply had to barged in from further up the East coast. To some extent, that probably limited population growth, but more importantly, it also meant that there were no mosquitoes. At the time, malaria was one of the biggest killers in the West Indies, but Port Royal was spared that scourge. That one fact is why we are communicating today in English and not Spanish. Morgan and his Buccaneer allies brought Spain to her knees in the Caribbean, but he is scarcely mentioned in history. This book could change that; that is why it was written.

CHAPTER 1

Isla de Vaca, 2 January, 1669
Off the southern coast of Haiti

Morgan awoke at six bells, or seven a.m., just as the sun was rising. Every half-hour the bosun added another bell to the cycle, so that seven thirty would be seven bells and eight o' clock would be eight bells. The smell of green coffee being roasted aroused him in a sensual way; no bargaining, no ultimatums, just a seductive smell and immediate satisfaction with the first sip. Twelve hours of uninterrupted sleep had renewed his energy and enthusiasm for the task at hand. He looked down at his toe and cautiously flexed it; no pain, no redness. God, it was good to be alive. Morgan sat on the edge of the bed and looked out the large transom windows in his cabin. Slowly he began to plan his day, but the lingering effects of the opium made it hard for him to focus on details.

"Caleb!", shouted Morgan, craving a strong cup of coffee. Within seconds the cabin door opened and Caleb stepped silently over the threshold.

"Sir?"

"Toffee," said Morgan smacking his lips desperately trying to wet the stale cotton in his mouth. "Coffee…bring a pot."

"Right away, Sir. Doctor Browne was very insistin' that you drink water, Sir. There's a pitcher by your bed, Sir."

"Fine, Caleb, just get me some coffee," said Morgan, rolling his eyes. Morgan realized at once that Browne was right. Gbessay, the obeah woman in Port Royal, had been over the signs of dehydration a number of times with Morgan, but this time he did not have the luxury of a penthouse suite in Port Royal in which to recover from another attack of gout. He was to lead a party of 900 men in an attack against the most powerful country in the world in the next few days. His head started bobbing up and down as he thought of this. "So here I am, sitting in a cabin…the Captain's cabin, in a British Man o' war, the Commander of a fleet, for God's sake! I haven't peed since God knows when and my mouth…Christ! Time to wake up, me boy," he whispered.

Morgan moved to the nightstand and poured a generous glass of water and downed it. Then another, and another. The House of Morgan—excess, he thought, as he waited impatiently for Caleb to appear with life-sustaining coffee.

There was something gnawing at his gut that was just below the surface of awareness. Morgan often imagined that some mornings upon awakening he had not returned to his body in quite the right way; there was hollowness to all that he experienced the remainder of the day. In some indefinable way, this morning was similar because of a slight feeling of unreality, but strangely different. There was terror deep inside him. He could feel it, but he could not determine the source of the terror. Suddenly it came to him—it was that damned dream again, no doubt amplified by the opium he consumed the night before. Hung by the neck twice by the Spaniards and both times the rope had snapped, leaving him very much alive. Gbessay had told him that the dream meant that he would cheat death twice on this cruise, but even if she was right, it did very little to quiet the screaming voices inside his head. He drew in a deep breath and exhaled slowly as he imagined that he was safe and protected. The terror left him just as Caleb opened the cabin

"Coffee's 'ere, Sir." Caleb placed the silver tray on the Captain's table and quietly left the room.

Morgan sat at his table and uttered a silent prayer of thanks for the freedom of motion that comes naturally to those with joints that are without pain. He poured a generous cup of thick Jamaican coffee that had been roasted only minutes before. Each sip was a splash of heaven. He had grown accustomed to this bean which had been grown on the north shore of Jamaica about 3,000 feet above the town of Trelawny. He had first tasted the bean two years before at a wealthy merchant's house. Morgan had been so impressed that he had made inquiries about where the beans had come from and the following day he contacted the owner of the plantation and arranged to buy it. It was only four acres, but it produced enough coffee to supply Morgan's meager needs and turn a slight profit on the remainder.

Ever so gently, the *Oxford* began to move. Morgan could hear the anchor chain being hauled through the hawsehole on the bow of the ship. His pulse quickened. Somewhere in the deep recesses of his mind, Morgan produced an image of the *Oxford* run aground on a reef, slowly breaking up. His heart pounded heavily in his chest. God! How am I going to explain this! he thought.

Be like water, he heard in the back of his brain. He took a deep breath and slowly let the air out. His heart slowed down and the panic began to dissipate. Look at your assets, he thought. Collier was in command of this ship and he knew her limitations. Captain Bigford would certainly have sounded the passage around the island; otherwise the *Oxford* never would have hoisted anchor. Morgan had a powerful urge to be on deck, but he checked the impulse. Trust. It was all about trust. Everybody on deck knew that Morgan had awakened, because they had seen Caleb deliver the coffee to his cabin. If Morgan appeared on deck for such a trivial maneuver, Commander

Collier would be put in an embarrassing position. Better to stay below and have breakfast.

Morgan cursed himself. He had been in this passage perhaps 15 times before, at least five times in command of a boat, and had never bothered to sound the bottom. Ah, the life of a freebooter in command of a shallow-draft boat, he thought.

On deck the mood was one of cautious elation. The crew was well rested and every man was excited about the festivities planned for this evening. At the same time, however, there was an unspoken fear of running aground. The original English crewmembers aboard had spent precious little time in the tropics and there was a general mistrust of warm shallow waters that nurtured reefs. The new Buccaneer crewmembers were quite comfortable with Caribbean waters, but they were troubled by the *Oxford*'s deep draft and saw it as a great liability.

"Fly the fore course, Lieutenant Thatcher," said Collier to his Midshipman. Within seconds the lowest square sail on the foremast was unfurled and it filled with the steady on-shore breeze. Collier felt the rudder dig in and smiled as he took control of the *Oxford*. Fifty yards ahead was the "*Serpent*," a twenty-two foot sloop manned by Captains Bigford and Balfor. Although the *Serpent* was sailing with only a jib sail, she was doing a steady four knots, while the *Oxford* was barely doing one. Collier was happy with the *Oxford*'s progress. If she went aground at this speed, it would be a simple matter to float her off on the next tide, or lighten the payload and do it immediately. In either case, the *Oxford* would not break up.

The trade winds were blowing a steady eight knots and the *Serpent* hoisted her mainsail as she sped ahead of the *Oxford*, showing Collier the deepest passage to the island. Once there, the *Serpent* did an about face and sailed rapidly toward the *Oxford*. Collier saw the *Serpent* turn a mile away and drew out the brass tubes on his telescope a little too eagerly. The scope snapped into two pieces as the stop on one of the tubes gave way. "Bugger me!" he shouted. Almost immediately, three other officers moved toward him with telescopes extended in their hands. Collier smiled at Kessenger, who was the ranking Lieutenant, and exchanged his broken telescope for Kessenger's. "Thank you, Lieutenant Kessenger. Would you be kind enough to have that attended to," said Collier motioning to the brass tubes in Kessenger's hands.

"Right away, Commander," said Kessenger, who disappeared below decks.

Collier extended the tubes on Kessenger's telescope slowly and peered at the *Serpent* in the distance. In the inferior English optics Collier could see Balfor taking a long draw on a demijohn of rum and then passing it to Bigford. Scanning the coast to the west, Collier could see that three sloops from the fleet had already dropped anchor off the eastern tip of the island, well away from the French ship. He trained the scope on the *Serpent* again and watched as the two Captains passed a demijohn back and forth several more times.

A demijohn was a glass bottle that was covered with woven wicker. The Buccaneers prized demijohns both as canteens and storage containers for spirits. Morgan had been importing demijohns from France for years, but had recently begun to trade with Portugal, because the glass was thicker and had fewer bubbles. This secondary business was essential for Morgan because of his wine interests. When a shipment of wine arrived from France, the hundred–liter oak barrels were taken to a warehouse, where they were kept cool until they were called for. It was rare for someone to buy an entire barrel, because once opened, the wine would oxidize in just a few days. Most people would send their servants to the warehouse with empty demijohns, which were then rinsed and filled with fresh wine. Even with the wicker covering, there was inevitable breakage and Morgan was quite happy to sell replacements.

The *Serpent* was bearing down close-hauled on the *Oxford* with Balfor, the handsome mulatto ladies-man, tending the tiller. Bigford was sitting on the windward rail, his immense weight barely keeping the boat from capsizing. Twenty yards and closing on a collision course, Collier collapsed the telescope and gritted his teeth, "This is going to be a squeaker," he muttered. Everyone on deck was silent as the boat continued its insane course. At the very last moment, Balfor eased off the tiller while Bigford dropped his pants and bent over, much to the delight of the crewmen who applauded enthusiastically.

"Reminds me of mi' first wife, but she 'ad more 'air. Portoge' she was!" shouted one of the mates. The deck erupted in laughter as the *Serpent* narrowly missed the aft end of the *Oxford*. Morgan heard the commotion and came on deck. Collier explained to him what had just happened. Morgan let out a chuckle. The English Lieutenants, who stood close by in their sweat-soaked blue uniforms, were astonished by Morgan's levity. They had been anticipating orders for a court martial, or a flogging, or a demotion at the very least. Collier and Morgan were well aware of what must have been going through the minds of their officers. It was time for some fun. Morgan gave a secret wink to Collier, who nodded imperceptibly.

"Commander Collier," said Morgan as he turned to walk away. "If those two fools make another pass at this ship, have them shot dead."

"Very well, Captain," said Collier with a straight face. Collier had been the recipient of the same kind of torture for the last several months and it was gratifying to be able to dish some of it out. He finally understood that it was not malicious, but rather a way of shaking up reality as you perceive it to be, in order to give you a broader understanding of the entire picture. It was a way of giving you more freedom. Being "English" was nothing more than a set of arbitrary limitations. Collier was pleased with himself that he had forsaken the Naval uniform in favor of the much more practical Buccaneer dress. Just then, Kessenger came up on deck and told Collier that his telescope would be ready in less than an hour. Collier motioned Kessenger closer.

"We are going to have a bit of fun with the 'blue-sweats,'" whispered Collier. In a soft monotone, Collier gave Kessenger his instructions. Kessenger walked slowly away and looked back at Collier pleadingly.

"Do your duty, Lieutenant Kessenger," shouted Collier harshly, successfully suppressing his laughter.

Kessenger walked slowly away with his head bowed and found the over-weight Sergeant of the Marines next to the fo'castle, sweat dripping from his saturated red coat. Kessenger motioned the Sergeant over to the starboard rail, then spoke softly in the man's ear and walked away.

Moments later two Marines appeared on deck with their long guns and walked briskly to the starboard rail and took note of the rapidly advancing *Serpent*, perhaps 100 yards away and closing rapidly. Both of the Marines cocked their long guns and rested them on the starboard rail of the *Oxford*, awaiting the arrival of the *Serpent*. The three English lieutenants became quite agitated by this spectacle and one of them approached Commander Collier, who lounged beside the helm feigning indifference to what transpired on deck.

"Commander, might I have a word with you about the *Serpent*," said Lieutenant Owen, the ranking officer of the watch.

"Certainly, Lieutenant, but keep it brief," said Collier who was studying the ship's log.

"Surely you cannot, with a clear conscience, carry out the Captain's order, Sir," said Owen with a look of astonishment on his seventeen-year-old face.

"What would you suggest I do Lieutenant? Have them flogged? Flogging is such a nuisance! First you have to assemble the men on deck, which means an entire watch has to be roused from sleep, then you have to administer the punishment, then a team has to clean up the blood, and esperit de corps is shot to hell for days afterwards. Hanging is sometimes even worse, because you can never be sure that the head is not going to pop off completely, which can get very messy indeed!"

"But, Sir..." Owen looked over at the starboard side of the ship and could see the mast of the *Serpent* approaching. He ran to the rail and looked over the side. Fifty yards in the distance he could see the *Serpent* barreling toward the *Oxford*.

Not to be outdone by Bigford, Balfor was standing on the mainsail boom leaning back against the inflated sail. Balfor was naked and equally inflated, yelling, "Birdie, I need you Birdie." To the uninitiated, Balfor looked quite insane. Owen ran back to Collier.

"Sir, that man is naked!" exclaimed Owen.

"What man?" Collier asked absently, studying a chart.

"The Negro, Sir."

"You mean Balfor?"

The two men approached the starboard rail, which was covered with crewmembers, who were shouting oaths at the on-coming vessel. Every time that Balfor said "Birdie", the crewmembers would tuck their hands in their armpits and flap their elbows making chicken noises.

The three Lieutenants were utterly confused by what they saw and stayed as close to Collier as they could. Standing in the direct sun, their coats were now drenched with sweat. They glanced nervously at each other; each secretly hoping that one of the others could sort out what was happening. Even Collier seemed to be enjoying the drama before them, although he never flapped his arms.

"Fire on my orders!" shouted Collier. Word had gone round the ship—to everyone except the low ranking officers--that the Marines were firing unloaded muskets, so the crewman began shouting oaths. "Kill the bastard papists!"

Owen tried once more to reason with Collier and said, "Please, Sir, this man is insane!" Owen made the mistake of pulling on Commander Collier's arm in the height of his passion to save poor Balfor. Collier did not say a word, he simply looked down at the shorter officer and raised his eyebrow, flared his nostrils and took a deep breath, leaving no doubt in the young Lieutenant's mind that he had made a serious mistake touching a superior officer. A repeat offense could prove lethal. Collier turned away from Owen and studied the *Serpent*, which was now thirty yards away and had fallen off the wind so that she was now running parallel with the *Oxford*, but in the opposite direction. Balfor was still standing on the boom with his back against the mainsail, calling for "Birdie", his earlier tumescence significantly reduced, no doubt due to the alcohol.

More than anything else in the world, Wallace wanted to go back below decks and avoid what was about to happen. Wallace was a good head shorter than the two men who dragged him above deck to the rail. It was pointless for him to resist. The crew cheered the arrival of Wallace and he was mightily embarrassed. Balfor saw him at the rail and screamed, "Birdie! Thank God, you have come to save me!" The crew cheered and flapped their arms. The *Serpent* was now dead even with the *Oxford*, about twenty yards off her beam.

"Aim your weapons and fire!" shouted Collier. The young lieutenants beside him gasped as the Marines pulled their triggers simultaneously. There was the initial click of the flints striking home and then a brief pause before the deafening roar of their long guns. The crew cheered.

Bigford, who was at the *Serpent's* helm and Balfor, who was standing on the boom, were not in on the joke and they reacted poorly. Bigford pulled the tiller toward him and the *Serpent* lunged toward the *Oxford*. Balfor dropped to his knees on the boom and attempted to jump into the water, but before he had time to react, the *Serpent's* bowsprit jammed into the side of the *Oxford* and sheared off. The force of the impact swung the *Serpent* abruptly to the right so that it was now parallel to the *Oxford*, headed in the same direction. Balfor and Bigford were both thrown over the starboard rail into the water, unharmed. If

Balfor had reacted more quickly and jumped before the impact, he would have been crushed between the two boats.

"Man overboard!" shouted Owen.

"Belay that order," Collier said calmly.

"But Sir, those men have been shot!" protested Owen, with the other two lieutenants nodding in agreement.

"Those muskets were unloaded, Lieutenant Owen. We were just having a bit of fun." Owen looked at his compatriots hoping for a glimmer of understanding, but they were equally confused.

"So it was all a joke, Commander?"

"Yes it was, Lieutenant Owen."

"But I don't understand, Sir, who was the joke on?"

"You, Lieutenant Owen." Owen looked at his friends again, but they shrugged their shoulders. The crewmen within earshot of the conversation had the good sense to walk away and not laugh openly. Collier looked over the rail again and saw that Balfor and Bigford were safely back on deck of their damaged boat, no doubt inspecting themselves for bullet wounds. It would be a simple matter for them to jury-rig a fore stay for the mast and then set sail for the island, only a mile in the distance.

"Let's take a walk, lads." Collier led his understudies back to the helm and relieved the helmsman. Even at one or two knots, there was an undeniable excitement being at the helm of a ship. Collier was enjoying himself.

"The first order of business is to take off those damned coats. Look at you! You are drenched!" Owen was about to register a protest, but his two companions were eagerly pulling off their sweat-soaked coats and Owen did likewise. He was amazed how sensuous the trade wind felt when it hit his thin cotton shirt.

Slowly, the *Oxford* crept northward toward the anchorage on the north coast of Isla de Vaca. Collier had a broad smile on his face as though he knew some secret the others did not share. Every thirty seconds, or so, he would make an almost imperceptible correction on the large wheel before him, but for the majority of the time, his hands were by his side as he surveyed the expanse before him.

Cow Island, or Isla de Vaca, was a Mariner's dream. There was lush vegetation and high mountains that promised an abundant supply of fresh water. No wonder that the majority of raids launched upon the Spanish Caribbean ports originated here.

The three young Lieutenants were uncomfortable with the long silence that followed. Collier stood at the helm with a huge smile painted across his face, softly humming a tune. Owen finally summoned up the courage to speak.

"Will that man be punished, Sir?"

"What man?" said Collier distractedly.

"Captain Balfor, Sir."

"What on earth for?"

"Conduct unbecoming, dereliction of duty, destruction of fleet property, Sir."

Collier looked over at the three young Lieutenants and realized that each one of them had a look of righteous indignation on his face. His initial impulse was to slap them and send them below. The look of contempt on Collier's face soon gave way to a smile again as it dawned on him that barely nine months ago he too had been in the service of His Majesty as a Lieutenant, sent to spy on the Buccaneers. His transformation was now complete, but only because his teachers had been patient with him.

"Lads, blow a kiss good bye to the world you came from. It does not exist here. Every man on this ship is here because he chooses to be, not because he was hit over the head in a London pub and dragged away by a press gang." Owen was still incensed, like a bull with his head lowered, hoofing the ground prior to a charge.

"But, Sir! The man was naked with…a hard-on, Sir." Owen's two compatriots, who were a year younger and a bit shorter, stood with looks of utter horror on their faces, preparing to run if Collier responded aggressively.

"I know, I know. He was kind of cute," said Collier fluttering his eyelids. There was a nervous moment and then the four of them began laughing and the spell was broken. What a blissful relief it was to have the tension lifted. In some strange way, the bonds of friendship had been forged between these four men, as they had been countless times before on other ships far away from home. The fifteen-year-old Thatcher, who had innumerable freckles, owing to his Irish ancestry and too many hours of sun, was suddenly free to ask questions.

"Sir, I do not understand the joke. Can you explain it?"

"The Captain was playing with the three of you, that's all. Word circulated through the ship that it was all in fun and you were the only ones who were not in on the joke. You handled yourselves well and the men respect you for trying to save Bigford and Balfor." The three young Lieutenants beamed with pride. "On the down side of things," continued Collier, "there is a hidden message here, which is that the three of you have insulated yourselves from the rest of the crew. Even the other midshipmen did not tip you off that it was all a joke. Of all people, they should be your allies."

"But, Sir, what about discipline?" said Owen. "The crew is unruly…even the captains are behaving like mad dogs!"

Collier's rebuke was swift. "Lieutenant Owen, you may want to temper any future comments about your superior officers with a modicum of restraint, although I happen to agree with you. If this had been a Ship of the Line under English command, we would presently be arranging a Court's martial. But the fact of the matter is that we are part of the Buccaneer Fleet and English rules simply do not apply here. Discipline is required only when a man is ordered to do something he does not want to do. Every man on this ship has volunteered for this cruise. We do not hold guns to their heads. We simply share the profits with them and with a bit of luck, most will never need to work again.

"Lads, we are at war with Spain. In the days to come you will see bloodshed and torture. But for now, just enjoy yourselves and give everybody else the same freedom. The primary Buccaneer law is this: *"no victim, no crime."* If you can just keep that in mind when you are dealing with the men, it will make everybody's life much less complicated."

The three young officers kept silent as they pondered their Commander's words. Using the "no victim, no crime" axiom as a yardstick to measure the days events, it did indeed seem that what Balfor and Bigford had done was in no way a criminal act. Just as it had for Collier a few months before, the English reality bubble had burst for the three lieutenants.

The baby-faced Comstock finally worked up the nerve to speak. "Why was Captain Balfor calling for 'Birdie', commander?"

"He was calling for Wallace, the man they dragged up on deck. Wallace is the ship's whore."

"Ship's whore, Sir?" Comstock said, his face turning a crimson red. "I don't understand, Sir."

"Mr. Wallace is a knob-licker, twenty to thirty men every night, except Sundays, of course," said Collier matter-of-factly. Owen and Thatcher kept silent as Comstock kept asking questions with a look of utter disbelief on his face.

"But, Sir, how do the men make him do such…unspeakable things?"

"My understanding is that Birdie requires very little in the way of prompting," said Collier, who was beginning to enjoy himself at the expense of poor Lieutenant Comstock. "To Birdie, the *Oxford* is like a floating brothel in which he can exercise unlimited lust. The man has prolific appetites and he has a cadre of dedicated followers." Comstock was still in a state of disbelief.

"Sir, you mean that he actually likes what he does? I mean that he doesn't accept money?"

"I would be happy to make some inquiries for you, Lieutenant." Once again Comstock's face was flushed red. Owen and Thatcher were giggling, unable to contain their laughter.

"That is not what I meant, Sir," said Comstock as if he had been wounded. A few moments later the laughter subsided, but many questions remained. Owen was the first to re-start the inquiry.

"Sir, why has there been no action taken against this Birdie fellow? And why do they call him Birdie?" asked Owen.

"What is Birdie's crime, Lieutenant Owen?"

"Buggery, Sir. There was a prohibition against it in the articles we signed in Port Royal."

"Lieutenant Owen, I am not a legal scholar, but I think that most people would agree that buggery involves an altogether different orifice. But let's get back to issue of what a crime is. Remember no victim, no crime. Who is the victim in this case, gentlemen?" There was a brief pause as each of the young officers tried in vain to come up with a victim. "Just as I thought. All three of you are steeped in the most incredible cultural hypocrisy the world has ever known, except for all the others, of course." The three young men looked at each other and shrugged.

Collier studied the rapidly approaching coastline. The *Oxford* was almost to the eastern tip of Isla de Vaca and on the opposite north side of the island he could see three masts above the low hills. That would mean a ninety-degree turn to the left just passed the tip of the island and a short run of fifty yards doing a beam-reach, still with the one sail. Another ninety-degree left turn would put the *Oxford* next to the French ship at which point the anchor could be dropped. Any remaining breeze would back-wind the sail and set the anchor.

"This just might be the most beautiful anchorage in the world," Collier said under his breath.

Sir?" asked Owen.

"Nothing Lieutenant. Just happy to be alive."

"Sir, could I ask one more question?" asked Owen.

"This will have to be the last one, but ask away."

"Sir, why do the men call him Birdie?"

"You haven't figured that one out yet, huh? Very well, start naming birds," said Collier.

"I am sorry, Sir, I don't know what you mean," said Owen.

"Just name some birds. I will start with 'eagle.'"

"Oh, I see, Sir. Osprey."

"Keep going! Lads, join in!"

"Kestrel."

"Blue bird."

"Robin."

"Swallow."

"Stop right there, Lieutenant Thatcher. I believe you have solved the riddle."

CHAPTER 2

Immediately after the *Oxford* dropped her hook, a launch was placed in the water that contained four sailors, two gunny sacks full of charcoal, one cask of rum, two empty water casks and two very unhappy pigs. It was going to be a sand pit roast and by a little past noon every person on the lee side of the island would be involuntarily salivating. Having caught bait fish earlier this morning, several of the sloops were departing for the south coast of Haiti, just a few miles from their present position. Some would fish along the weed lines for dolphin, while others would troll a couple of miles off the coast for mackerel and tuna.

Morgan left his cabin with a bottle of good Madeira and stood next to Collier amidships, resting on the port rail. They studied the lines on the French merchant ship that was anchored about seventy yards away. She was narrower in her beam than most Merchantmen, which meant that she had been built for speed at the expense of payload. She was deeper in the water than one would have anticipated, if indeed, she was outward bound.

"Fast boat, Harry. We could use her," said Collier.

"My guess is that she is homeward bound, judging by how deep she is sitting in the water. That means that she would be resistant to the idea of joining us. The question is why is she here? When she commandeered the *Westin* she was just as close to Jamaica as she was to here. Something is terribly wrong here. We are going to need some sober gunners and grapplers tonight."

"I will arrange it, Captain," said Collier.

"Could you also arrange to have this bottle of Madeira delivered to the Captain of that ship?"

"I will do it myself, Captain. I want to get a sniff of her close up."

Just then a body whizzed past by them within inches and splashed in the water below. Sailors were jumping off the yardarms into the water sixty feet below. Morgan shook his head in disbelief.

"I can't believe that I used to do that," said Morgan, who smiled and walked back to his cabin with a noticeable limp.

Morgan sat down at his table and opened the ship's log. Quill in hand, he perched his foot on a chair with a pillow and began to write in the log. He described the unnamed ship swinging at anchor next to the *Oxford* in some detail. What was she doing here? he wondered. Caleb entered the cabin after a soft knock on the door.

"Pardon, Sir, will you be needin' lunch, Sir?"

"I am hoping that the Captain of that ship next to us will invite me over, but in the meantime, I could use a fruit plate." Gbessay would be proud of me, thought Morgan.

"Very good, Sir."

"By the way, could you fetch the ship's surgeon?"

"Right away, Sir."

Morgan studied his elevated big toe. He tentatively moved the joints and while not exactly painful, there was enough discomfort to assure him that another attack was coming. The tenor of the rest of the cruise would be set tonight and Morgan felt that he could not afford to be perceived as infirm, or weak. He would be expected to party with his men, and he would, but tonight he planned to avoid drinking contests and any other sort of excess. Toes can change behaviors, albeit temporarily.

"Conk, conk," said Browne at doorway.

"Nah who dat," said Morgan in response. It was one of the few times they had a chance to practice their Patois. They had had this conversation at the doorway perhaps a hundred times before and each time it varied slightly.

"Nah me."

"Nah me, who," said Morgan. It was their standard joke. When people "knocked you up", i.e., "came to call," they expected you to recognize their voices.

"Nah me."

"Your muddah no give you name?" asked Morgan.

"Me muddah give me plenty 'tings. When I go ungry, me muddah provide for me. When I go tire, me muddah let me sleep. Sweet muddah, I never forget her."

"Ya muudah a sweet dumplin', I wan' poke her!"

"To god, you would be standin' in a line," shot back Browne. Then it was over. Browne stepped into the cabin and examined Morgan's elevated toe.

"On balance, I would say you are probably going to live, although I have to admit that I have lost most of a rather substantial inheritance at the tables."

"As always, you have served me with a medical miracle and made me want to dance with joy, except that my fochin' toe is dangling precariously in the bowels of hell," said Morgan. Just then Caleb entered the cabin to deliver the fruit plate to Morgan. The conversation kept going full speed.

"Sorry Captain, anything more than three syllables and I get terribly confused," said Browne. "You see, I am just a country doctor, and the vermin I have so far encountered at this latitude were never mentioned in the texts I studied, present company excepted, of course." Morgan chuckled and somehow felt relieved.

"First of all," Morgan said in a bold voice, "I would like to remind you that keelhauling is an art form that requires a considerable amount of practice and the crew would benefit from the exercise. Of course, it would be interesting to test your endurance. However, at the present time we are anchored in a secluded cove in the process of celebrating a landfall and the beginning of an extraordinary adventure."

Caleb moved slowly toward the door and exited the cabin. Assured that the threats that Captain Morgan made were directed toward the ship's surgeon and not himself, Caleb relaxed and hovered outside the cabin door, making mental notes of the conversation that transpired, adding, once again, to the mythology that became the legend of Sir Henry Morgan.

"You are quite correct, Captain. It would be an indefensible tragedy if the festivities were interrupted. I believe I may be able to lessen your pain shortly after sunset tonight. The infusions require twenty-four hours to complete."

"Not acceptable, Doctor Browne." There was no mistaking Morgan's tone. The playing was over. "I will have my tea and I will have it now."

"Very well, Captain, but I cannot guarantee the potency of the draughts."

"How many are there?"

"Six, Captain."

"I will have one every two hours until the pain is gone. I would like you to prepare another six for tomorrow."

"I am your humble servant, Captain," said Browne as he walked toward the open door. "By the way, I am going to sharpen my saw, just in case."

"Thank you, Doctor Browne," said Morgan, softly chuckling. Browne nearly knocked over Caleb as he leapt over the threshold. For an instant the two men locked eyes and Browne shook his head as if the end was near for the Captain. Browne made his way below to the galley, while Caleb oozed out on deck, telling tales of keelhauling and imminent amputation to eager listeners.

CHAPTER 3

"What do you suggest we tell him? That she choked on her vomit?" Eschol Tarrante was a practical man. Celeste had, in fact, smoked too much opium and had had her fair share of Jamaican rum the night she died. A panic-ridden inhalation with a mouth full of vomit was a death sentence everywhere in the world. When Tarrante spoke there was always a hissing sound. He frequently drooled because his lower lip was gone. He always had a small towel at hand to absorb the embarrassing spittle that leaked out through his bottom teeth.

A few years ago Eschol Tarrante had been considered one of the handsomest and most eligible bachelors in the Caribbean. He stood a little over six feet and had very fair skin and piercing blue eyes. He was a "quim loadstone," or "pussy magnet," who could walk into a room and nearly always leave with the most beautiful woman there. Women did not want to spend the rest of their lives with him, necessarily, but they did want a chance to be impregnated by him to insure that their offspring would be close to perfection. They may not have consciously thought that, but there is a strong genetic pull on the heart of a woman that draws her inexorably toward a certain man.

He was in no way the consummate lover. Once alone in a room with one of his lover-victims, Tarrante stripped them bare and verbally attacked them, often spanking them before he bent them over and filled them with his seed. There was no comfort afterwards and they were left to their own devices to achieve satisfaction, while he beat a hasty retreat from the room. The truly amazing thing was that women would compete with each other for his selfish love, most of them being repeat-customers.

Captain Ruppert took another draw from his pipe. He looked over at the *Oxford* through one of the starboard windows in his cabin and squinted his bird-of-prey eyes. My God, he thought, what a huge ship! The *Oxford* stood ten feet higher in the water than his ship. One salvo and we are history, he thought, time for appeasement.

"They undoubtedly have spies in our ranks, just as we have in theirs," said Ruppert. "Morgan may already know that she is dead, so there is little point in trying to lie about that fact, however, he cannot possibly know the manner of her death--only you and I know that particular detail."

"I suggest we stick to the facts and simply eliminate the troublesome parts. Belly pain followed by fever and collapse," hissed Tarrante.

"Agreed. I suppose we have no choice but to entertain Morgan for a space of time. I would prefer that we do it this afternoon, rather than tonight. I want all interactions with their crew severely curtailed. No alcohol is to be consumed until after sundown tonight. Discussions concerning our cargo are strictly forbidden. I will send the Admiral a thank you note for the mediocre bottle of Madeira and invite him for a mid-day feast. Any other business?" Terrante shook his head, and dabbed his mouth as he silently left the aft cabin, his eyes on the floor.

Cancer is a strange, unpredictable thing. It can lie quiescent for years and then take off like a wildfire, leaving only destruction in its wake. Such was the case with Eschol Terrante's lip. Over four years ago the ship's surgeon had noticed a small non-healing ulcer on the skin just below the lower lip a little to the right of center. He recognized it as a cancer and recommended immediate cautery with a red-hot poker. In true Tarrante fashion, he ended up screaming at the surgeon that he was a low-class failure who had had to escape from France to avoid pending legal action. The surgeon, who was in the Caribbean because he could afford to be, was not taken aback. He recognized Tarrante's diatribe for what it was; a grief reaction. The surgeon simply shrugged his shoulders and walked away.

It was about two years later when the cancer began to grow at an alarming rate, quickly engulfing the lip to its full thickness. It was also spreading downward toward the chin. Tarrante had gone from "most eligible bachelor" status to "monster" status in three months. Oddly enough, the first person he consulted in the matter was Gbessay, the obeah woman, whose reputation as a healer had reached him years ago. She had told him, "De only medcine can fix dat is fire." Terrante was once again in denial and wasted another four months seeking out herbalists who failed to improve his condition.

One night Terrante finally gave in. He knew what he had to do to save his life and he summoned the ship's surgeon. After several draughts of rum and laudanum, Tarrante was taken below decks and placed on the carpenter's bench. His head was placed in a wooden block vise so that he could not turn it and a leather strap was placed over his forehead so that he could not lift upward. His ankles were bound and two rotund seamen lay over top of his thighs. One man was placed on each arm and the surgeon explained how to hold the arms without dislocating them. Tarrante was out cold. The ship's surgeon studied Tarrante's lip with the aid of a lamp and wondered if he could do less damage with a knife, but he knew it would be a bloody proposition. He vaguely remembered that there was an artery somewhere in the area, but he could not pin down the exact location. If he cut through the artery and was unable to tie it off quickly, Tarrante could easily die. The poker was the only solution. Red-hot iron would generally seal off all of the smaller vessels and virtually guarantee that no infection would follow.

The trouble was that patients tended to be less than enthusiastic about the pain.

The ship's surgeon raised his demijohn and took a generous mouthful. He rotated the poker in the steel brazier and sparks popped in anger. He called for four lamps to be lashed to the beam above the table. Another draw on his demijohn and he was ready. Tarrante's mouth was agape in his opium coma and a wooden block was placed between his teeth.

"Hold tight, now," the surgeon said in French. He picked up the poker in his right hand and grabbed Tarrante's lower lip with his left hand. The flesh sputtered and smoked and Tarrante suddenly came to life. It was not the present burning pain that drove him now, but the entire collection of all of his previous pains, which had brought him to this point. He bit down on the bite block and lifted the two men holding his arms slowly off the ground and then gently set them down again. There was no further struggle, just the hiss of air moving through his dilated nostrils.

In less than a minute the job was done. Tarrante immediately slipped back into his opium dream world and he was released from his bonds. A pillow was placed behind his head and a folded blanket was inserted underneath his backside as two shipmates lifted his pelvis off the table. He spent the night on the carpenter's bench free from the pain that had been his constant companion for as long as he could remember.

The following day Tarrante awoke in severe pain, but it was not his lip that bothered him, it was his chest and shoulders. He had torn thousands of muscle fibers during his delirious lifting the night before. Inhibitory mechanisms that normally prevented such destruction had been temporarily suspended and now he had to pay the price. It would be days of agony with each movement of his upper torso. Tincture of opium suddenly began to call to him and he answered.

With the passage of time, Tarrante became increasingly irritated by the remnant of his left lower lip. It frequently went into spasm and the remainder of the time it just flopped downward toward his chin. Finally he had had enough. He summoned the ship's surgeon and instructed him to cut off the remainder of his lower lip. With the aide of a significant amount of opium, which he no longer swallowed as a tincture, but now smoked, he subjected himself again to the red-hot poker. This in no way improved his already volatile mood, but it was finally over with.

Tarrante's sexual appetite had been substantially reduced by the opium he now smoked on a daily basis, but he still longed for an occasional romp with one of the whores in Port Royal. At such times, he would instruct one of his officers to procure an acceptable woman for the night, sometimes two, or three. The ladies were told that they would be the companion of a high official, whose identity must remain anonymous. Therefore, no light would be allowed in the room, not even a candle. This arrangement worked out well for several months until Tarrante let his guard down and fell asleep beside one of the ladies. When she awakened in the morning and looked over at him she let out a yelp and grabbed her clothes and ran for the door. Tarrante was awakened by the yelp and saw the look of horror in her eyes when she opened the door. She looked back as she ran over the threshold, slamming the door behind her. Tarrante had been devastated by the experience. That was six months ago and, since then, his spirits had gradually worsened.

Captain Ruppert was afraid of Tarrante, who stood a almost a foot taller than the Captain and, even under the influence of opium, was a far superior swordsman. Tarrante still obeyed the Captain's orders, but he often mocked the Captain behind his back. Ruppert knew that it was only a matter of time until Tarrante challenged him for control of the ship. Ruppert had spent many hours with Tarrante and he no longer had an automatic revulsion to Tarrante's monstrous face. The remainder of the crew, however, had never grown accustomed to Tarrante's appearance. That kind of fear does not support leadership; it destroys it.

Nevertheless, there was a relative stability among the crew. That gave Captain Ruppert some time to evaluate his present circumstances. He had forty-two-hundred ounces of silver ingot in the hold of his ship, the *Cor Valant*. That might entice an otherwise benign Morgan to seize his ship, present contents included, and sail it back to Port Royal as a prize. Indeed, Morgan might seize the *Cor Valant*, or *Brave Heart*, simply to settle an old score, i.e., Celeste. That was the trouble with Morgan—he was impossible to predict. That fact had been demonstrated a number of times before, much to the chagrin of the Spaniards.

Ruppert had paid close attention to every ship that was anchored off the shore of Isla de Vaca. He had searched in vain for a boat that was close to his own in configuration. The only thing close to *Cor Valant* was a sixty-five-foot cutter that sported sixteen cannon. She was a beamy thing that would not hold to the wind well and, of course, she could barely turn out five knots in a gale, un-loaded, with a freshly scraped bottom. Definitely, not in the same class. How to transform the *Cor Valant* from a virginal debutante into a diseased whore in the next few, very few, hours?

Ruppert called for "Pa' Jean," which was a nickname for his first officer, Patrick Jean. It was such a pleasure to deal with this man instead of Tarrante. There was never any second-guessing of his orders, no veiled threats, just some simple philosophical observations that never failed to make the Captain smile. Unfortunately, Tarrante was still in the aft cabin lounging in a comfortable chair with the back pointed toward the door.

"Captain?" Pa' Jean said from the cabin door.

"Come in and have seat," said Ruppert. The Captain's eyes darted to the chair facing the aft windows. Back and forth his eyes went to the chair, until Pa' Jean gave an understanding nod that the chair was occupied. Pa' Jean took a seat at the Captain's table and looked to Ruppert for direction.

"I want you to find the ship's carpenter and have him make some bung-stoppers four inches in diameter. Next, I want you to have, say five four-inch holes drilled in the hull, near the keel, on the side opposite the *Oxford*. You must then attend to the number of planks showing to the *Oxford*. Let water in through the new holes so that two planks are submerged, re-plug the holes and have the water pumped out. Do this twice a day. Always keep enough water in the hold to keep our cargo covered."

"Let me assure myself that I understand what it is that you want Morgan to see: A ship that is taking on water with bilge pumps manned continuously. An unattractive prize for a fleet that is about to begin a cruise," said Pa' Jean, a little shy of six feet and muscular.

"Precisely."

"I will arrange to have the bilge pumped from the starboard side so that the *Oxford* can see our labors."

"You think like a Captain. One last thing; have the carpenter make a plug for my head and instruct the men to use it as the need arises. We want this ship to smell horrible."

"Understood, Sir," said Pa' Jean as he stood up from his chair to leave.

"Please ask O' Donte to come to my cabin." O' Donte was the ship's surgeon. He got his nickname, "The Tooth" from the appearance of his two front teeth, which were huge.

"Right away, Captain."

Moments later the carpenter's mate appeared and asked permission to measure the hole in the captain's toilet. Next came O' Donte, who was motioned inside the cabin by Ruppert.

"You wanted to see me, Captain?" O' Donte was the surgeon who had used the red-hot poker on Terrante's lip.

"Yes, I have an assignment for you. I want you to pay a visit to the *Oxford's* surgeon. I want you to fabricate some sort of illness that will make Morgan reluctant to come aboard. Ask their surgeon for advice and see if they have any medicine for it. How is your English?"

"Passable, Captain."

"Another thing I would like you to do is ask for a couple of volunteers to eat a large meal to be followed by tartar of emetic. I want this to happen the minute Morgan's launch leaves the *Oxford*. Have them wretch their guts up on deck and sweep the mess into the scuppers, but don't rinse it off. Let the perfume linger so that Morgan can appreciate it. I want them wrenching over the side when he ties up to us."

"Very well, Captain. Will that be all?"

"Don't be overly dramatic about the illness. I do not want them to suspect a ruse. Once you pick out the disease, inform the crew so that they can act the part. By the way, give this invitation to one of the officers. Let's hope he will decline the invitation." O' Donte stepped forward and took the folded parchment from Ruppert. The parchment was folded into thirds and held together with a red wax seal. The words "Captain Morgan" were written in a sloppy script. After O' Donte departed, Tarrante turned his chair back toward the table and sat down.

"You are the clever one," said Tarrante and then dabbed his chin. Privately, Captain Ruppert was not optimistic about their chances. There was bad blood between the two Captains and Morgan could easily seize their ship under a number of pretexts. On the other hand, Ruppert had sailed with Morgan many times in the past and those excursions had been profitable and friendly. The really troubling question for Ruppert was how much pain had Morgan experienced with the loss of Celeste? Equally important was the boarding of the *Westin* and whether, or not, Morgan knew about it. Ruppert gritted his teeth and slowly bobbed his head as he thought about how easy it would have been to just pay silver for the goods they took from the *Westin*. Because of that oversight, there was a good chance they would all hang. The crew seemed to sense this and they were very subdued, no doubt planning their escapes if the *Cor Valant* were boarded.

Chapter 4

"It's the ship's surgeon from the Frenchie boat, Sir," called the midshipman to Commander Collier. "He says he wants to have a word with Doctor Browne." The small skiff was side-tied to the *Oxford*, while they awaited Collier's orders. The skiff was thirteen feet long and had a single sail that propelled it at a good six knots with enough room for the skipper and two passengers. In contrast, the *Oxford*'s launches required six oarsmen for propulsion at a measly four knots.

"Bring him aboard," said Collier. "Kindly inform Doctor Browne that he has a visitor."

O' Donte climbed the rope ladder clumsily and was winded when he came on deck. The crew was silent as they studied the short Frenchman, sizing up his clothing, his general appearance and the parcel he carried. His wide-brimmed hat with a feather was strangely out of place, but the *Oxford*'s crew had not seen the horrors of Tarrante's face, nor could they appreciate the fact that O' Donte had figured out that sunlight had caused Tarrante's cancer. O' Donte studied the crewmen as well, looking for signs of scurvy, pox and skin cancers. He handed the folded parchment to the Midshipman who helped him regain his balance on the deck. Browne arrived and extended his hand in greeting.

"Richard Browne, the *Oxford*'s surgeon, welcome aboard." O' Donte shook his hand eagerly.

"Michelle Mitterand, ship surgeon of *Cor Valant*. Your acquaintance is good. My men call me O' Donte," he said smiling.

"That certainly fits. Would you like to come below and have a spot of tea?"

"My pleasure, Sir."

Knowing that Morgan would want a full report of what had transpired between the two men, Browne decided to behave as the perfect English gentleman and get the Frenchie shit-faced. He thought that the galley would be the perfect place since, even with the ports open, it was ten degrees hotter than any other part of the ship. Cool white wine was the perfect antidote to the heat and it was delivered directly from Morgan's personal cache. Who could resist? To top things off, Cyrus Jones would pass his pipe around, while he fixed the mid-day meal and produced baskets full of fish balls, occasionally interjecting apothecary insights. The light was dim in the galley and it took a few minutes for their eyes to adjust.

O' Donte set his parcel on the table and passed it over to Browne. The package was wrapped in oilcloth and Browne knew what it was before he began to open it. The smell was unmistakable; jesuit's bark, or chincona as the natives called it. The bark was native to South America and it contained high levels of quinine which could stop even a severe case of malaria, or "bad air," in its tracks. Browne picked up the parcel and placed it before his nose. He inhaled deeply as Jones set two glasses on the table and began to pour a cool chardonnay. O' Donte sniffed at the wine and downed the glass.

"This is an exceedingly generous gift, Doctor O' Donte." The parcel weighed well over a kilogram and, given the fact that one aristocratic family in England had a monopoly on the chincona bark trade, it was worth about five years salary for the average tradesman. Jones re-filled O' Donte's glass and produced a pipe that he lit with a broom straw.

"Our luck has been good and we find a Spanish ship. She had supplies of many bark. We help them relieve the burden," said O' Donte, smiling. O' Donte took a draw on the pipe. Browne translated what O' Donte said into French and realized that it was much more eloquent. Browne decided on a new stratagem.

"I miss the sound of our native tongue," said Browne in fluent French. His governess had been a Parisian teen left homeless after her family had been taken by a burst of plague. Browne had spent over ten years with Brigitte before he had been shipped off to boarding school at the age of twelve. In the English countryside one rarely has a chance to speak French and that left Browne with a Parisian sixteen year-old fluency, female at that. Over the years that followed, Browne had engaged every French-speaking person he could find in order to broaden his language skills, but in a country that was at war with France more often than she was at peace, the opportunities were scarce. Although Browne was fluent in French, he never learned to speak "man French," which was designed to keep a wall between mature males and everyone else, including females and adolescent males. It was simply another language that all mature males spoke, having gone through adolescent angst and the process of learning to cuss appropriately.

"This is a pleasant surprise," said O' Donte, who was visibly relaxed. "Do I detect a Parisian accent?"

"You have a good ear, my friend. I was born in Paris and lived there for my first twelve years. My father was a diplomat and he was recalled to London." Jones refilled their glasses. "A few months later my father returned to Paris and I was placed in an English boarding school. What a nightmare." Browne realized he was getting tipsy and the story that he was concocting was getting complicated. He had actually never been to France, but the stories that Brigitte had told him over and over during the decade they had spent together would provide him with a framework to create a phantom childhood. All that he needed to do was just stay sober. Browne stood up from the table and took a large mouthful of wine. He walked behind O' Donte toward the table with the fish balls and spit the wine silently back into the glass. He grabbed the basket of fish balls and poured his glass of wine down the copper galley sink. He winked at Jones who smiled back. Browne sat back down at the table and slid the basket of fish balls over to O' Donte, whose glass, noted Browne, was empty.

"Surely you have been back to Paris since that time," said O' Donte, who reached for the basket. Jones filled their glasses again.

"After I completed my education, there were certain pressures placed on me that made a return to Paris impossible." Such a vague statement served to increase O' Donte's curiosity about Browne. Just then Lieutenant Owen called down from the top of the stairs.

"Doctor Browne, the Captain would like a word with you."

"I am on my way, Lieutenant," said Browne rolling his eyes, making O' Donte smile. "Please make yourself comfortable. I will be back momentarily," he said to O' Donte, filling both their glasses. Browne picked up his wineglass and stood up. He passed the glass to Owen at the top of the stairs and said softly, "Drink up, dear boy, it is the best wine you have ever had." Owen smiled and shrugged his shoulders in resignation as he raised the glass to his lips.

When Browne entered the aft cabin he was relieved to see that Morgan's foot was on the ground. Morgan and Collier were sitting at the table discussing the substantial leak on the French ship.

"If we take her she'll have to be careened for repairs and that could set us back days," said Collier.

"True enough," said Morgan motioning for Browne to have a seat, "but if we loose track of Ruppert now, we will never have another opportunity to apprehend him. He would never dare show his face again in Port Royal." Morgan looked at Browne and said, "What do you have for us?"

"Nothing yet. I am softening the little bastard up with some of the wine you so generously provided. When he first came on board he was extremely nervous. He is sickly white. I am going to need a little more time with him."

"You are going to have to speed things up a bit. We have been invited to a luncheon and I would like you to come with us," said Morgan, pointing to the open parchment in the center of the table.

"I would be delighted, Captain. Maybe they will have some decent wine," said Browne with a snicker.

"Get to it, Browne. Be ready to depart in half an hour."

"Thank you," whispered Owen, as he passed the empty glass back to Browne, who nodded and descended the stairs. In the dim light of the galley, Browne caught his hip on the corner of a table and let out a string of profanity. O' Donte, who was obviously very tipsy, began to chuckle as Browne danced around the room holding his left hip. Browne finally sat down at the table and closed his eyes for a few seconds.

"Did you study ballet as well as medicine? You are very light on your feet," said O' Donte. Both men laughed as Jones, who was not in on the joke because he did not speak French, filled their glasses. Browne sipped and O' Donte gulped. Browne decided it was time to extract some information from his new friend.

"When you came aboard today I sensed that you had some problems aboard your own ship. How may I be of service to you and your ship?" Browne deliberately slurred his words to approximate O' Donte's level of intoxication.

"It is true that we have some mysterious gastrointestinal ailment among the crew. It seems to come and go in unpredictable cycles. Sometimes the men vomit blood. I was wondering if you had ever encountered such an illness. Can you make any recommendations with respect to medicine, like tartar of emetic…" There was a pause as O' Donte gathered his thoughts. "What I mean is the opposite effect; something to calm down their intestines and the vomiting. We have tried opium, but it only seems to make the vomiting worse." Browne caught the frustration in O' Donte's face after he said, "tartar of emetic," but he wasn't sure what it meant. He decided to play along.

"It is strange that you should mention that, because I heard that many of Morgan's men came down with a similar illness during the Portobelo raid last year. Were you anywhere near Portobelo?"

"No, not at all. We were well to the north." O' Donte caught himself before divulging the location of his ship's landfalls. "Besides, I was there in Portobelo and treated Morgan's men as well as my own. This is a totally different process."

"Perhaps I might have the pleasure of examining one of your patients. It seems that I will be joining the Captain on a visit to your ship in just a few minutes," said Browne.

"I would be most grateful."

"Can you tell me where you were when the first case occurred," said Browne, hoping to get some small piece of information.

"Actually, we were here. It was about three months ago."

"Very well, you can give me a more detailed account when we get to your ship. In the meantime, I must admit that I cannot place your accent," said Browne, who had decided to avoid direct questions and engage O' Donte in casual conversation in the hopes of dropping his guard.

"I am from Pessac, just south of Bordeaux. My family has been in Pessac for seven generations, intimately associated with wine, of course. I was the black sheep and became fascinated with natural history and medicine. I began a practice in Bordeaux and was fairly successful, but I soon became bored and eventually became a ship's surgeon on one of my uncle's boats." Browne listened attentively as the story unfolded. "At first I spent my time on short runs in the Bay of Biscay, but once I had proven myself, I was placed on the larger ships that did commerce in the Americas, primarily Boston. On my third trip we headed south to pick up a load of rum in Barbados and that is when I realized that I wanted nothing more to do with the cold of Bordeaux, or Boston."

"I know the feeling well," said Browne as he took a draw on his pipe. What he said to O' Donte was true. Browne was fed up with the dismal English countryside and the smell of the open sewers in London. Jamaica was a paradise in comparison, with its fresh fruit, tropical warmth and an endless supply of adventure. Both men stared at the table in front of them and were glad for the silence that followed, however short-lived it was.

"Captain's launch being pulled along side, Doctor Browne," shouted Lieutenant Owen down the companionway.

It was simply astonishing how well armed Morgan was as he left his cabin and stepped on deck. He wore a short bulky coat, which contained a pulper in each side pocket and a small pistol in each padded shoulder. In the waist of the coat were two braided wire cables the diameter of an index finger that could be withdrawn in a split second to deliver punishing blows to anyone approaching from either side. Finely woven silk on the inside of the sleeves insured that the coat could be dropped in an instant if there was a chance of submersion, which is what worried him most. But there was a cost associated with the hidden protection; heat gain and sweat. Morgan chose a wide-brimmed felt hat with a coarsely woven top to help eliminate heat. Naturally, there were two thin tempered steel daggers in the brim. The pants were coarsely woven hemp, cut at the knee, with a readily accessible dagger on the side of each thigh. His boots were unfashionably short, but they were cool and managed to conceal three daggers each, small but lethal in the right hands. In the event that etiquette dictated that he remove his coat, there was a finely balanced throwing knife accessible in a small pocket stitched in his shirt at the base of his neck. He had spent hours learning to throw the knife and used to joke that if he ever lost his fortune he could always make a living doing a road tour back in Wales.

With this strange assortment of iron weights, Morgan took his first tentative steps on deck. A hundred eyes were on him as he felt his way to the port rail, where Browne was starting his descent down the rope ladder to join O' Donte who sat in the bow of the launch. Browne caught the heel of his right boot in the ladder and several midshipmen and deck hands peered over the side to evaluate the situation. Morgan, who was by this time was also at the rail, looked back at the deck hands and smiled with a raised eyebrow, as if to say, "Another landlubber, posing as a sailor." That one eye contact galvanized over a hundred men to follow him into a battle that was to last three months. Finally, Browne freed himself from the ladder and continued his descent. By now, all of the second watch and third watch were on deck to observe the festivities.

Morgan stepped over the side before Browne reached the bottom of the ladder. As he did so, captain's pipes were sounded, which always made Morgan feel uncomfortable. Morgan made a mental note to have that formality eliminated from his official comings and goings, but in the meantime, he had to negotiate the weight hidden in his clothing. Mercifully, he had chosen a pair of boots with a small heel. There was a loud snap as Browne's boots hit the seat of the launch. Morgan was just below the rail, out of sight. Morgan let out a wail, which the crewmen interpreted as Morgan falling off the ladder and landing in the launch. The *Oxford* listed to port as the crewmen ran to catch a glimpse of their injured Captain. Morgan climbed up two steps on the ladder, a head above the rail and raised his eyebrow.

"Made yer look!"

The crewmen let out a sigh and began to laugh. Once again, Morgan had put forth a small token of humanity and insured that his crew would follow him anywhere he chose to go.

CHAPTER 5

Commander Collier stood on deck with his telescope held to his eye, peering over at the French ship as the captain's launch pulled away from the *Oxford*. The water between the two ships was unusually calm and he was intrigued as the French ship began to sink. First one plank disappeared below the water line and then another. By the time the launch pulled up to the French ship, she was four planks deeper in the water, then suddenly it all stopped. Collier observed two sick seamen heaving their guts up over the side as the launch approached. Odd, thought Collier, the water is flat calm. He checked the planks again and there was no change. The bilge outlet had not changed, just a constant flow. He felt nothing but pity for the poor bastards who manned those pumps below decks. He moved his telescope to the Captain's launch, which had kept a distance from the French ship. There seemed to be some negotiating going on between the launch and the French ship. Finally, the launch pulled away from the French ship and headed toward Isle de Vaca. Once the launch was out of earshot, Collier noticed that the men who had been vomiting on deck were suddenly gone.

"Remind me not to eat French food," he mumbled under his breath.

"Sir?" asked Owen who had been standing silently beside Commander Collier.

"Nothing, Lieutenant, I was just commenting on the dangers of French cuisine."

"Yes, Sir, I quite agree. Those men seemed terribly sick, at least until the Captain's launch pulled away."

"You noticed that, did you?"

"Yes, Sir, I did. What is even more peculiar is the way she drafts. She is five planks deeper in the water than she was this morning. About an hour ago I thought she was sinking, but then it all stopped, Sir."

"Lieutenant Owen, how old are you?"

"Seventeen, Sir, I just had my birthday last week."

"Midshipman Owen, you have just been promoted to Lieutenant. I will inform the bursar and your pay, or shares will be increased commensurately. You will continue to observe and report directly to me."

Owen stood there frozen. He had a rush of emotion, but he could not find the proper way to express it.

"By the way, Lieutenant, get rid of that uniform. That is an order."

"Yes, Sir. Thank you, Sir," was all that he could squeeze out as Commander Collier turned and walked away.

The Midshipmen were addressed as "Lieutenant," but they were actually a step below until they passed an exhaustive examination. That was the English system, but it simply did not apply here. Collier was well within his rights to give an on-board promotion. Add to that the fact that Owen had been doing all of the navigating since leaving Port Royal. The other midshipmen made so many errors that they were completely unreliable as navigators.

Morgan stood by the pit in the sand that was being loaded with the last of the charcoal. Next, a layer of rocks would be placed on top of the glowing charcoal and then the gutted pig with intact skin would be placed on top of the rocks and then buried with sand. Eight hours later sailors would be eating the legendary "Vaca lavish," the traditional meal that signaled the start of a lucky cruise. Morgan exchanged pleasantries with his men and then started walking down the deserted beach on the north shore of Isla de Vaca. Browne and O' Donte had gone into the dense woods in search of medicinal plants, so that left Morgan alone and quite content.

Morgan caught a mirror flash from the French ship, which was about a half mile away. He looked to his left and saw the small skiff that had delivered O' Donte to the *Oxford* playing in the surf. Her skipper would raise the boat up in a swell and dart outside just as the wave began to break. One false move and the boat was kindling. Naturally, Morgan wanted to try his hand at it. The mirror flashes continued and finally the skipper of the skiff waved and headed back to the French ship. Morgan estimated he had at least twenty minutes before the skiff could return to the ship, load the Captain and first mate and transport them to the island. It was just enough time for a good swim.

Morgan saw a palm log in the sand just ahead and walked over to it. He carefully laid his coat over the log, then his shirt, pants and boots. Twenty pounds lighter and carefree as a four year old, he ran toward the water until he was knee-deep, then dove forward spinning, finally sending up a huge cascade of water as his back slapped an on-coming wave. He smiled as the cool water tickled the hair on his arms and legs, and sent his balls on a short journey to warmer climates. He swam forward a short distance just beyond the small breakers and rolled on to his back with his ears slightly submerged below the water. The familiar clicking noise of the Caribbean waters soothed him much the same way as the frogs did on land in Jamaica. Peace.

A musket shot in the distance sharpened the wits of the Marines, who had rowed Morgan's launch to the island. The demijohn of rum and the dice were cast aside as the six men rose and grabbed their muskets. Their leader realized that the bare limestone cliffs behind them made it impossible to tell from what direction the shot had come, so he began to look in all directions. He spotted Morgan almost at once, floating in the water. Even at a distance of 75 yards he could clearly see the unusual coat draped over the palm log. He was certain the motionless body in the water was Morgan and after a few seconds he sounded the alarm

"The Captain 'as been 'it!" he shouted. He pointed to the two men nearest him and said, "The two of you sound an alarm, then reload and head up into the hills there," pointing to the cliffs directly above Morgan. "The rest of you come with me.

One Marine pulled the trigger on his musket and a second later the thunderclap boom rang out. The second Marine started counting and cocked his musket, "Thousand two, thousand three." Bam, went the second musket and within sixty seconds another launch was being lowered into the water beside the *Oxford*.

Rational thinking was not a tool that was utilized that day. The two Marines re-loaded and began to sprint up a trail that went in the general direction of the cliffs above Morgan. Browne and O' Donte began sprinting down the trail, once Browne had recognized the distress call.

Four Marines and two pig roasters were sprinting down the beach toward Morgan, who was still motionless in the water, completely oblivious to everything above the water, but totally captivated by the sounds *in* the water. It was one of the most peaceful moments of his life.

The two Marines had run about fifty yards up the steep rocky trail before they were completely winded. Silently, they both swore oaths to themselves that they were going to lose weight, as they bent forward with their hands on their knees. Suddenly they heard the sound of footsteps rapidly approaching from uphill. They both took cover and raised their muskets. Browne, who was in the lead, never heard the clicks as the Marines cocked their muskets.

"Halt!" shouted the Marine on the left side of the trail. Browne did his best to comply, but as he dug his heels into the gravel trail, the ground gave way and he slipped and fell on his ass, continuing to slide down the hill on his back. The musket ball that had been aimed at his chest missed him by two feet. The younger Marine on the right took aim at O' Donte's midsection and pulled the trigger. There was a brief delay as the ignited powder in the pan hissed its way toward the barrel. In that space of time the winded Marine took a much needed breath and the muzzle of his gun raised up so that when the ball finally roared out, it struck a glancing blow on the side of O' Donte's right temple. It was not a lethal wound, but O' Donte went down with a thud.

It is astonishing how effective military training can be. The well-seasoned Marine, who had fired at Browne, had already charged his musket with powder and placed a cloth wad with a ball on top in the end of the barrel and was extracting the ramrod from the underside of his musket. Browne had never had any military training, but he had had an older brother. His initial disbelief turned into a murderous rage as the tortured fragments from his childhood merged to save the adult .The Marine had nearly extracted the ramrod when Browne jumped to his feet. Browne placed both hands on the vertical musket and gave a tug. The Marine let go of the ramrod and with both hands pulled back on the musket with all of his might. Browne let go of the musket and grabbed the ramrod as the Marine fell backwards on the ground. Browne took a giant step forward and raised the ramrod. Browne saw the Marine pull his leg back and before the boot delivered a direct hit to his groin, Browne spun on his heel and as the rotation completed, he delivered a sound blow to the Marine's neck. The Marine let out a yelp and dropped his musket, both hands at his neck.

Browne was not content. His next blow struck the Marine in the center of his crotch. Reflexively, the Marine turned on his side, with legs pulled up to his chest, letting out a guttural moan. Browne delivered several more blows until he heard his sobbing mother say, "Please stop, Doctor Browne. Please stop!"

Browne paused, ramrod raised for another strike. Why would mother be calling me Doctor Browne? Suddenly, Browne passed through the waist-deep water of childhood into the ever-present fog of the adult world and realized that he was out of control and had work to do. It was the young Marine's voice that had been calling him back.

"Oh, shit!" said Browne as he looked up the trail and saw the sobbing young Marine with O' Donte's head in his lap. There was blood everywhere.

When there is an injured person with a wound, it is incredibly difficult to estimate how much blood has actually been lost. To the young Marine that fired the shot that almost killed O' Donte, it must have seemed like gallons. Browne dropped the ramrod and took two paces uphill, before he turned to and walked back to the older Marine lying on the ground. On some level Browne knew that the injured Marine would seek his revenge and Browne was sorely tempted to kill him and be done with it, but for the moment it seemed better to deal with a little fear than a lifetime of guilt. Browne bent over and picked up the ramrod and then walked over behind the Marine, who was still in the fetal position. Browne placed the tip of the ramrod squarely in the center of the Marine's back and pushed a little to elicit a response. There was none, so Browne bent down to whisper in the man's ear.

"I have decided to let you live. But I just wanted to let you know that if you get within ten feet of me, I will nail your balls to the stern of the *Oxford* and drag you back to Port Royal. Nod if you understand."

There was no response from the Marine, so Browne jabbed the ramrod in deeper. Suddenly the Marine's head began bobbing rapidly. Second in command of the Marine detachment assigned to the *Oxford*, this poor bastard's reputation would never recover. Browne could hear the talk Below decks already: "Tried to shoot the ship's surgeon, he did, but Doctor Browne got hold of his ramrod and nearly beat 'im to death! I seen it with me own two eyes!"

Browne picked up the musket next to the motionless body before him and started walking uphill toward the next mess that he needed to clean up.

Morgan was completely oblivious to the activity around him. He was trying to regulate his breathing so that he could get by on four breaths a minute. A forceful breath out and he began to sink, but a rapid breath in and he bobbed back to the surface. One thousand one…

The two pig roasters had pulled ahead of the four Marines from the *Oxford* in an insane race down the beach, and once they were even with Morgan on the beach, they ran into the water and dove into a small breaker. They swam rapidly toward their injured Captain. The four Marines stayed just above the water line ostensibly to protect their shoes and gear, but the reality was that none of them could swim.

As the first pig-roasting Buccaneer approached the lifeless body in the water, Morgan sensed something big approaching him. Human physiology being what it is, Morgan's pulse rate went from sixty to one-hundred-twenty in less than a second as the term, Shark! raced through his mind. The blood flow to his skin was immediately diverted to his muscles. His penis, which had teetered on a fairly substantial incipient erection, now took on the dimensions of a dung beetle. Hit on the first pass! raced through his mind. It was widely believed at the time that if you were in the water with a shark, the shark would typically come in for a couple of close-up contacts before it decided to take a bite out of you. If you were lucky enough to strike the shark in the face on the first pass, he would likely go on to easier prey.

With his nervous system geared up for attack, Morgan opened his eyes and practically came out of his skin as he saw the Buccaneer reaching over to pluck him out of the water. Morgan lashed out with a powerful hook that caught the Buccaneer on the side of the head and knocked him senseless. Without hesitation, Morgan made a mad dash for the beach and happened to catch a wave that was beginning to break. He kicked hard and gave a good stroke with his hands and was shot forward toward the sand. As he rode the wave in, Morgan was perplexed by the presence of the four Marines on shore. And who was the man he had just hit in the head? "Is this a mutiny?" he whispered. "Impossible!"

Morgan reached knee-deep water and stood up to take stock of what had just happened. He glanced back from where he had come and noticed a second Buccaneer apparently helping a dazed man come ashore. The Marines standing at the water line seemed confused, rather than menacing. Morgan stood naked on the shoreline trying desperately to figure out a reasonable explanation for what he saw, but nothing made any sense.

"Sergeant, a word," said Morgan as he walked past the four Marines toward his clothes. The Marine followed him dutifully toward the palm log. Morgan pulled on his knee-length britches and with his head tilted, looked at the Marine.

"We was tryin' to save ya, Sir!"

"What do you mean, Sergeant?" said Morgan, pulling on his shirt.

"We 'eard a musket shot, Sir. We looked around and saw you floatin' in the water and…well, I thought you 'ad been 'it, you see."

"Very well, Sergeant," he laughed. "It is all beginning to make sense now. I assure you that I am unharmed, but in the last minute I have heard a gunshot and a man scream up in the hills to the right of us. I suggest that you take your men and proceed in that direction."

"'Appy to oblige, Sir," said the Marine Sergeant, bowing as he left.

When Morgan had finished dressing, he looked up just as the French skiff buried its bow in the sand. The skipper of the craft lowered the small sail as two officers jumped off the bow into the dry sand. Morgan studied the men in the distance and noticed that the larger of the two appeared to have no lower lip.

Browne bent down to inspect the wound on O' Donte's right temple. The musket ball had taken a swath of skin and muscle with it, but more importantly, it had also taken a portion of the temporal artery. Blood was spurting from both sides of the wound. Overcome with guilt, the young Marine sobbed as he watched Browne tear a strip of cloth from the bottom of O' Donte's shirt. Browne wadded up the cloth and placed it on the wound.

"Hold this tightly against his head," said Browne. The Marine complied, grateful that he had something to do. Browne stripped off O' Donte's belt and placed it over the dressing, removing the Marine's hands in the process. Browne cinched down on the belt until the bleeding stopped. O' Donte moaned and opened his eyes. He was dazed, but very much alive. The young Marine sighed in relief and stopped his sobbing.

"This man is going to be just fine. Go over and take care of your friend," said Browne motioning toward the senior Marine. O' Donte sat up abruptly, freeing the young Marine. Browne was able to catch about every fourth word when O' Donte began swearing, as only a Frenchman can do. O' Donte turned his rage on Browne, who was close at hand. The Frenchman was sitting in the center of the trail with his fist raised at Browne, who struggled to glean some useful swearwords. But it was all too fast. With his sixteen-year-old-girl French, Browne was able to understand the words, "mother," repeatedly, "dog," and "donkey," occasionally, with a regular, "English dog."   In the midst of his scatological tirade, O' Donte picked up a handful of dirt from the trail and hurled it at Browne, who saw it coming and turned away.

"Mate with yourself!" said Browne, frustrated with his incompetent French vocabulary. He repeated the phrase silently to himself several times and then began to laugh. It was the type of laughter that only occurs when you have just had a near-death experience and survived it. It was unstoppable, all-consuming. As he headed down the trail, Browne glanced back at O' Donte, who sat in the center of the trail with the belt on his head, shouting obscenities at no one in particular, and the laughter increased to the point that Browne could barely walk. He continued down the trail, giving the older Marine he had nearly beaten to death a wide berth. He had gone about a half mile and had finally gotten control of his laughter, when he met the four Marines coming up the trail.

"Are you 'urt, Sir?" asked the Marine in the lead, who could see the blood stains on Browne's shirt. The second Marine also advanced toward Browne, while the two in the rear raised their muskets and scanned high and low for as yet unnamed enemies. There were more shots in the distance and all four of the Marines were spooked.

"I am fine," said Browne, who began to laugh again, "but there are two injured men up the trail." Browne studied the four Marines , who were deadly serious. He realized that they probably thought he was insane and the last thing he wanted was a Marine escort down the hill, so he pulled himself together. "There is one injured Marine and one injured ship's surgeon. It will probably take all four of you to get them down the hill."

The four Marines darted up the hill and Browne kept his laughter in check until he was out of earshot and then it all began again. He replayed the image of O' Donte sitting in the middle of the trail over and over, until he had to sit on a rock on the edge of the trail to rest. Finally the laughter subsided and Browne could breathe easily again. Then the real work began.

In the oxygen-saturated recesses of Browne's mind, there was a sudden recall of the "fake pull on the musket," the extraction of the "ramrod," and the pivot of his hips when he saw the boot coming for his groin. Tears welled up in his eyes as he tried to decide whether he had done these things as a result of the "training" his brother had given him, or had his brother actually been there with him—possibly in control of his body. It was a subject that he could never discuss with his brother, who had died two years before in London, while Browne was out at sea. Browne had not received word of his brother's passing until six months later when he returned to port.

If the passion is great, the memory formed is forever. Such was the case for the men on the beach of Isla de Vaca, on January 2, 1669. A number of shots rang out, perhaps thirty in all, which drew everyone's attention to the sandstone cliffs inland from the beach. The vegetation began to tremble and then panicked cattle, running at full speed, jumped over the edge of the cliff and began their slow-motion descent to the rocks below. Morgan stared transfixed at the scene before him. He did a quick inventory of the drugs he had consumed recently that included colchicine, a cup of rum, make that two cups of rum after breakfast, tobacco and the residual opium in his system from the night before. "Is this an opium dream?" he asked himself, aloud. He looked back toward the surf and saw the two pig roasters staring at the hill equally perplexed. Morgan looked back at the cliffs and as the last cow went over the edge, he noticed several Buccaneers standing at the top of the cliffs looking very pleased with themselves. They waved down to him and he waved back, still not quite believing what he had just seen. Suddenly, he realized that the preceding drama was a stroke of brilliance.

Shooting the cows inland and packing them out to the beach was one of the most laborious tasks imaginable, as Morgan knew all too well, having done it himself for three seasons in his youth. Driving the cows toward the beach and then stampeding them over the cliffs would save the Buccaneers hundreds of hours of back-breaking toil. Morgan made a mental note to find out who had dreamed up this scheme.

Suddenly there was a commotion up the beach involving the two recent French arrivals and some Marines, who were carrying an injured man. Morgan cocked one of his pulpers and walked briskly toward the fracas.

Dante could not have devised a more compelling drama than the one being acted out on the beach. The Marines had deposited O' Donte in the sand at the water's edge, and Browne was removing the belt around the man's head, trying to inspect the wound. O' Donte sat there passively while Browne tried to get a glimpse of the wound. The high pressure arterial bleeding began again and Browne quickly replaced the pressure dressing. Captain Ruppert and Tarrante had seen the furrow in O' Donte's right temple and they became agitated, asking O' Donte over and over what had happened. Browne cinched down on the belt and O' Donte, who had been silent and passive up to this point, let out a whimper and began to swear again, as nearly as Browne could tell. Captain Ruppert took a few steps backward when Tarrante drew his foil and grabbed Browne by the collar and flattened him in the sand. Ruppert hoped that one of the Marines would challenge Tarrante and kill him, so he stood in the background, as Tarrante became more aggressive. Tarrante was leaking spit through his uncovered lower teeth, but he did not seem to care. He shouted commands in French to have his comrade carried to the skiff on the beach, but aside from Browne, who was lying in the sand trying to fight the giggles, nobody could understand him. The Marines present were hesitant to intervene, largely because of their earlier mistakes. Morgan approached the scene and had no hesitation whatsoever.

Morgan saw his ship's surgeon being held flat on his back in the sand by a madman with a foil. Make that a madman with a foil and no lower lip. Morgan cocked his second pulper, which caught everyone's attention.

"On your knees, asshole," said Morgan softly, in crisp French. Morgan had learned how to say that phrase in five different languages without a trace of an accent. With two menacing pistols pointed at his head, Tarrante decided to obey the command and seek revenge later. There was also the added incentive of the four Marines, who had belatedly raised their muskets and drawn a bead on his chest. Ruppert prayed that Tarrante would do something stupid and get himself killed in the process, but it was not to be.

Browne attempted to stand, but he began laughing again and looked up at Morgan and mouthed the words, "Sorry," on hands and knees. Morgan had been in similar situations himself and he raised his eyebrows and bobbed his head, as if to say, "I understand what you are going through."

Morgan saw that his Marines had taken control of the situation, so he calmly un-cocked his pulpers and placed them back in his coat. He looked at the young Marine, who had helped carry O' Donte down the trail, straight in the eye.

"Come with me," he said

Morgan and the young Marine took a position just out of earshot and Morgan asked the boy to explain what had happened up the hill. The young Marine commenced his tale and spoke so rapidly he had finished almost before he had begun. Morgan counted over ten mea culpas during the story. The boy was obviously consumed with guilt and Morgan tried to ease his pain, pointing out that he would have done the same thing in that particular situation.

Morgan put his arm over the boy's shoulder as they walked back to the group assembled on the beach. Tarrante was still on his hands and knees in the sand with muskets pointed at his back and head by deadly serious Marines. Morgan instructed the Marines to escort Tarrante to the French skiff while he took Captain Ruppert aside. After a few clumsy exchanges, it was apparent that neither man was competent enough in the other's language to say what needed to be said. Morgan looked back and saw the Marines escorting Tarrante across the sand. He located Browne, who was standing up and evidently in control.

"Doctor Browne, a moment of your time, please," said Morgan. Browne walked up to the two captains dreading what was coming next, but he was pleasantly surprised when he realized that all he had to do was translate.

"Doctor Browne, would you be kind enough to tell Captain Ruppert that I am terribly sorry for what happened to his ship's surgeon. It was an accident that never should have happened."

Browne relayed that sentiment and the tension was markedly diminished. Browne relayed back to Morgan that Ruppert said that, "These things happen, from time to time." Morgan was relieved.

"Please tell the captain that I would be most honored and pleased if he and his officers would do me the honor of joining us for a celebration aboard the *Oxford* tonight at sunset." Browne completed the translation and Ruppert smiled.

"Please tell your captain that the honor is mine. It would be a privilege to attend your celebration."

Back in his cabin, Morgan stood while Caleb helped him out of the heavy coat. God! What a relief to feel human again, thought Morgan, who walked over to his rum barrel and drew a half-cup.

"Captain?"

"Come in Collier," said Morgan. Collier stepped over the threshold with Owen behind him.

"Captain, I brought along Midshipman Owen, who has just been promoted to lieutenant."

"Congratulations, Lieutenant. I like your clothes." Owen was dressed in knee-length pants and a loose-fitting sailcloth shirt that seemed to add twenty pounds to his slender frame.

"Thank you, Sir."

"Lieutenant Owen has made some remarkable observations today, Captain," said Collier. "Perhaps you would tell the Captain what it was that earned you a promotion."

"Of course, Sir," said Owen, nervously. "I came on the dawn watch and noticed that the French ship was sinking, Captain."

"Go on, Lieutenant Owen," said Collier.

"Well Sir, the ship was four, or five planks deeper in the water in the space of twenty minutes. Then suddenly it all stopped and the crews began pumping."

Morgan took a gulp from his mug and said, "What do you think it all means, Lieutenant?"

"I think the Frenchies are letting water in deliberately, Sir."

"Yes, but why?"

"I can only speculate, Sir, but in conjunction with other observations, I believe the Frenchies are trying to make her seem undesirable."

Morgan slipped off his boots and placed his foot on the table. "Caleb," Morgan shouted.

"Sir," said Caleb poking his head in the door.

"Fetch the Ship's Surgeon, if you please." Caleb departed silently. "Lieutenant, why do I keep feeling that I have to drag information out of you? Just gather up your bullocks and tell me what you think. This is not the Inquisition."

"I will do the best I can, Sir," said Owen, whose mind went totally blank.

"Lieutenant Owen, please proceed," said Morgan in a bored voice. Collier nodded to the young lieutenant, as if to say, "You are among friends."

"Think of the water, Sir. The French ship let in about 20,000 gallons of water in about twenty minutes. Then it suddenly stopped. How can that be?" Browne appeared at the threshold and listened. "That amounts to 1,000 gallons in a minute's time. That works out to 16 gallons per second, Sir. Suddenly, it all stops. Why? How?" Collier was impressed by the line of reasoning, which had gone considerably farther than the simple observations Owen had shared with him on deck. "The only logical conclusion is that the Frenchies have deliberately made one or more holes in their hull and have complete control of its flow."

The conversation stopped as Browne entered the cabin and inspected Morgan's foot. "Hmm," was all he said and then departed.

"Please continue, Lieutenant," said Morgan.

"Well, Sir, I noticed that as you approached the French ship two men appeared on the starboard rail and began vomiting. Once you were out of sight, the men went below decks. Nobody has vomited over the side since, Sir."

"Commander?"

"The Lieutenant's logic is captivating, Captain," said Collier. "I observed the same theatre as Mr. Owen and I can think of no other explanation."

Browne appeared with two cups of colchicine tea. Browne handed Morgan a mug of tea.

"I think that I may be able to shed some light on the vomiting," said Browne. "With the assistance of your wine cellar, I was able to coax their surgeon to give up some meaningful information. He slipped up and said, 'tartar of emetic.' That would certainly account for the vomiting."

"Gentlemen, thank you for your insight," said Morgan. "Commander, a word." The others cleared out of the cabin hastily. Morgan downed half a mug of tea and then limped over to his keg and filled the mug with rum. "Help yourself, Collier."

Collier selected a clear glass from the cabinet and filled it to the rim with the tan-colodred rum and then joined Morgan at the table. In the silence both men unwound after the day's events, nursing their rum, glad to have a short rest. From experience, Collier knew that Morgan was hatching a plan and that it would be unwise to interrupt him. So Collier studied Morgan's toe, that was propped up on the table. It didn't look too bad this time, thank God. Morgan pulled himself back into the present and took a gulp from his mug.

"What are your thoughts about the French ship?"

"I expect they are the same as yours, Captain," said Collier, who could never bring himself to call Morgan, "Harry." "We should take her tonight after sunset."

"Go ahead and organize it. I would suggest sending orders to the Captains of our four biggest ships soon, because we only have two hours to play with. The nature of the mission is to be kept confidential until the launches are in the water. Send my launch with six, or eight Buccaneers, *no Marines this time!* What do you think about Owen commanding the launch?"

"I was going to suggest it, Captain. The beauty of the plan is that the Frenchies are anchored directly in front of the pig roast. There will be dozens of boats surrounding them all night, carting men and supplies back and forth."

"Just be sure that the men are sober and that they get to their guns quickly, because I don't want to have my cabin blown apart in the melee."

"Consider it done, Captain. Will there be anything else?"

"Yes. Have their officers thrown in our brig when they come aboard."

"I will see to it personally, Captain. Dark thirty."

"Dark thirty, Commander."

Pocket watches in the seventeenth century were notoriously inaccurate and could gain or loose more than an hour in a twenty-four hour period. Every watch would have a slightly different reading than all of the others and so there was no point in synchronizing them, because in a few hours they would all be different again. However, the watches were reasonably accurate over short periods of time. Virtually everyone could agree on when the sun touched the horizon and then it became a simple matter to add thirty minutes to whatever time showed on the face of the watch.

Morgan stretched his arm across the table and picked up the second mug of tea. He could already feel the effects of the first cup as the stabbing pain began to subside, but he knew what the night had in store. He downed the mug and limped back to his keg and filled the mug half full of rum. Better take it slow, he thought.

"Caleb!" he shouted.

"Sir?" said Caleb, practically jumping back in the room. Good, thought Morgan, he hasn't had a chance to blab anything to the crew.

"I will have my bath now."

CHAPTER 6

The smells coming from the galley stoves were intoxicating as the other ship's Captains began to arrive aboard the *Oxford*. One by one the launches tied up beside the *Oxford* and the Captains climbed up the tortuous hemp ladders, while the boson played Captain's pipes. Unlike Morgan, the other Buccaneer Captains generally got a kick out of the English salute. There were two fiddlers on deck dueling each other much to the delight of the evening watch. The rest of the crew was ashore dancing in front of a huge bon fire. Morgan emerged from his cabin cleaned and spotless, and walked to the port deck, where the Captains were being welcomed. "Welcome aboard, Captain," he said countless times, but he kept hearing gunshots from the beach. Finally in exasperation, he walked over to an assemblage of Midshipmen on the fore deck and selected one with a telescope.

"May I?" said Morgan as he jerked the telescope from the Midshipman's hands. He glanced at the beach and was astonished to see two ship's cannon being dragged in the sand in front of the bon fire. It appeared to be a contest of some sort. Four men were tethered to each cannon and then a pistol would sound and the teams would pull for all they were worth for approximately fifty paces. The winners would unleash themselves and raise their arms in victory. Then they were handed large mugs of rum, which they downed without stopping. "I'll be damned," said Morgan under his breath. It was sunset and he looked at his watch.

"Thank you," said Morgan as he handed back the telescope.

Morgan walked back to the reception line and saw Collier doing the honors.

Silently, Lieutenant Owen slipped over the rope ladder on the starboard side of the *Oxford*, joining eight other heavily armed companions in the Captain's launch.

"Captain Kessenger, welcome aboard," said Collier with pipes blaring. Kessenger caught Morgan's eye and both men smiled. Morgan whispered in Collier's ear, "Who authorized the cannons on the beach?"

"Captain Balfor, welcome aboard. I trust your manhood remains intact." Balfor smiled and nodded at Collier as Captain's pipes played again. Balfor was too drunk for word play, but he did manage to keep his balance. Collier moved closer to Morgan. "I did, Captain. The men asked if they could have two cannons on the beach to do tests of strength. I agreed to let them do it, but in return, they had to point the cannons at the cliffs and fire one shot each at dark thirty."

"Impressive, Commander," said Morgan, smiling from ear to ear.

"Welcome aboard, Captain Ruppert," said Collier, who waited for the two officers who accompanied Ruppert, and then led them to a group of four Buccaneers with pistols drawn and cocked. The Buccaneers led the three men down the companionway, but as he began his descent, Tarrante glanced back at Collier and gave him a look that raised the hair on Collier's neck. It was the stuff that dreams are made of. Bad dreams.

Jones sent up dish after dish of delicious appetizers from the galley. First it was garlic puffballs. The Buccaneers who had driven the cows over the cliffs had gone inland a fair distance and discovered hundreds of fist-sized puffball mushrooms, which were white and meaty inside. They had also brought back fresh-water snails that Jones had steamed in a wine sauce and placed back in the shells. What an irony, thought Morgan as he bit into one of them.

Collier began leading the fleet Captains into Morgan's cabin, where they were seated, tightly packed, at the Captain's table. The last to enter was Morgan himself. Collier urged him toward his seat and looked at his watch.

"Ten minutes, and counting, Captain," said Collier, looking at his watch.

Ruppert sat on the floor of the small cell, unable to comprehend what had happened. Tarrante, on the other hand, was on the offensive in the oppressive darkness. He checked the riveted thick iron strips that enveloped them for signs of weakness, but could find none. The door was vulnerable, but only with a large pry bar. There was none in sight. Their only hope was the guard at the top of the companionway, who was listening to the fiddlers on deck. Tarrante had noticed the guard's smell on the way in and had guessed that the man had been drinking all day.

"How is your English, Rene?" whispered Tarrante to the third man of their company.

"I can make myself understood, but I would starve as a translator."

"That will be good enough. Here is what we need to do." Tarrante explained his plan to Rene and then told Captain Ruppert to stay out of the way, or Tarrante would beat him senseless. Rene took his position in front of the door with his legs spread wide. Tarrante was directly behind him on hands and knees, ready to pounce.

"English, I need rum," said Rene. There was no response.

"English, I need rum!" shouted Rene. The Buccaneer at the top of the stairs turned his attention to the brig below deck and began to descend the stairs.

"English, please, I need rum." The Buccaneer held a mug in his hand and raised it as he approached the cell.

"What's it worth to ya, eh?" said the jailer in a cocky tone.

"I have eight Reales." That got the jailer's attention. Two weeks pay for a mug of cheap rum.

"Show me," said the jailer. Rene held the coin in his hand and put his arm out through one of the six-inch holes. The jailer approached, but Rene pulled his arm back quickly.

"First rum," said Rene.

"Not on your life, Frenchie. Toss the coin out first." It was an impasse. Rene *had* to draw the jailer in.

"En meme temps," said Rene, unable to come up with the English words.

There was a pause and Ruppert blurted out from the back of the cell, "At same time." The jailer nodded his head and slowly approached the cell with his mug extended. Rene shot his hand through a higher opening this time, forcing the jailer a few inches closer. All that Rene had to do was grab hold of the jailer's mug-hand and pull it inside the cell. Rene had been holding his own arm back about three inches, so that when the jailer extended his arm toward the cell, Rene lunged forward and grabbed the jailer's right wrist and pulled for all he was worth. The mug clanged on the metal door and Tarrante bolted upward between Rene's legs. Rene was thrown to the left violently, but managed to keep hold of the jailer's arm, which was now completely inside the cell up to the arm pit. Tarrante thrust one of his massive arms through an opening at waist high, the other at chest high. He grabbed the jailer's clothing with animal force and gave out a guttural groan as he jerked back, smashing the jailer's face against the metal door. The jailer's knees gave out and there was a sickening pop as his shoulder dislocated. Rene felt like he was going to vomit, but he continued to hold the jailer's arm. Tarrante pushed the jailer away from the cell door and pulled him back into it with a violent burst. It was hard to tell if the cracking noises were the bones in the jailer's face, or his neck.

Tarrante rifled through the jailer's pockets until he found the keys. In a few seconds they were free from the cell. Captain Ruppert and Rene ran toward the stairs. Ruppert looked back to see where Tarrante was and saw him picking up a small oil lamp. Ruppert was stunned as he saw Tarrante descending another flight of stairs deep into the heart of the *Oxford*.

They were halfway up the companionway when Ruppert said, "He is going to blow the magazine. Get on deck and jump in the water." Just then there was a loud explosion and Ruppert stopped and held his head. But then he realized it was cannon fire in the distance. Rene was now several steps ahead of him. Rene burst out of the companionway with such ferocity that an alert Buccaneer challenged him to stop. Rene kept running and took a ball in his back just before he made it to the rail. Ruppert waited at the top of the stairs until the crew converged on the lifeless body. There was another cannon shot and while everybody's attention was drawn to the shore, Ruppert walked slowly to the stern of the *Oxford* and dove over the side.

The chink of the grappling hook was partially masked by the sound of the second cannon fire on the beach. Owen's man had landed the hook beautifully on the starboard side of the aft rail. Owen's hands were sweating and he was grateful for the knots tied at one-foot intervals. He made it to the top and signaled the seven other men to climb. The hook from another launch had been thrown widely and landed with a metallic clank just an inch away from Owen's foot. Owen picked up the grappling hook and placed it to the port side of the stern rail directly above the boat that had thrown it.

"You're set," he whispered down to them. "Climb!" Owen kept low and looked forward to see if the Frenchies had posted sentries. He could see none. All of the French crew appeared to be gathered on the bow of the ship, watching the festivities on shore. Owen could see other Buccaneers climbing up the hemp netting amidships, keeping low. The men from his launch had all made it up to the aft deck. He ordered four of them to locate the ship's cannons and stand guard over them. From the other launch, he ordered two men to go below and look for stragglers. The remainder moved forward slowly toward the group of Buccaneers assembled amidships.

There was a musket shot and then Owen heard a loud splash coming from the direction of the *Oxford*, but there was not enough light to see what it was. He pushed forward silently with his men. Suddenly, there were two massive explosions, separated by about a half a second. The first was big enough to rattle the French ship, but the second was impossible to comprehend. The *Oxford* had been blown to pieces and everybody on the ship *had* to be dead. In a few moments debris began raining down on them. The Buccaneers gave up all pretense of secrecy and congregated on the poop deck. Nobody said a word. Finally Owen, the youngest man there, took charge.

"Men, we need this ship now more than ever. Let's take her for the Captain!" Owen cocked his only pistol and raised his cutlass. He and the other men ran en-mass toward the drunk Frenchmen on the bow of the ship. There were no shots fired, no limbs severed. The French knew they were out-manned and simply surrendered. A hale of debris started to rain down on the men and everybody ran for cover. Some of the wood debris was still aflame and it became like a scene from hell. Lieutenant Owen issued orders for a bucket brigade to be formed and directed the remaining men to shackle the prisoners and throw them into the hold of the ship.

Owen peeked his head out of the companionway and surveyed the deck. There were several small fires on deck, but what caught his attention was the mainsail tied to the top of the mizzenmast. The amount of debris falling was substantially reduced now and it was time to act.

"Two buckets on deck now!" he shouted. The initial smoky glow of the mainsail now had flames licking upward. Seconds later two Buccaneers rushed up the stairway with their buckets in tow, heading for the beam rail, which was mercifully only six feet above the water line. As the two men pitched their buckets over-side, two more men came up the stairway and did likewise. Lieutenant Owen was directing traffic on deck and with only two buckets worth of water the mainsail was completely doused. Next, they focused on the remaining flaming wood fragments on deck. Owen climbed ten feet up the starboard ratline and surveyed the remaining canvas. He could see no glows, or flames, but he was still not satisfied.

Nevertheless, there was time for him to take a deep breath and check himself for wounds. He had heard hundreds of stories about men not realizing they were severely wounded until hours after a battle. Owen patted himself down and decided that he was not injured. He also realized that his bladder was so distended that he was going to piss his britches if he couldn't unbutton the flap on the front of his pants in the next three seconds. He fumbled with the flap buttons while hanging in the rigging, but at the very last second his plumbing made contact with the night air and the stream that burst forth almost made it over the rail. There was, of course the mid-stream involuntary shiver and the subsequent urge to paint the sky, so he let it fly. That is until a voice said, "You'd do that to one of your shipmates?" Owen looked down and saw a drenched man climbing up over the side of the ship, exhausted.

Any competent Marine architect will invariably place a ship's magazine in the center of a ship, below the waterline, where there is the greatest possible protection. The *Oxford* was designed in just such a way by the Pett family, which had been building ships for the Royal Family since the time of Henry VII. One might assume that when a magazine exploded it would wreak havoc in all directions equally. Such is not the case. The keel of a ship and the underwater portions associated with it act very much like an elongated parabolic mirror. The portions of the hull below the water line were almost impervious to the explosion. The five-inch-thick hull of the *Oxford* was supported by water, which, for practical purposes, is incompressible. So when the explosion occurred, the massive energy released was directed upward, straight upward and the hull itself was not injured. The bulkhead in Morgan's cabin also managed to deflect a substantial amount of energy upward. In fact, everyone in his cabin survived the blast. They were stunned, to be sure, but no one was mortally wounded, that is until the mizzenmast crashed down on top of the cabin. Fortunately, it was just off-center. Everyone on Morgan's side of the table was ejected into the water, alive. Those on the other side of the table were crushed by the weight of the massive pine mast.

When the explosion happened, Morgan reflexively took in a deep breath. Unfortunately, the air he breathed in was searingly hot and full of sulfur. When the shock wave hit a fraction of a second later, it blew him out of the cabin, and also knocked the wind out of him, saving the deep parts of his lungs as he exhaled forcefully. The explosion also temporarily blinded him and deafened him. The flash burns on his face were quenched when he entered the water less than a second later. He opened his eyes and swam with every ounce of strength he had toward the hazy orange light on the surface. There had been a time not so long ago, when he too had been jumping from the yardarms of tall ships, crashing deep into the water and feeling the agony of his oxygen-deprived lungs as he fought his way to the surface. He could feel the drag of his clothes in the water, so he imagined himself naked, with plenty of air to spare when he reached the surface.

He came very close indeed, but he didn't quite make it. There was a dull thump as Morgan's head hit the bottom of a boat and he knew he was done for. He could feel himself ebbing away as the reptile part of his brain gained control and demanded a breath. It didn't matter what the breath consisted of; it simply *had* to breathe in. That was the point when Morgan mercifully lost consciousness.

Lieutenant Owen fastened his pants as best he could and started making his way down the hemp ratline. He arrived in time to help the exhausted Buccaneer safely on to the deck. Suddenly, he heard voices coming from the water below and realized there were more survivors. How in God's name could anybody have survived that explosion? He wanted desperately to act, but he was not sure what to do. One thing was for sure; he had neglected to do something more important than attend to the survivors in the water. Then it came to him; "fire in the sailcloth!" There were also the prisoners to deal with. He wanted desperately to give orders to somebody who would have them carried out, but there was no chain of command. Just then, two of the bucket men happened by to offer assistance.

"You two, climb to the top of the masts and check for fire in the canvas." Owen scanned the deck for other men, but found none, so he ran to the open aft hatch and yelled, "I need every available man on deck! There are survivors in the water!" Men started pouring out of the hatchway like ants defending their colony. Owen saw one of the *Oxford's* carpenters and said under his breath, "how the hell did he end up here?" Cummings was in his mid-fifties and sported a long gray ponytail. He walked with a pronounced limp, but was energetic. Owen took him aside.

"Mr. Cummings, I will need you here. I am placing you in command of the guard below. Keep four men with you and have them sleep in two-hour shifts. I want you to mix some creosote with sand and jam the shackle locks. Give the prisoners as much rum as they can drink. We need to keep them down for the night." Cummings eyes lit up.

"'Appy to oblige, Sir."

"Thank you Mr. Cummings. Please go below and send up any men you can spare." With that, Owen ran to the beam rail and looked over the side. There were six men in the launch below.

"Christ!" he said aloud. "Belay that! Do not cast off!" He screamed. The men in the launch looked up at him uncomprehending. Owen called down, "We need two men per launch to make room for survivors. There are five launches tied up to this boat. Spread the men out!" They seemed to understand and Owen directed his attention to the men in the rigging. They were climbing down, slowly. If they had spotted a fire, they would be sprinting down the lines, thought Owen.

Suddenly it dawned on him. I am playing bloody chess! Trying to stay three moves ahead of my opponent! Owen smiled at the revelation and shook his head in disbelief. Then there was the horror of the stories he had heard about shipboard explosions. Men impaled with everything from slivers to yardarms. "Christ, what are we going to do with the survivors," he said aloud. "How many are there?"

Five more men appeared on deck and approached Lieutenant Owen for orders. He was temporarily paralyzed, as if in a fog. Tears welled up in his eyes as he saw the belly of the *Oxford* rising up in flames. He could plainly see the surface of the water between where he stood and the *Oxford*'s funeral pyre, and he recognized dozens of men clinging to debris in the orange light. From somewhere deep within his brain there was a voice that said, "Three moves ahead!"

Owen did a quick survey of the men before him and chose the most promising of them for his next move.

"The four of you find launches tied up to this ship. Two men per launch. Go to the far side of the *Oxford* and look for survivors. You," he pointed to a familiar face he could not identify, "remain here." The four men scattered. Owen addressed the man he had kept behind.

"Once the fire on the *Oxford* goes out we are going to need light. Take charge of the two men in the rigging and round up as many lanterns as you can. Scour the ship, if you have to, but get me some light."

Lieutenant Kessenger had his arms over one of *Oxford*'s yardarms that was floating in the water midway between the burning hulk and the *Cor Valant*. He had a high-pitched ringing in his ears, which made communication with the other men beside him impossible. He patiently ran his fingertips over his face trying to locate small pieces of glass that had embedded themselves in his skin during the explosion. In the red glow he smiled like a mad man, amazed that he was still alive. He noticed a dull thud in the yardarm and felt something brush past his thigh. He reached down in the water and felt cloth. He tugged on it and realized it was a man, who had apparently hit his head on the yardarm while surfacing. He tapped the man next to him on the shoulder and pointed down to the coat he had pulled above the surface. The man was exhausted, but seemed eager to help. Together, they hoisted the body between them up on the yardarm, first to the chest. Then by rolling the yardarm, they managed to place it directly in the abdomen. The other men grumbled as they were knocked off the yardarm, one by one.

Kessenger hoisted himself up next to the unconscious body and slapped it on the back. Then he grabbed hold of the man's hair and yanked backward, insuring that if the man took a breath, it would be air and not water that entered his lungs. A violent wrenching followed, then there were tentative gasps, followed by more wrenching. Finally, there were perhaps five deep breaths and then the man went limp.

The stern portion of the *Oxford*, which carried the bulk of what cargo remained, suddenly dropped into the water then dragged in the remainder of the intact hull with her. In less than thirty seconds she was gone. She had been an elegant lady and everyone who witnessed her death felt a sense of irreparable loss. For a brief time there was only blackness and men were crying as they clung to the only portions of her that remained, in the warm waters, just to the south of Hispanola.

CHAPTER 7

Captain Ruppert muscled his way up out of the water into one of the launches tied up to the stern of his ship, the *Cor Valant*. He rested momentarily and then grabbed the base of the transom porthole of his aft cabin. He hoisted himself up and slid through the small porthole. Moments later, two Buccaneers shimmied down the bowline of the launch and untied her. Ruppert remained absolutely silent in his cabin until the Buccaneers rowed the launch away.

Ruppert had been formulating a plan as he swam from the *Oxford* to the *Cor Valant*. There was no question in his mind about what Morgan had planned for him; trial for piracy in Port Royal and then a public hanging. Tarrante had realized the same thing, of course, which was why Ruppert was in the water now, contemplating his tenuous future. Still, he reasoned that there were a number of things he might be able to do in order to save his own skin.

The most immediate thing was to get rid of the drenched formal clothes he was wearing and change into something that would help him blend in with the Buccaneers. He opened his cabin door a crack so that he could hear if someone was approaching. He quickly stripped off his clothes and put on his most casual knee-length pants along with a simple white cotton shirt. In the darkness, he felt around his nightstand and located two loaded pistols. Next, he got down on his hands and knees and reached deep into the nightstand until he located a hidden compartment that contained a hundred gold Duchats in a felt bag with a draw string. He placed the bag into his right front pocket. The bag weighed a little over four pounds and, coupled with the weight of his pistols, it would become a major liability if he had to swim ashore.

Ruppert noticed that the light coming through his cabin door was becoming progressively brighter. He peeked outside and saw Buccaneers tying lamps in the rigging of the yardarms. He knew that he would have no difficulty getting from his cabin to the ship's hold, lights, or not. In fact, this new development meant that there would soon be hundreds of people on deck tending to the wounded. Certainly everyone who knew him had been killed when the *Oxford* exploded. With any luck, he should be able to move about as he pleased. He felt around the forward bulkhead until he found his keys. There was a small chance that he could free what remained of his crew and overpower the Buccaneers. He would then be in control of the biggest ship in this anchorage.

Before he left his cabin, Ruppert tied his hair in a ponytail and unhooked the lamp that hung in the center beam above his head. He walked confidently along the deck near the port rail, periodically glancing over the side. He grabbed a belaying pin and placed it in his shirt. He looked to his right and saw that injured men were being hauled up over the rail in an improvised sling. The injured men were being placed on thick layers of sailcloth and Ruppert wondered where it had come from. He looked up at the rigging above him and realized that the lower yardarms had been stripped to make beds for the wounded.

"We are fucked," said Ruppert softly, realizing immediately that his ship could not be spirited away without sails. He simply shrugged his shoulders and kept walking. The next thing that occurred to Ruppert was that if he could free his crew, they could probably overpower another boat. There were twenty to choose from. They would all be lightly manned, as most of their crews would be engaged in recovery operations. Ruppert looked over the side and saw his launch with the sail intact. She could carry four men on a calm day, but he had twelve men to look after. She would be the "fall back" option, if he could not free his men.

Silently, Ruppert descended the stairs in the companionway and waited for his eyes to adjust to the dim light. In the distance he could make out his crewmen who were shackled by their wrists. One man was raising a demijohn to his lips for a drink, while the others appeared to be passed-out. Ruppert moved closer, looking for a guard. He slipped the belaying pin out of his shirt and noticed one of his men sitting upright playing with the lock on one of his shackles. It was O' Donte, with a large bandage on his head. Ruppert moved toward a stack of oak barrels lashed to the lower deck. The flurry of activity on deck muffled the creaking boards beneath his feet. Ruppert moved to the edge of the barrels so that he could see O' Donte. One of his men stirred and sat up to take another draw on the demijohn in front of him. There was the sound of chains rattling and O' Donte stopped fiddling with his shackles and pretended to be asleep.

Finally, O' Donte opened his eyes and began working on his shackles again. He looked up regularly, directly at the barrels. Ruppert caught O' Donte's attention and raised his belaying pin. O' Donte smiled and looked directly at the guard on the far side of the barrels. O' Donte raised one finger and then leaned his head to the side and closed his eyes. When their eyes met again, Ruppert raised one finger and tilted his head with his eyes closed. Ruppert looked at O' Donte, who then nodded his head.

Ruppert moved forward and looked around the front side of the barrels, then pulled back. The guard was sitting up against the barrels with a musket in his lap, which was not cocked. There was, however, a bayonet fixed to the musket pointed in

Ruppert's direction. Ruppert moved back behind the barrels and began his attack from the other side. He raised the belaying pin and took two steps. There was a dull thud and then the guard went limp. Ruppert pulled out his set of keys and walked over to O' Donte.

"Nice of you to join us, Captain," whispered O' Donte.

"It looks like one hell of a party. I will have you out of here in no time," said Ruppert selecting a key from his ring.

"Don't bother, they have plugged the locks with creosote. I have gotten one of the hinge pins loose on this shackle. Take a look." Ruppert's forty-year-old eyes would not cooperate. He went back to center of the hold and grabbed the lamp. O' Donte had managed to drive the hinge pin on one of his shackles about halfway out. The other pin seemed solid. Ruppert picked up the lamp and began rummaging through a tool chest on the other side of the cargo hold. He brought back a mallet and a rusted steel nail.

"Hold the shackle right on the edge of this board." Ruppert raised the mallet and hit the head of the nail. There was a metallic click as the shackle snapped open and fell on the deck. "Let's try the other one." Two strikes and the other shackle opened. Ruppert picked up the pieces and examined them.

"Who made these things?" whispered Ruppert.

"I believe they are Spanish."

"It figures," said Ruppert. "Let's get out of here." One of the drunken sailors suddenly sat up.

"Captain, you have come to rescue us," he shouted. Without a word, Ruppert raised the belaying pin and knocked the man senseless. Ruppert and O' Donte waited silently to see if the outburst had attracted any attention. Apparently, it had not.

The two men ascended the stairs and surveyed the deck. There were about thirty injured men on the deck and there were still men being pulled up over the side. Ruppert glanced over the rail to see if his boat was still there and was delighted to see a two-masted bugalet, side-tied to the *Cor Valant*. Ruppert nudged O' Donte and pointed to the boat. It would be a rough go, but two men could handle her if they used the fore sails alone. The pair walked briskly toward the bugalet and began to climb over the side.

"It's the Captain," a man shouted in the distance. Ruppert froze. He turned to see what was coming his way, but all hands were on the other rail as Henry Morgan was pulled out of the water. Ruppert and O' Donte slipped quietly over the side and lowered themselves onto the deck of the bugalet. There was not a soul on board, so Ruppert raised the fore sail as O' Donte untied the bowline. The westerly trade wind was brisk and pushed them out of harm's way in less than a minute.

CHAPTER 8

"I'll need a lamp," said Browne as he kneeled down to get a better look at Morgan. The men were slipping the sling from underneath Morgan, who lay motionless on the wooden deck. Several lamps arrived and Browne placed his ear directly in front of Morgan's lips. There was air moving. Browne ripped open Morgan's shirt and noticed a lacy purple rash on the abdomen and chest.

"Shit," said Browne, "livedo reticularis. I'll need four men." Livido reticularis is an ominous sign that can signal impending death. Fresh corpses always have livido because purple, oxygen-starved red blood cells accumulate in the capillaries and can be seen through the skin.

"Here, Sir. What are your orders?" Browne looked up and realized that thirty men had assembled to watch the fate of their Captain ensue.

"Drag him further back and place him on that sail," Browne motioned with his hand. Once there, Browne said, "Strip him naked. We have to check him for wounds. You there," he said to a tall man who seemed eager to help, "go below to the aft cabin and find some clothes…something that doesn't smell bad."

Browne watched carefully as his Captain was undressed, all the while looking for wounds and then it dawned on him; there were three dozen sailors watching what was happening.

"You men there," he fanned ten fingers at them. "Go and help the others. We have plenty of men here." There was no response. "Do it now!" screamed Browne and the men broke up instantly. Browne's teeth began chattering. He could never remember being this cold. He had only been in the water for twenty minutes, or so. How could this be happening?

"These are tropical fochin' waters," he said, teeth chattering away. "At least I won't have to deal with that asshole Marine sergeant."

"I am sorry Sir, I could not understand you," said the midshipman beside him.

"Nothing Lieutenant. Do you suppose you could arrange a team to go below and find blankets…anything to keep us warm?" Browne was struggling against a tremendous urge to get into a fetal position on the deck.

"Of course, Sir!"

Browne struggled to remain in control. Now his arms and legs began to chatter. He tried desperately to keep an eye on Morgan, but he had lost control of his body. He sat on the deck and shivered uncontrollably. From a time long ago, Browne remembered his mother stripping off his clothes after he had fallen through the ice in a small lake behind their house in Wales. He had fought briefly and then surrendered as the warm wool blanket enveloped his body.

"Lieutenant," he whispered. "See that all the men who were in the water are stripped and given blankets."

"Aye, Sir," said Lieutenant Owen. Browne lapsed into unconsciousness and started convulsing.

"Mr. Jenkins! Go below and fire up the galley stove. You men there, take Doctor Browne down to the galley and see that he is stripped and given blankets. Keep him near the stove." Owen then turned his attention to Morgan. There were no major wounds that he could see, so he had him wrapped in blankets and taken to the galley with Browne.

Owen ran below decks to see just how big the galley actually was. Jenkins was standing in front of the stove, which he had filled with kindling. He had a powder horn on a table beside the stove and he would pour a small amount of gunpowder in his hand and then toss it into the firebox. A huge flame would then roar in the stove and spread more fire to the kindling. It was already getting very warm.

"Not to worry, Sir, she's roarin' now!" said Jenkins.

"Nice work Mr. Jenkins," said Owen, who was visibly relieved when Jenkins put the cork back in the powder horn. Owen sized up the galley, which was small by any standards, and figured that six more men could be fit into the room if they were lying down, perhaps fourteen more if they were sitting up. Owen looked up and saw four men bringing Browne through the aft doorway. They set him on the floor, sailcloth beneath him. Thankfully, his convulsions had stopped.

Back on deck, Owen did a quick survey of the casualties. There were forty two in all, a few with missing limbs, at least three dead, and the rest seemed to have minor injuries, but all were suffering from hypothermia in the eighty degree trade wind. Owen shook his head in disbelief as the sweat rolled off his forehead. Just then the freckled Lieutenant Thatcher tugged on Owen's sleeve.

"I was on shore at the pig roast. I came as quickly as I could. What happened?"

"Focus on now. We can talk about what happened for the rest of our lives, but there are men dying here. Gather up a team and go below and find some clothes. Strip the prisoners if you have to, but get some dry clothes up here." Thatcher hesitated, uncomprehending. "I will explain later, just get to it!" said Owen in an exasperated tone. Thatcher gathered up a dozen men and went below without a word.

Owen was irritated by what he saw on deck. There were dozens of men wandering around watching their shipmates die. He decided to put them to work.

"You men there, we need your help!" The men surged forward. "I want two men with each injured man. If their clothes are wet, you must strip them bare. You will find some blankets by the fo'castle. Wrap them up. If they can walk, run them through the galley. Form a que."

Owen ran below decks to the galley again. He noticed that the stove was red hot on top.

"Mr. Jenkins, please find someone else to attend to the stove. I need you for more important things. We are going to usher injured men into this hell hole you have created to warm them up. Crowd as many men in the galley as you can and give them five minutes, or so and then bring in the next group. Understood?"

"Perfectly, Sir."

Owen looked down at Morgan, who stared vacantly back at him without any expression on his face. "At least he is alive," whispered Owen, who was sweating profusely. Morgan's color had gone from purple to a lobster pink. His greedy skin was soaking up heat and delivering it to the interior of his body.

The first group of walking-frozen entered the galley and Owen was literally pushed out of the door on the fore side of the cabin. Owen stared, uncomprehending. Every man in the room was wrapped in a blanket, but they shivered uncontrollably and their teeth chattered. Doctor Browne had been right. Owen looked back to check on Browne, but there were twenty men in blankets blocking his line of sight.

The deck was still littered with bodies. Some were undoubtedly dead, but surely some were alive and needed warmth to survive. Owen tried to think about what he should do, but he was tired and his mind refused to focus and instead went to the molasses cookies that his grandmother had baked for him when he was a child. Owen yawned several times, but he forced himself to remain awake. Thatcher, who was coming into his own because he was normally awake at this time of night, sat down beside Owen, hoping that he could pry some information out of Owen about the explosion.

"I cannot make my brain work. You are going to have to take over for a couple of hours," said Owen. It was not a suggestion; it was a command.

"I will do my best," said Thatcher who was terrified and excited at the same time. "What should I do?"

"The men on deck are going to die if they are not warmed up. Figure out a way to keep them dry and warm them up," said Owen, who then closed his eyes and went to sleep.

Thatcher was terrified and had never felt more alone in his life. He shook Owen, but there was no response. "I have to think," he said to himself. Heat. Where is there heat on this boat? The galley! Thatcher dashed twenty steps over to the galley and saw a group of men being led inside and another group departing. He saw the red-hot stovetop and realized that Owen had already thought of this option. He leaned up against the cabin house that stood four feet above the deck and covered the galley. Where else is there heat produced on a boat? His backside was up against a window that acted as a solar light source for the galley and he was uncomfortable. "Hot! Heat! This is heat." He considered tying men to the side of the cabin, but quickly rejected the idea. He felt the top of the cabin house and it was uncomfortably warm. "That's it!" he shouted. He surveyed the top of the cabin and figured he could put twenty to thirty men on top, if they were tightly packed. He ran out to the fore deck and saw at least twenty uninjured men tending to the wounded.

"Men, I want you to form a party and transport the injured men to the top of the galley cabin. Keep them on the sails so that they will not be burned. If a man is dead, leave him on the deck." Thatcher's voice was uneven and anything but compelling. The men hesitated, even though Thatcher had rank on them. Thatcher sensed the hesitation and was enraged by it and stiffened.

From somewhere deep inside of him came an animal command, "Do it now, damn you!" Then came a flurry of activity, with a body being placed on the roof over the galley every thirty seconds. Thatcher wanted to make sure that he was doing the right thing and so he went to the galley roof and placed his hand on an unoccupied spot directly over the galley stove. He pulled it back immediately as the molten tar used to seal the space between planks scorched a patch of skin on the heel of his hand.

"Carr...ist!" he shouted, shaking his hand. Just then, a man was placed on the roof in front of him and there was just enough light to see that the man's jaw and nose had been blown off. Tears welled up in Thatcher's eyes and he wanted to stop...stop everything, but then the pain in his hand was suddenly gone and he regained control of his fears.

"Men! Make sure that every man is placed on at least four layers of sail cloth. Every man needs to be turned every five minutes, or so. Sing a short ditty and turn your man." Thatcher moved to other parts of the galley roof and found that they were considerably cooler than the place he had burned his hand.

Morgan opened his eyes and stared ahead. He was under the table in the galley and all that he could see were bare feet and legs walking past him. "Where the hell am I?" he mumbled. He was drenched in sweat and threw off his blanket. He attempted to sit up, but he struck his head on the table above him and went into a hideous coughing spasm. The men walking past him paid no attention. Finally the coughing subsided, but not before he had emptied the contents of his lungs and stomach on to the floor. He sat up again, slowly this time, struggling for breath. Gradually he relaxed and his breathing returned to normal. The bare legs continued to pass by and he was confused. The thought occurred to him that he had died and gone to hell. God knows it is hot enough, he thought. He noticed movement under a table opposite him, as he struggled to see through the endless legs in front of him. A man sat up and Morgan realized it was Browne, who appeared dazed.

There was a break in the sea of legs in front of him and Morgan dashed out on hands and knees to the other table. He was winded when he got there, after traversing perhaps eight feet. Then came another coughing fit, not as bad as the previous one, but it was enough to make him vomit again. Finally the coughing stopped, and Morgan sat upright and slowly caught his breath. Browne began gently slapping him on the back, but didn't say a word. Morgan turned around and looked Browne squarely in the eyes and smiled. Browne smiled back and nodded his head, as if to say, "Everything is all right."

"Do you have any idea where we are?" whispered Morgan. Browne seemed not to hear the question; his tongue was darting back and forth in his mouth pushing his cheeks out, as though a bumble bee was trapped inside, trying to get out.

Browne looked up at Morgan and said, "I've bitten the hell out of my tongue. Must have had a fit!"

"Sorry about your tongue, but do you have any idea where we are? Or why men keep running through here in blankets?"

"What is the last thing you remember?" said Browne. Morgan hesitated before speaking.

"I remember Jones bringing me a mug of tea and then a very bright light. Then I was deep in the water and I hit my head on the bottom of a boat. Can we get out of here?"

Both men were drenched in sweat as they made their way up the stairs, wisely carrying their blankets with them. Morgan was completely out of breath and had to sit down on the deck. He was seized by another coughing spasm that made him vomit, this time with streaks of blood amongst the mucus.

"Die, ya bastard," shouted Browne. It was a strange sort of humor, that only a Welshman could appreciate. In due course, the coughing fit subsided and Morgan managed a good laugh. The humor was short-lived as the two men surveyed the deck around them. A launch tied up to the bow had just unloaded its cargo of injured men and dead bodies.

"Men! Don't bother with dead bodies. We can pick them out tomorrow. Concentrate on the living! These are your shipmates and they are counting on you to be strong and vigilant!" shouted the freckle-faced Thatcher. His delivery would have been better if it had been an octave lower, but the two tired crewmen groaned and lowered themselves back into the launch, resigned to their fate.

Morgan raised his thick eyebrows and said, "Not bad for a Midshipman. Do they teach them that stuff in some Navy school?"

"Harry, he is making it up as he goes along, just like the rest of us," said Browne absently, as he surveyed the injured bodies strewn on top of the deckhouse. Despite the eighty-degree temperature, the fifteen-knot trade wind chilled Browne to the bone. His teeth were chattering and he pulled his blanket tightly over his shoulders. "We had better get below and find some clothes."

Captain Ruppert's cabin had been ransacked by the Buccaneers, who had been looking for clothes and blankets. Browne felt around in the darkness and found the bed stripped bare and the small closet completely empty. Morgan joined in the search and stumbled on a sea chest that had been overlooked. Morgan felt around inside the chest and realized it was full of winter clothes.

"Browne, try these on," said Morgan, passing along a shirt and pants. Both men topped six feet, but they managed to outfit themselves tolerably well with clothes designed for the shorter Captain Ruppert. Morgan also found a bottle of brandy in the chest and took a large gulp before passing it over to Browne.

"I am going back on deck. You should stay here and get some rest," said Browne.

"Not on your life. I am coming with you."

Lieutenant Owen felt refreshed after a brief nap. Mr. Jenkins had informed him that they were running out of kindling for the galley stove and Owen had instructed him to begin breaking apart furniture to use as fuel. Midshipman Thatcher forced himself to check on the man with the mutilated face. Mercifully, the man had died, as had most of the other men with serious injuries. Tears welled up in Thatcher's eyes as he pulled a blanket up over the dead man's face.

Morgan was out of breath at the top of the stairs. He began to cough again as Jenkins led another group of twenty men in blankets into the galley for a warm-up. The eastern sky had a reddish glow heralding the dawn of a very depressing day ahead. Morgan could feel the warmth of the galley air rising through the stairwell and he stayed there as Browne went on ahead to check on the wounded. Morgan saw Lieutenant Owen talking with one of the wounded men on top of the galley roof twenty feet ahead.

"Lieutenant Owen, report," shouted Morgan. Owen hurried over to join Morgan at the top of the stairs. The sun was just beginning to creep above the eastern horizon.

"How are you feeling, Captain?"

"I feel like a mule turd that was run-over by a carriage wheel, Lieutenant," said Morgan, who was finally able to see the carnage on deck. "How many dead?"

"Upwards of sixty, Sir. We have lost seven in the last hour. We stopped pulling bodies out of the water, so that number will be higher."

"What of my officers?"

"I was just speaking with Commander Collier, who is in good shape except for some burns on his neck and shoulders. Captain Bigford was almost cut in half by the mizzen mast. His body is over there," said Owen pointing to the fore deck. "Lieutenant Kessenger has several splinters in his groin and legs, but is otherwise unharmed. Sir, there were several men whose faces were so severely injured that I could not identify them."

"Of course, Lieutenant. See what you can do to arrange some food for the injured men on this boat. Please pass the word that all able-bodied officers are to meet here at noon today. I will also need a list of the dead and injured."

"Aye, Sir."

Tables and chairs were being set up on the aft deck of the *Cor Valant* to accommodate the officers. Nobody wanted to be below decks—not after last night. Cyrus Jones had been standing next to Morgan when the *Oxford* exploded and he was thrown out into the water without any injuries. He swam to the *Cor Valant* and found his way to the galley, which was always a place of comfort to him. His clothes were wet, but he hunkered down in fore portion of the cabin and wedged himself between a couple of barrels, where he managed to stay warm. He was grateful when Jenkins had stoked the fire in the galley. Despite the hordes of naked men wrapped in blankets being paraded through the galley throughout the night, Cyrus Jones had slept soundly. He awakened at dawn with a powerful desire to cook. He began opening cabinets one by one, occasionally letting out a spirited, "Oh, that's nice," when he found a familiar spice. He sized-up the galley stove and realized that he was going to have to be creative. Lieutenant Owen entered the galley and began a conversation with Jones.

"Mr. Jones, we have ninety injured men on deck who require food. In addition, we have approximately thirty officers who will be assembling at noon. See what you can do."

"I will need assistance, Sir."

"Tell me what you need."

"I will need four assistant cooks and adequate kindling for the stove," said Jones, who was actually hoping for two assistants. "I will also need two-hundred eggs, greens and a side of beef from the beach. We could use another galley, Sir, so as to make bread and cakes."

"I will do my best, Jones."

The rigging of the *Cor Valant* was covered with clothes that were soaking up the morning sun. Browne had completed an assessment of the wounded and made a mental note of the things he needed to attend to. Two shattered legs needed to come off and one exploded eye would have to be removed this morning. Browne was in a panic; all of his medical instruments and herbs were now at the bottom of the Caribbean Sea. O' Donte must have had some supplies, he thought. With that, he went below and began rummaging through sea chests and cabinets in the officer's quarters. Within minutes he had found a chest full of medical instruments and a locker with over a hundred types of herbs. Browne smiled as he realized that he was now better stocked than he had been aboard the *Oxford*. There was only one problem; he could not find any laudanum, or opium. It would be unbearable to amputate a leg without laudanum. He continued searching until he came upon large sea chest with a sturdy lock on the front of it. The chest was bolted to the deck and the lock held firm against Browne's improvised pry bars. He gave up and went back to the chest with the instruments. He opened the top and began placing containers of herbs in the chest and then closed it and slid it to the bottom of the stairs.

Up on deck, Browne found Lieutenant Thatcher standing next to the galley drinking coffee.

"Lieutenant, would you be so kind as to locate a carpenter and have him open the locked sea chest in the officer's quarters? There is also a sea chest at the bottom of the stairs that I would like to have brought up to the galley."

"Happy to oblige, Sir."

"By the way, you and Lieutenant Owen are to be congratulated for keeping the men warm last night. You saved a great many lives, my own and the Captain's included.

"Why thank you, Sir," said Thatcher, flushing bright red.

"Have the bodies placed on a sloop and we will go out to sea this afternoon and have a proper burial," said Commander Collier. Owen began to speak, but thought better of it. Both men stood at the starboard rail and looked to the west. There were still bodies and debris everywhere. A small boat tied up to the *Cor Valant* and the two crewmen began passing up baskets of eggs.

"Sir, this may not be the best time to bring this up. I know you are in a lot of pain with your burns and all."

"Speak your mind, Lieutenant."

"Sir, the men are stripping the dead of their gold," said Owen, hesitant to say more.

"Go on, Lieutenant."

"Well, Sir, they are cutting off fingers to get the rings off," said Owen, who was suddenly nauseated.

"*Hmm*," said Collier. "You are an officer in charge of these men. What do you plan to do about it?"

"I think we should put a stop to it, Sir."

"I agree that it is bad form, thoroughly disgusting, in fact, but what is the crime? Who are the victims?"

"The dead are the victims, Sir," said Owen vehemently.

"That is where we disagree, Lieutenant. The dead have no possessions and they have no pain. In fact they have no bodies. How can they be victims?" Owen was becoming angry and frustrated by this line of reasoning.

"What about their dignity, Sir?"

"Dignity is for the living, not the dead."

"So what you are saying, Sir, is that we are going to sit by and do nothing?"

"Lieutenant, if you think that it is wrong to cut the fingers off of dead bodies, then don't do it! Look at the broader picture. In a few hours, we are going to bury these bodies at sea. They are going to be eaten by sea creatures; everybody knows that.

Does that rob them of dignity? We are going to read from the bible and commend their souls to the deep. Will that change anything? Let's say that we placed a screen below the bodies and came back in a week. The screen would be full of gold jewelry. Would it be proper to harvest the jewelry, or should we send it to the bottom of the sea?" Owen was tired and could think of no further arguments to support his cause, so he just remained silent and watched in the distance, as the men in the launches continued to pull the bodies out of the water.

"Presents," said Browne, reaching into the sea chest in front of him. He pulled out several large flower buds and handed them over to Cyrus Jones, who smiled as he placed the buds under his nose and inhaled deeply.

"Ah, there is nothing sweeter that the smell of Indian hemp," said Jones. "You have just made my day, Sir." Jones now had five cooks assisting him in the galley. It was a good time for a rest break. Browne handed him a container full of colchicum.

"You may want to make a draught, or two for the Captain."

"Easily done, Sir," said Jones, loading his white clay pipe. He popped a broom bristle free and moved over to the stove. Jones took a deep hit and passed the pipe over to Browne.

"The way I sees it, Sir, colchicum saved me life."

"How is that, Mr. Jones?"

"Call me Cyrus, Sir. I was passing off a cup of it to the Captain when the *Oxford* went up. If I 'ad been in the galley when she went off, I would 'ave been blown to pieces. Tiny pieces." Jones re-lit the pipe.

"It is funny that you would mention that, because I had every intention of stopping by the galley and picking up a cup for the Captain myself. I had been smoking a bit of herb and completely forgot. Could you load that pipe again?" Both men began to laugh.

"If you are not in a hurry, Sir, I could fix you some breakfast."

"Actually, I *am* in a hurry. I have to go chop off a couple of legs. I never eat beforehand."

"I don't see how you do it, Sir."

"Well, first you take a knife and cut down to the bone. Then you pick up the saw..." Jones was holding his side and gasping for breath. Browne joined in and soon had to find a chair. The thing that kept them going was the looks on the faces of the five cooks, who apparently thought that both men had gone completely insane.

Browne finally regained control and went back to the sea chest. He pulled out the bone saw and headed over to the galley sink, where he took a brush and used seawater to get rid of most of the rust on the blade. He dried the blade on his pant leg and checked the teeth for sharpness with his index finger. "Hmm," he said. This caught Jones' attention and he moved closer to inspect. Browne went back to the sea chest and rummaged around until he found a file. He went back to the sink and placed the blade on the edge. He gently began filing the dull teeth, one at a time.

"If you want to be a 'two-minute-man,' you have to be able to cut through two lower leg bones in less than fifteen seconds."

"A 'two-minute-man,' Sir?"

"That's right, Cyrus. Two minutes, start to finish."

"I am no sailorman, Sir, but if you are telling me that you can take a leg off and 'ave it sowed up in two minutes...well, Sir, I would not believe it unless I seen it with me own two eyes."

"That can be arranged, Cyrus. It appears that my assistant was killed in the explosion. How would you like to be my new assistant? You can still cook, of course."

"Why, Sir, I would be delighted. When do I start?"

"In about an hour, I should think. Wait. Why not now? Here, let me show you how to sharpen this saw."

"Commander! A word, if you please," shouted Morgan, who was standing at the aft rail. Morgan had been pacing on the aft deck and was alarmed that he could only take ten steps, or so, before he became totally winded. He continued to cough up clear mucus as though his lungs were trying to flush out any remaining seawater.

"How are you feeling, Captain?" asked Collier.

"I have seen better days. Do we know how it happened?"

"Do you remember a musket shot right before the explosion?"

"Yes, now that you mention it."

"Well a few hours ago we pulled a mate out of the drink, who reported that he was the one who fired the shot. He said that one of the Frenchies came up out of the hold and ran for the side. He said that he shot the man in the back, as he was about to jump over the side. I would assume that if one man made it out of the cell, they all did. My question is, why did the Frenchie run to the side through a group of men who were sure to recognize him? Why not keep a low profile and wait for a more opportune moment? He must have known that the magazine was going to blow any second and he panicked."

"Sounds plausible," said Morgan.

"There is more. One of the Buccaneers who was attached to the boarding party, swears that he saw a man jump off the port rail of the *Oxford*, just before she blew. He had looked up because of the sound of the gunshot. Late last night, we discovered that the guard covering the Frenchie prisoners on the *Cor Valant* had had his skull caved in by what was probably a belaying pin. One of the Frenchie prisoners also died of a similar head wound. Lieutenant Owen, in a moment of pure brilliance, had the men put a mixture of sand and creosote into the shackle locks."

"Why? Why did he do that?"

"He wasn't sure how many keys there were, or where they were."

"You are absolutely right. It was a brilliant move." Morgan nodded his head in admiration.

"The plot thickens. The men found a set of wet clothes in the Captain's quarters, which we think belonged to Ruppert."

"Wait a minute, Browne and I both changed clothes there last night," said Morgan.

"We figured that out. There were three sets of clothes in that cabin. By the way, your clothes should be dry. I suggest that you change into them before the men flog your haberdasher." Morgan looked down at the cuff of his pants and realized that they were halfway up his shins.

"Actually, this is the latest Paris fashion. I think you are jealous." Collier smiled.

"Quite so. I shall instruct all of the men to follow your example. Meanwhile, one set of shackles had the hinge pin driven out with a nail. We assume that at least one Frenchie was liberated by the evil Captain Ruppert. Furthermore, Captain Bigford's boat tied up to the *Cor Valant* after the explosion. The boat has not been seen since."

"You have to love the little bastard. What are the odds that he could have pulled this off?" said Morgan.

"Slim indeed, Captain. He is the very epitome of cunning, courage, and murderous intent. Perhaps we should inform the Vatican and see about getting him canonized."

"The Vatican has never canonized a living person. Have him killed first, then inform the Vatican."

"I will attend to it presently, Captain. Have you spoken with Owen about the numbers?" Collier looked grim.

"How bad?"

"We left Port Royal with nine-hundred-twenty-nine men aboard twenty different vessels. At present, we have seven-hundred-eighty-four able-bodied seamen, ourselves included, but I still have some concerns about you. Are you absolutely certain that you have not experienced a growth spurt?" said Collier pointing down to the cuffs on Morgan's pants, that rose halfway up his shins. "It is commonly seen in men who have African lovers. Do you have an African lover, Captain?"

"How many?"

"Ninety bodies have been pulled out of the drink, Captain. We are going to have a memorial service in the afternoon on the far side of the island."

"Count me in. How many injured?"

"Seventeen men will never cruise again, but they will probably survive."

"That leaves thirty four unaccounted for. I am astounded that the number was not higher. That magazine was full to the brim. How do you account for it?"

"Over three-hundred men were on shore."

"Of course," said Morgan, rubbing his chin. "How many know the numbers?"

"Just the three of us," said Collier.

"Let's keep it that way for a while. You realize that an attack on the plate fleet is impossible now."

"Of course. But I am not the one you need to convince. I do not report to the Crown. I have not corresponded with my family in the better part of a year."

"Relax, Collier. I was not questioning your loyalty, for crissakes. I was simply pointing out that we are going to have to change tack. The *Oxford* was a major disaster and we are going to have to make up for it, somehow. What is that godawful noise?"

"I believe that Doctor Browne is attending to one of the injured men." Collier pulled out his watch and noticed water under the crystal. "It should be over within another sixty seconds, or so."

"The carpenter has opened the chest, Doctor Browne," said Lieutenant Owen, peeking his head into the galley. Browne and Jones were devouring their second plate of scrambled eggs.

"Chest? What chest?" said Browne.

"The locked chest in the officers' quarters." Browne looked puzzled.

"Yes, of course. What was in it?"

"I am not sure, Sir. It looks like tar wrapped in waxed paper." Browne's eyes lit up.

"Let's go have a look, shall we?" he said to Jones. Jones smiled, knowingly.

The sea chest was unharmed. The carpenter had been able to pick the lock. Inside the chest were dozens of neatly stacked cubes of opium, individually wrapped in waxed paper.

"My God, Sir! There must be fifty pounds here," said Jones. Browne reached down and picked a cube from the chest and placed it under his nose. He inhaled deeply and then passed the cube to Jones, who did the same. A silent smile passed between the two men. Browne placed the cube in his pocket.

"Lieutenant Owen, would you be kind enough to have this chest unbolted from here and transferred into the Captain's quarters? A new lock, or perhaps a key to the old one would be most appreciated."

"I am sure something can be arranged, Dr. Browne." Owen was getting testy. He was working on very little sleep and people kept giving him things to do, primarily because he always got them done.

"By the way Lieutenant," Owen was expecting another assignment. 'Have you had any breakfast? Why don't you have Comstock cover for you while you catch a nap?" Owen smiled and was relieved that somebody cared about how beaten up he was.

"Maybe I will, Sir. Thank you."

"No, Lieutenant Owen, thank you."

CHAPTER 9

"I would prefer to work on deck where the air is fresh and the light is bright," said Browne. "Have the table moved from the galley to the area in front of the forecastle. Have the men smoke as much opium as they can. When they have passed out, we can start. I would prefer to have men holding them down, so get some volunteers. I cannot stomach tying a man down."

"How many, Sir?" said Jones

"How many what?"

"Men, Sir."

"We have two legs and an eye."

"Not that, Sir. How many holders will we be needin'?"

"Four, or five, I suppose," said Browne. "I am going below for my instruments and the brazier. Do the other cooks know how to make fish balls, Cyrus?"

"I reckon not, Sir. Them was me own creation."

"Of course," said Browne, salivating and sorely disappointed. With that he went below.

Several mates were recruited for the task at hand and within minutes the improvised surgical suite was assembled and the patients were brought on deck in stretchers. Two men brought up the brazier and placed it on a stand down-wind from the table so that the patients would not catch on fire from the sparks that flowed out in the trade wind. Cyrus had a broom brought up from the galley and asked for some clay pipes. It was then that he realized that Browne had the opium and he went below to find him.

Cryus Jones found Browne in the galley sharpening a knife by the sink. He was using an oil stone with a fine grain, lost in his work, sweeping the blade to and fro on the glistening surface. He paused briefly and put the edge of the knife to his thumb pad. He seemed satisfied and licked the hair on his left forearm. He dragged the edge of the blade over the moistened hair and was satisfied with the bald spot that he had created. He looked up at Jones and said, "We are ready."

"Sorry, Sir, but we are *not* ready. You see, you have the opium in your pocket."

"I do?" Browne fished around in his pockets until he found the cube. "By God, you are right!"

Jones went back on deck and packed the pipes. He knew the power of opium and he had one of the mates light the pipes for the three patients. Jones instructed the mate not to inhale any smoke, but by the time the pipes had been loaded for the third time, the mate was on his back on the deck. The patients were in a light coma, but the mate managed to keep his eyes open and just smiled. Browne arrived and showed Jones how to place a tourniquet on a leg. One man was assigned to hold the wooden stake to prevent it from unwinding. Browne noted the dusky color of the broken leg and was satisfied with the tourniquet's placement and tension.

"Would someone be kind enough to summon Lieutenant Comstock," said Browne. The baby-faced Comstock was from a rich family and Browne assumed, rightly, that he had a watch.

"Doctor Browne?" said Comstock.

"Do you have a pocket chronometer, Lieutenant Comstock?" asked Browne as he placed a poker into the brazier. He then took a pair of scissors and began trimming the pant leg just beneath the tourniquet.

"I do, Doctor Browne."

"Would you do me the honor of timing my work?"

"It would be a pleasure, Doctor."

"Thank you, Lieutenant. If you could just count off five-second intervals." Comstock nodded his understanding. Browne removed several more instruments from his inherited sea chest and laid them out in the order they would be needed. "What is this man's name?" asked Browne.

"Baker, Sir," offered one of the mates.

"We will need one man to lay over Mr. Baker's hips. We will need another to bend his good leg back beneath him, so that he cannot shift his weight, then one man on each of his shoulders." The men moved into position and Browne was satisfied. "As soon as that poker is red-hot we will begin."

"What I want you to do, Cyrus, is man the poker. When I cut through the skin you will notice some spots that are seeping blood, or pumping blood. Simply touch the poker to them and they will stop. Then replace the poker in the brazier. We need to keep it red-hot."

"I will do my best, Sir."

"There are three arteries that we will have to attend to; the anterior and posterior tibials and the peroneal. I used to ligate them with cotton thread and then wait a few days for them to go through putrefaction and simply pull them out, but a German surgeon taught me a trick. You can grab these small arteries with a clamp and pull until you tear them and they snap back into the muscle. This stops the bleeding and does not result in putrefaction." Mates began collecting on the aft deck to watch the show.

Jones looked down at the horribly disfigured lower leg. The normally straight tibia was wavy in its last half and the foot pointed directly to the side, as if it had been attached to a different human being. The toes were black—dry gangrene. Browne checked the man's teeth and saw that they were sound. He instructed one of the mates to put a wooden bite-block into Baker's mouth.

"Lieutenant Comstock, we will begin on your mark," said Browne. "Men, hold the leg up so that I can make my first cut on the back of the leg." Browne placed his twelve-inch knife on the surface of Baker's calf so that he could sever it in one quick up-stroke.

"Ten seconds. Five, four, three, two, go!"

Baker struggled against the men holding his shoulders and exhaled as he took his wrath out on the bite block. Browne made the initial cut through the calf muscles and then made deep longitudinal cuts on each side of the tibia, thus freeing up the calf muscles so that they could be pulled forward over the bony stumps.

"Five seconds," said Comstock, revolted by the operation.

Browne cut through the skin over the tibia, mid-shaft, and exposed the bone. Next, he picked up an elevator, that looked like a shoe horn with a padded leather handle, and began loosening up the sheath around the bone by butting the instrument with the heel of his hand. He was able to slide the muscles and the sheath upwards about an inch and then instructed Jones to hold everything just where it was.

"Ten seconds," said Comstock, who was looking out to sea.

Browne set the elevator aside and reached for the saw. He wedged himself next to Jones, who struggled to hold the tissues up. Browne began sawing like a man possessed. Twenty passes and he was through the tibia. He re-positioned Jones and then went for the smaller fibula.

"Twenty-five seconds."

Finally, Browne was through both bones. He set the saw aside and reached for the knife. With two swipes he cut the remaining attachments and had the mates pull the amputated leg away.

"Forty-five seconds."

Browne scooped the calf flap up in his hand and placed it over tip of the exposed bones.

"You can let go of that, Jones. Get the poker ready." Browne seemed satisfied with the fit.

"Fifty-five seconds."

Browne picked up a pair of clamps.

"Loosen the tourniquet one turn." Browne dropped the calf muscle, which was twitching. He tried in vain to find the arteries, but the site was covered with blood and bone dust.

"One minute, ten seconds."

"I need a bucket of seawater, now!" shouted Browne. It was the one thing Browne had forgotten. Two mates jumped to their feet and ran for a bucket. "Loosen the tourniquet one more turn."

"One minute, twenty seconds."

Browne flattened out the calf flap and searched for anything that was pulsating. The men were crowding in for a closer look, realizing that something was amiss. Browne located the posterior tibial artery, which was shooting out a fine pulsating stream of dark red blood.

"Gotcha, you little bastard!" Browne placed the clamp and jerked his elbow back violently. He caught one of the on-lookers directly on the forehead and cold-cocked him. "A bit of room, men!" shouted Browne.

"One minute, thirty seconds."

It was going to be close. Browne held up the clamp and saw a small piece of artery in the jaws. Finally, the bucket came and Browne instructed one of the mates to pour half of it right onto the open stump. Browne found the peroneal artery and grabbed it. Everybody behind him jumped out of the way. His arm shot back again and the tortured artery snapped back, deep into the muscle.

"One minute, forty seconds."

"More water!" shouted Browne. There was an immediate splash. Finally he spotted the anterior tibial artery and clamped it. His arm shot back once again. "Poker, Jones," said Browne as he picked up the sail needle. There was a hiss and smoke, as Jones went along the edges of the skin.

"One minute, fifty seconds!"

Browne picked up the flap and ran the needle through it, then through the skin above it. He tied the knot rapidly, but did not trim the tails. He picked up another needle and rammed it home through the outside of the flap.

"One minute, fifty-five seconds."

Browne fixed the flap to the skin above and tied a square knot. He stepped back from the table and held his hands in the air.

"Two minutes, Doctor Browne," said Comstock, who was finally able to look back at the scene. There was a brief round of applause. Jones turned to whisper in Browne's ear.

"Is it finished, Sir? The skin is still mostly open."

"You have to allow for drainage. The bad humors have to find their way out."

"Of course, Sir."

"Lieutenant, could you send word when thirty minutes have passed? We will need to release the tourniquet."

"It would be a pleasure, Dr. Browne, so long as I do not have to be further exposed to this barbarity." Browne winked at Jones.

"One man's barbarity is another man's art, Lieutenant. You men there! Stop! Where are you going with that leg," demanded Browne.

"We was goin' to chuck it over the side, Sir."

"You will do no such thing! Bring it here at once!" The deckhand rushed over to Browne and eagerly passed him the dead limb. Browne winked at Jones again. "Mr. Jones and I are going below for breakfast."

"I was never much of a leg man, Sir," said Jones, trying to suppress laughter. Comstock's mouth dropped open.

"You there, on the tourniquet! Await word from Lieutenant Comstock and release the tourniquet on his command!" Browne hoisted the dead limb over his shoulder. "And whatever you do, don't let him kick the bucket." Browne swung the lifeless leg in the direction of the wooden deck bucket and knocked it off the table. There was a general gasp among the crew, as the two men went below. The fifteen-year-old Lieutenant Comstock was outraged by Browne's antics and stomped off in search of Commander Collier. The laughter did not begin until Comstock went below decks.

CHAPTER 10

The blistering tropical sun was nearly at its zenith and the Buccaneers were grateful for the cool trade wind, which had been so unwelcome a few hours before. There was a flurry of activity on the deck of the *Cor Valant* as the hands were transferring the dead to a sloop that was side-tied to the starboard side. Launches were coming and going, dropping off the Captains that had survived the explosion, along with their officers. Lieutenant Owen carried a ledger and did his best to account for the dead and the living.

Commander Collier knocked tentatively on the aft cabin door. He could hear snoring on the other side. He rapped louder, but there was no response. He looked back at his dark-skinned companion and shrugged his shoulders. He gently opened the door. Morgan was flat on his back with his mouth wide open.

"Captain?" Collier said softly. Then louder, "Captain!" There was no response, so Collier shook Morgan's bare foot. Morgan opened his eyes, but seemed dazed. He sat up and immediately began coughing. The coughing lasted for quite some time and both men wondered if it would ever stop, but finally Morgan hacked up a mouthful of mucus and spit it into a cup. Collier watched as Morgan struggled with each breath, his matted brown hair hanging down in his face. Despite his large-muscled frame, Morgan seemed somehow frail and weak. He was still dressed in the ill-fitting clothes he had been in since last night and he looked more like a vagrant than a Captain.

At length, Morgan opened his eyes and said, "What is it, Collier?"

"I have some documents to show you that were in with the ship's papers, but that can wait. You look like you are just back from a holiday in hell, Captain. We need to get you livened-up for the noon conclave." Morgan looked down at his clothes and smoothed his hair back, out of his face.

"You have a point, Collier, but since you mentioned hell, I wonder, have you looked in a mirror lately?"

Collier positioned himself in front of the mirror atop the chest of drawers. Morgan was right. Collier's face was beet-red with several large blisters. His eyebrows and lashes were reduced to stubble. The blisters on the right side of his neck had already popped and were coated with soot from his collar.

"Bloody hell," said Collier, studying his image in the mirror. "What do you say to a swim, Captain?"

"Commander, you have yourself a partner. By the way, who is your friend?"

"This is Captain Velasquez, who you promoted after a prolonged reconnaissance trip along the Spanish Main."

"Unbelievable! I cannot believe you are the same man! You look fit and healthy, and a hell of a lot friendlier without that hideous necklace." Morgan was referring to the necklace of sun-dried human ears that Velasquez had been wearing during their last encounter.

"You are too kind, Capitan," said Valesquez in a thick Castillian accent.

"Captain Velasquez has been a great help in deciphering the Letter of Marque that this ship has been sailing under. I think you will find it very interesting," said Collier.

"No doubt, but let's have that swim first, shall we? Feel free to join us Captain Velasquez."

"It would be an honor, Capitan."

Collier reached in his pants pocket and produced a silver bar that weighed about ten ounces. He set the bar on Morgan's table.

"What's this?" said Morgan, picking up the bar.

"Silver, I think. There were four-hundred-twenty of them in *Cor Valant's* hold. Owen found them this morning," said Collier.

"I like that boy more every day," said Morgan, estimating the weight of the bar in his hand.

"Pass me that pipe, will you Cyrus?" said Browne, studying the bones he had just dissected out of Baker's former leg. They were back in the galley again and the cooks were not happy about it, but Jones had seniority.

"He must have taken a hell of a blow to the lower part of his shin," said Browne. He took a deep inhalation on the pipe, held for a few seconds, then exhaled. "His tibia is shattered in five places and the peroneal artery was sheared in two. That is why the foot and ankle were so badly swollen. Say Cyrus, could you whip us up some fish balls?"

"Be 'appy to Sir, but the officer's mess is being served in just a few minutes."

"Oh, very well Cyrus. That should give us enough time to do the other leg." Browne took another draw on the white clay pipe and passed it over to Cyrus. "The eye is just going to have to wait," said Browne, exhaling a cloud of smoke.

Morgan grimaced as he dragged the turtle shell comb through his knotted hair. He struggled until the comb moved easily with each pass. He pulled his hair back into a ponytail and secured it with a short leather thong, then studied himself in the mirror. In his own clothes, a coarsely woven top with plenty of room to catch the breeze and a pair of tight breeches unbuckled at the knee, he looked very much the daring Captain Henry Morgan. There was a knock on his cabin door.

"Come!" said Morgan, irritated by the interruption. The door opened and Collier and Velasquez walked in, dressed in similar fashion to Morgan, but in addition, each man had a large floral-pattern scarf draped over the right neck, forming a cradle for a pistol on the left waist. It was a good system that avoided the "blowing your balls off with the pistol in your waist band" scenario and also offered a free shot to the back of you, should you need it. It was the very height of fashion, a creation of the freed slave Mrs. Kamara in Port Royal. She and her three daughters used a wax process to dye the finely woven cotton fabric that became known as gara.

"Captain, I brought that Letter of Marque. I think you should see it before you address the men."

"Who issued the Letter?"

"The Governor of Barracoa," said Collier.

"Just give me the highlights, will you," said Morgan, irritated.

"Of course, Captain. Here is the translation from the Spanish: 'That the said Governor did permit the French to trade in all Spanish ports, etc…As also to cruize upon the English Pirates in what place soever they could find them, because of the multitude of hostilities which they had committed against the subjects of his Catholic Majesty, in time of peace betwixt the two Crowns.' That is the substance of the letter."

"If there was any question about the legality of seizing this ship as a prize, this certainly settles the matter," said Morgan. "Captain, if you would be good enough to do a formal translation of the entire document, we can send it along with the prize crew to Port Royal."

"It would be my privilege, Capitan."

Collier felt as though he had been slapped in the face. Send this boat to Port Royal as a prize? Have you completely lost your mind?. Morgan sensed the anger that permeated

Commander Collier, but he had made his decision without Collier's consultation and he intended to stick to it.

"Commander, we can discuss the finer points of the prize later, but for now, a show of unity would greatly benefit our cause." Collier exhaled and decided to let the matter drop, at least for the present.

"Of course, Captain. By the way, Pulverin was very insistent on meeting with you at your earliest convenience."

"Fine. Shall we greet our guests?" said Morgan, opening the cabin door.

The aft deck was crowded with twelve small tables and when Morgan approached, the men stood up and removed their hats. The number of men who had dressings covering injuries of one sort, or another, shocked Morgan. He walked up to the assemblage without a word and circled the tables, looking each man in the eye, smiling and then moving on. When he had completed the circle around the tables, Morgan walked over to the table that had been prepared for him. He stood beside his chair.

"Brethren, take your seats," said Morgan. He remained standing until every man had seated himself. Collier was at his side and Morgan whispered, "Who pulled me out of the water?"

"Kessenger, Captain," whispered Collier into Morgan's ear. Morgan nodded his understanding and Collier took his seat. It was clear that Morgan was going to speak and the tables were silent.

"Brethren of the Coast, welcome. It is a solemn day in which we have all suffered the loss of friends and many is the time that friends have given us life. Today we have been spared the shroud, but soon it will come and cover us, one and all. When that day comes, let us pray that those who are left behind drink to our memory and fornicate most wickedly in the celebration of our passing. For the moment, fornication will need to be put aside for our return to Port Royal, but I heartily recommend that you partake of the wine generously supplied by the papist bastards who provided us with this lovely lady, the *Cor Valant*."

Every man stood and raised his glass.

"*Cor Valant*," said the men in a perfect unison that could never be duplicated during a march on a parade ground. This time, the men remained standing until Morgan was seated, thus returning the honor he had given them.

On Morgan's left was Kessenger, whose face and neck were covered in small scabs that had come from the flying glass particles during the explosion. Morgan took his hand and looked him in the eye.

"Thank you for pulling me out of the drink last night." All eyes at the table were now on Kessenger.

"I will be damned, Captain! If I had known it was you, I would have demanded an immediate field promotion!" There was laughter around the table. "Between you and me, Captain, I have no intention of reporting this to the Admiralty, but I believe that a case could be made for willful destruction of the King's property." The table grew silent. "In my opinion, the only portion of the *Oxford* that remained intact was the yard arm that I and seven of me mates was clingin' to. You came up from the deep blue with such force that your head split the yard arm and knocked the eight of us into the water!" Laughter erupted again. Morgan struggled for something witty to say, but he was overcome with exhaustion, so he just laughed with the others. More than anything, he wanted to be in his bed at the Golden Arrow. Rest would have to wait. There was still the remainder of this gathering and then the sea burial afterwards. He summoned a server and requested a pot of strong coffee. He would have to make due with whatever was available. He made a mental note to have the prize crew return from Port Royal with coffee from his plantation.

The first course was turtle soup with grated cheese and watercress on top. Next, a plate of fruit was served that included papaya and mango in a guava glaze. One of the cooks announced that there would be a brief respite before the main course was served and encouraged all the officers to try a most excellent dry white wine recently discovered in the ship's hold.

"Something must have frigged up in the galley," said Kessenger.

"Have you ever tried to cook a decent meal for fifty men on a galley stove?" said Browne defensively.

"What do you say we try some of that Frenchie wine?" said Collier, trying to defuse the conversation. It was at that point that Pulverin approached the table with a bottle of the recently discovered wine.

"May I pour for you?" asked Pulverin, filling Morgan's glass first.

"Merci, beau coup, Pulverin," said Morgan. Pulverin went around the table pouring three fingers into each glass, until the bottle was finished. Morgan savored his glass of wine and waited for Pulverin to make his move. Several people had left the table and Pulverin slipped into Kessenger's seat next to Morgan. Velasquez and Collier were on the other side of Morgan. One of the stewards placed a pot of coffee and a mug in front of Morgan, who nodded his thanks. Morgan waited for one of the men to open the discussion. In the distance, pipers were warming up for the funeral procession.

"Captain, this may not be the most opportune time to begin planning our next move," said Collier, "but you may want to hear what Pulverin and Captain Velasquez have been considering. As you mentioned earlier, a strike on the plate fleet is no longer possible."

"I am all ears, gentlemen, no offense to you, Captain," said Morgan snickering, as he reluctantly sipped his coffee.

"Maracaibo, Capitan," whispered Velasquez, who didn't get Morgan's pun. "It is a very reech city."

"I recall you describing a new fort at the mouth of the lake. How do you suggest we get around that?" Morgan's memory for detail was legendary.

"I have seen that problem, Capitan. The solution is simple. The fort is on island with many of sand hills. The water is perhaps three feet, with a sand shore. Boats can be landed."

"There is another problem," said Pulverin. "The Spanish keep a Man o' War inside the harbor. We are no match for them."

"When I go there two months ago, there were two large ships with forty guns. That was when I arrive. Five days later I go, they are not there," said Velasquez.

"It seems that the Spanish are over-extended. They may be rotating their fleet, or perhaps they are responding to intelligence, an impending invasion, that sort of thing," offered Collier.

"Hmm," said Morgan, downing a second mug of coffee. "Pulverin, you were with L'Ollonais three years ago when he took Maracaibo. What was the take on that raid?"

"Officially, we divided two-hundred-thirty-thousand pieces of eight. But the real value was much higher, because of the gems. Emeralds! Hundreds of them! The men had no idea as to their value, so the officers gave them a few pieces of eight for each one. In reality they were worth thousands." Morgan's mind began to race. The coffee had finally kicked in. The cooks began to serve the main course and people began taking their seats.

"This business stays between the four of us. Understood?" said Morgan. "Let me sleep on this and we will meet again tomorrow. Captain Velasquez, you will return to Port Royal with the prize crew and dispense some very incorrect information during a drunken orgy." Velasquez nodded his understanding.

At the mention of the prize crew, Collier had a visible pout on his face. Pulverin vacated his seat and Kessenger sat down beside Morgan. Let's get this over with, thought Morgan.

"We need to assemble a prize crew," he said to the table at large. "Last night, the Buccaneer fleet became indebted to the King for twenty-thousand pounds. Sending the *Cor Valant* back to Port Royal with a hull full of silver will cover most of that debt. At the same time, we will have a shallow-draft fleet that will allow us to do what we do best. Any questions?" Morgan looked around the table. "Good. It is settled. Please pass the word for Lieutenant Owen."

The thirty-foot sloop "*Spartan*" was side-tied to the *Cor Valant*. Owen had decided to have the shrouded bodies stacked on deck so that they would be easy to retrieve during the burial. He was beginning to regret that decision. He scribbled in his ledger. He multiplied the number dead, ninety four, times the average weight, say, one-hundred-fifty pounds. "Oh, shit! That is over fourteen-thousand pounds. All above deck!"

"Beg pardon, Sir?" said the mate next to him.

"Nothing, it is just that we have over three and a half tons on the deck. I wonder how much ballast she carries?"

"I couldn't tell ya, Sir."

Owen set his ledger down and walked to the rail. He peered over the side and could see three planks of freeboard. Next, he went below to get a look at the ballast stones in the hold. There seemed to be pitifully few. There was a good chance that she would capsize if she sailed close to the wind. "Damn!" He went back on deck and grabbed his ledger book.

"You are going to need to lash those bodies down."

"Aye, Sir."

Owen went back aboard the *Cor Valant*. The smells coming out of the galley were intoxicating and he realized that he hadn't eaten since yesterday. He asked one of the cooks for a small plate of food, but before he could take the first bite, Thatcher was tugging on his sleeve.

"The Captain is calling for you."

"Damn," said Owen. "Look, you will need to finish up for me. The *Spartan* is unstable and needs more ballast. Order some men to go ashore and get stones. You are going to need another sloop. Divide the bodies between the two boats."

"I will see to it," said Thatcher.

Owen dashed across the deck over to Morgan's table.

"You called, Sir?"

"Pull up a chair, Lieutenant. We were just talking about your performance last night. Well done, me boy!" The men at the table raised their glasses in salute. Owen was embarrassed and flushed red.

"I had a great deal of help. I will pass your congratulations on to the others. Thank you." Owen took a seat and opened the ledger.

"Do you have a final tally?" asked Morgan.

"I do, Sir. The crew of the *Oxford* consisted of three-hundred-twenty-six men when we left Port Royal. We currently have two-hundred-twenty-four able-bodied seamen from the original crew. Seventy-four men were recovered alive, sixteen of whom died of their injuries. Thirty-five bodies were pulled out. One guard was killed below by a head injury. There are seventeen men with disabling injuries, and thirty four missing and presumed dead." The table was silent. "I regret the loss of Captains Bigford and Aylett, and Midshipmen Fallows, Cooper and Hawking. At present we have seven-hundred-eighty-four able-bodied men, in nineteen remaining ships."

"There is no point in keeping the numbers secret any longer. It was a brutal night. Lieutenant, perhaps you could keep a list of the dead and injured and make sure that copies of that list are on the other boats. We will need to settle up with the widows when we return."

"I would be honored, Sir."

"Have you eaten, Lad?" asked Morgan.

"It has been a while, Sir." Within minutes, Owen had several servings of beef and dolphin in front of him, which he ate eagerly.

Morgan whispered in Collier's ear. "What do you say we let Owen take the prize back to Port Royal? God knows, he's earned it!"

"Suits me," whispered back Collier.

"Gentlemen, a toast to our prize-Captain, Lieutenant Owen." Owen raised the glass in his left hand in salute, while his right hand continued to shovel food into his mouth. Owen looked up because of the silence and realized that everyone was toasting him. His mouth hung open in disbelief. Kessenger slapped him on the back in congratulation and a huge chunk of food flew out of his mouth on to the table. Laughter erupted from the table and soon spread to the entire ship

CHAPTER 11

"Quite frankly, Cyrus, I have never done an eye before. The thing is, it should not be put off for too long because of the proximity to the brain. Eyes are said to 'wick infection into the brain.' The entire concept makes me bilious, but I think we can do it justice. Pass me that pipe, would you? Basically, all that you need to do is retract the lids while I cut the muscles and clamp the artery and nerve. Can you do that, Cyrus?" The galley went silent.

"Sir, I would be most 'appy to assist you in any way I can. But I am confused by the 'retract' business, Sir." Cyrus reloaded the pipe and tore a straw from the broom.

"Cyrus, I do not understand you." Cyrus passed the pipe over to Browne. The cooks in the galley were cleaning up, and after seeing a human leg dissected on the prep-table earlier, they were in no mood for any more "scurvy science".

"I am not a medical man, Sir. I understand apothecary and some Latin, but 'retract' is as foreign to me a 'bolen,' Sir." Browne grinned from ear to ear and put his hand over his mouth, secretly hoping that he was not going into one of the 'laughing fits,' that were thought to be associated with the consumption of indica, in particular.

"Cyrus," said Browne, scratching his chin. "Retraction means to pull. Latin, I think, from 'tracta'.

"Would I 'have to pull twice,' Sir? 'Re' means 'two,' or 'do again' ". Browne dipped his head in disbelief. Cyrus lit the straw again.

"Are you having me on, Jones?" Browne dropped the common denominator of professional names.

"I assume you want me to pull only once, Sir. No offense, Sir." Browne was on the razor's edge of laughter.

"Right, Cyrus. Pull one time, and keep pulling until I tell you to stop. Quite easy, actually."

'What should I pull *with*, Sir?"

"The retractors, Cyrus. They look like bent forks."

"Sorry, Sir. I think that something has gone terribly wrong, Sir. The way I understand it, Sir, you want me to put bent forks in a man's eye and pull, until you tell me to stop. That can't be right, Sir." Browne began tapping the underside of his chin and smiling again.

"Cyrus, I have had enough. We have to do the eye. Are you with me?"

"With all me 'art, Sir. I would never desert you in a time of need! But I was thinkin', do you suppose we could use bent spoons instead of forks, Sir?" Cyrus smiled and then winked at Browne. It was no longer possible for Browne to keep the indica laughter in check. Each spasm of laughter forced a portion of air from his lungs until he would rise up gasping for air, only to repeat the process, again and again. Cyrus was soon with him.

CHAPTER 12

The following day at noon, the four men assembled in the aft cabin of the *Cor Valant*. It was a small cabin in comparison to Morgan's lodgings aboard the *Oxford*, but it was quiet and the guard outside assured privacy. Out of habit, Morgan looked around for Caleb, who would have typically been snooping around to obtain bits of gossip, but Morgan realized with a pang of sorrow that Caleb had been among the "missing and presumed dead."

"Perhaps we could start with that island fortress," said Morgan unrolling a chart. "Can you point it out?" Valasquez and Pulverin studied the chart intently. The two men paused and looked at each other and shrugged.

"Capitan Morgan, where from you get this chart?" asked Velasquez.

"It was in Ruppert's chart table. All of my charts were blown to hell."

"So is French chart?" Velasquez looked over at Pulverin and raised his eyebrows. "There are many of problems, Capitan."

"Continue."

"The soundings, they are very wrong," offered Pulverin. Morgan looked over at Velasquez for confirmation.

"It is so, Capitan. Never did the cartographer who draw this chart enter the bay."

"Very well, then, let's see if we can tidy this up a bit. Collier, do you have one of your wads?"

"Always, Captain." Collier passed Morgan the thin sliver of graphite encased in the rosewood holder.

"See what you can do with this," said Morgan, passing the wad over to Velasquez. Pulverin began an animated discussion with Velasquez in Basque, which Morgan and Collier could not understand. Finally, Velasquez tentatively began to print on the edge of the chart. There were several "oows" and "ahs" as Velasquez continued writing.

"Capitan! This is good," said Velasquez, very excited. "You have more? I would like very much to give one my son."

"It can be arranged, Captain, but we need to proceed with the chart."

"Of course, Capitan." Once Velasquez got the hang of the wad, he began marking feverishly on the chart, aided by the prompting of Pulverin. At one point the two men almost came to blows over the location of some shallow areas, but within the space of ten minutes, the French chart had been re-designed. Pulverin insisted that the disputed areas be marked. Velasquez accommodated him in order to keep the peace.

Morgan studied the chart in the silence that followed, occasionally drawing on his white clay pipe. Collier was looking over his shoulder.

"Are you sure about this channel? It seems impossible," said Morgan, who was perplexed by the serpentine passage marked on the chart.

"It is so, Capitan. In my little fishing boat, I run aground maybe twenty times. I pretend I am drunk to avoid suspicion from the castle and the big boats. You see why the pilot is in high esteem, yes?" Morgan looked at Pulverin for confirmation.

"I am not certain about the passage," said Pulverin. "It was three years ago. I can tell you our boats also went aground many times. Before our leaving, L' Ollonais secured a pilot. Our boats were much deeper in the water, you see," said Pulverin.

"How far would you say it is from the island with the fort to the center of the channel?" asked Collier, who, after seeing the soundings on the newly configured map, was glad to be rid of the *Cor Valant*. Velasquez turned to Pulverin and began a rapid exchange in Basque. The two men came to some sort of an agreement.

"No more than three-hundred yards. The fort was not built until recently. She has perhaps ten thirty-six pounders." The fort would have to be taken before the channel could be entered. It was the cost of doing business.

"Tell me about the troops. What were their nationalities?" asked Morgan.

"The officers were Spanish. The troops were very ugly! Some Gypsies, Italians and French," offered Velasquez. "It was the opposite in Cartagena—all the troops were Spanish there."

Morgan smiled broadly and Collier gave him an inquisitive look.

"Cartagena is one of the main distribution points for the Plate Fleet. The Dons station their best troops there and leave the scum to look after the smaller cities. Our general strategy is to spook the troops and get them to run. They are not bound by any sense of honor, so at the first sign of trouble, they will often desert their posts and head for the hills. I am thinking that if we sent Captain Velasquez into Maracaibo just ahead of our appearance, he could scare the hell out of them. 'L' Ollonais is back with ten ships just outside of the harbor!', or something like that."

"It would be such fun, Capitan!" said Velasquez.

"I thought L' Ollonais was dead," said Collier.

"He probably is, but who cares? The Dons think of the Freebooters as demons. Literally. They call me 'El Diablo', which is Spanish for 'The Devil'. Some think that because we are demons, or evil spirits, if you will, we cannot be killed. Wait until they hear about the *Oxford* exploding! Only a spirit could

survive such a thing! Odds are, they are going to run like hell."
The men were giddy with excitement.

"I just had a thought," said Collier. "Once we make it through the channel their ships cannot follow us, because of their draft. The entire lake is ours as long as we want it!"

"Exactly. We can take our time. The only problem is going to be getting back out, but we can cross that bridge later. We need to have several contingency plans, but I think Maracaibo is the prize. Thank you for your assistance. It goes without saying that only the four of us know this discussion took place." Morgan made eye contact with each man and all of them bowed their heads slightly to acknowledge understanding. "Captain Velasquez, please remain behind, as the others return to their duties."

"Of course, Capitan Morgan." Collier and Pulverin filed out of the cabin dutifully, both a little disappointed that they were not part of the conversation that began with their departure.

Morgan felt parched, so he opened the cabin door and asked the guard to find a bottle of the white wine that had been served the day before. When he returned to the cabin, Morgan found a chair and remained silent for several minutes. Velasquez seemed content with the silence, so much so, that Morgan became uncomfortable. Morgan had used this test a hundred times before. It was the perfect "tabula rasa", or blank slate, upon which men wrote their worst fears. Velasquez was the one in one-hundred persons who seemed to have nothing to write on the empty slate. He was calm. Very strange, reflected Morgan, who had seen many men lose their composure in the same circumstances.

"My friend, I have some good news and some bad news," said Morgan. "The good news is that I want you to meet a woman and make love to her. The bad news is that she is somewhat less than attractive. Her name is Veronica Sanchez. She works for John Starr at Lovingo." Velasquez was obviously not enthralled by the news. "Her family consists of two children and her parents, who are being held captive in Caracas. When she supplies information to the Dons, her family is treated well. We have intercepted many of their communications." Velasquez sighed and awaited further bad news. "We have been supplying her with information for months, in the hopes of using her to our benefit. It seems that time has come."

There was a loud knock at the cabin door and Morgan attended to it, while Velasquez digested the information he had been given. Morgan returned with a bottle of wine and two glasses. He poured two generous glasses of wine and passed one to Valasquez. Velasquez took a gulp of the white wine and began massaging his temples.

"If you have any particular fetishes, she has the capacity to make you very happy," said Morgan. "You may actually enjoy yourself, so don't pout." Velasquez smiled and drained the rest of his glass. Morgan hovered over the chart silently, studying the coast of Central and South America. "Hmm," he said. He took a pair of dividers and began measuring distances from several of the largest ports. "Come here and look at this." Velasquez positioned himself on the opposite side of the table. Morgan picked up a piece of thin spaghetti and placed it deeply into a lighted candle, until it began to burn. He slowly withdrew the spaghetti and then drew the flame into his pipe.

"Cartagena will be the perfect decoy. It is the closest large port to Maracaibo. If we can convince the Dons that we are going to hit Cartagena, they will almost certainly pull every ship out of Maracaibo," said Morgan, pointing to the chart with the stem of his pipe. Velasquez nodded in agreement. "When you were on your cruise, did you happen to remove any crosses from Cartagena?" Morgan referred to the rampage that Velasquez had gone on after his son had been victimized by a priest.

"Si, Capitan. Four ears, also. He was my first Bishop! The man was pig and die like pig, but was very generous! He give me the biggest of crosses and a ring with ruby that was so big as a grape! The priest with him, he die well, but give me small cross, with no emeralds." Velasquez had spoken matter-of-factly about the carnage and then seemed lost in thought.

"That may well work to our advantage. As I understand it, Veronica was excommunicated by the church and she absolutely hates the Don's. When she hears that you were an assassin working for the Freebooters, she is going to come apart!" Morgan cast his eyes upward. "This is beautiful! Be sure you wear one of the crosses!" Morgan refilled their glasses, laughing.

"A toast, Captain," said Morgan raising his glass. "The riches of Maracaibo! May they soon be ours."

"The reeches," said Velasquez raising his glass. Velasquez held Morgan's eyes with a piercing stare and a broad smile on his face. It was the beginning of a new friendship and an adventure that would change the course of history. And both men knew it.

"Pass the word to the others that we shall meet tomorrow for breakfast."

"Si, Capitan," said Velasquez. He pointed to his stomach and said, "Revuelto." Morgan smiled.

"Me too," said Morgan in Spanish.

CHAPTER 13

"You are going to have to make a decision, Sir. Fish balls, or eye balls. I can't do both," said Cyrus standing in front of the galley stove. Browne was sitting in front of the prep table cutting apart the eye that they had removed a few hours earlier from an old salt named Bookbinder. The previous day they had waited too long and the opium had worn off and Bookbinder had begun to vomit. His shipmates transferred his hammock to the taffrail so that Bookbinder could simply heave over the side of the hammock into the scuppers. It seemed to go on for hours. Eventually, Cyrus made him some tea from the indica buds and sweetened it with honey. Bookbinder was instructed to take a small sip every ten minutes and it had worked exceedingly well. Today's strategy was to give Bookbinder the tea *before* the opium and there had been no recurrence of the vomiting.

"Cyrus, quit clowning around and come over here! You have to see this."

"Yes, Masta. Should I bring the forks, Masta?" Browne began to laugh.

"Fork yourself, Cyrus. You could bring that pipe of yours.

"Yes, Masta." Browne had opened the eye with a knife and nailed it to the prep table, so that it was wide open. There was a thick, gelatinous goo leaking out of it. Browne held a lens over top of it, inspecting every square inch in the light supplied by the clear glass in the galley roof above. Cyrus took a deep breath and then and passed the pipe to Browne, who gave him the lens in return.

"What am I looking for?"

"First, look at the lens, that roundish white thing in the front."

"I have it, Sir."

"That is the lens of an eighty-year-old man. It is completely opacified. He was already blind in this eye."

"I don't feel quite so bad about the forks now, Sir."

"Look more closely now, Cyrus. The very back part of the eye," said Browne pointing with the tip of his knife. "Do you see the hole there?"

"It is clear to me, Sir."

"It appears that this Bookbinder fellow had some debris penetrate his eye and pass into his brain."

"Indeed, Sir! What does that mean, Sir?"

"The back of the eye is supported by a bony sphere that is thinner than an egg shell." Browne took another puff on the clay pipe with the long stem. He waited a long time before he replied. "If it had been hot metal, or shot, he probably would not supperate. But it was probably wood, since that is what I found inside the eye."

"Indeed, Sir. What, exactly do you mean by 'supperate'?"

"The generation of pus, Cyrus. It is a bad sign, especially in the brain. Take this lens and look carefully at the gelatinous fluid." Cyrus took the lens and scanned the specimen. He patiently looked, but could find nothing worthy of note.

"Look for fine pinkish hairs, Cyrus. They are everywhere." Cyrus looked again and finally found them.

"I see them now! What is it, Sir?" Cyrus was excited by the discovery, like a child on Christmas day.

"Worms, Cyrus."

"In 'is bloody eye, Sir? That is the most revoltin' thing I've ever seen!" Cyrus set the lens on the table and backed away. "I pray it is not catchin', Sir."

"I do not believe so, Cyrus, otherwise we would all have it. I saw this same process in a Virginia slave. He had an eye gouged out during a fight with another slave. The plantation boss sent word to Harcourt—the local physician—while we were in the middle of a dinner at the great house. Candied yams, pheasant and rack of lamb. It was an excellent night, up to that point. Harcourt did not bother with the retractors and laudanum was expensive and in short supply. Needless to say…" Browne's eyes began to tear up and he sat quietly until the emotion passed. Cyrus decided that nothing he said would make the situation any better, so he picked up two mugs and went over to the rum barrel. He sat one of the mugs on the table in front of Browne.

"That ought to take the edge off, Sir." Cyrus took a sip from his mug and then placed a bud in the pipe. He walked back to the stove and ladled out some fish balls onto a steel rack. He lit the pipe and returned to the table. Browne was studying the eye again and sipping his rum.

"The thing is, we opened the eye the next day in the bright sun. I was pitifully hung over. Harcourt had a very powerful lens and we could see the worms moving. And by the way, the lens in the slave's eye was completely opacified." Cyrus passed the pipe to Browne.

"What does it all mean, Sir?."

"I am not sure, Cyrus. I asked Gbessay about the disease and she was very familiar with it. She called it, 'river blindness'. She said it only occurs in Africa. Do you happen to know if Bookbinder was ever on a slaver?"

"Now that you mention it, Sir, I believe he was. I think there were about ten men on the *Oxford* who had been rescued from a slaver that had refused to strike." To "strike colors" was to lower your flag as an act of surrender to a superior ship.

"Tell you what, Cyrus. Why don't we have some fish balls and then go and see Bookbinder. At some point, it would be interesting to examine the other men from that slaver."

"If they are still alive, Sir."

CHAPTER 14

The Galley fires were burning and the smell of bacon and fresh bread permeated the ship. Lieutenant Owen ordered the prisoners brought up one at a time so that they could be washed in seawater with the deck pumps. Three guards were assigned to them now and during each changing of the guard, the men were required to inspect the shackles. Velasquez and Collier were sipping coffee at the chart table, readying themselves for breakfast with Morgan. The boson struck eight bells and Collier took the weights off the parchment chart, which immediately rolled itself up. He slipped the tie back on and then headed toward the aft cabin wordlessly, with Velasquez in tow. Directly ahead of them a canvas bag crashed onto the deck and both men, who had been deep in thought, jerked involuntarily, simultaneously reaching for their pistols. In an instant there was a sharp snap behind them as Pulverin's boots hit the deck. He put pistols hard into each man's back. Collier and Velasquez froze.

"Your money, or your wives!" he shouted. "On second thought, the money will be sufficient," came the words in a thick French accent.

"Pulverin, you asshole! Stop behaving like a five year old!" screamed Collier, who had taken a pinch of fabric on his rump and held it outward. He began to walk stiff-legged as though he had filled his pants. The crewmen who were within earshot were rolling on the deck. Pulverin had spent the night on his sloop and arrived rested and playful. The three officers continued walking aft until they reached Morgan's cabin. Collier rapped on the door and then opened it.

"Welcome to my humble house, gentlemen. Naturally, the most liberal use of the word 'gentlemen' was intended," said Morgan sitting at the small table.

"Bon jour, Captain."

"Buenos dias, Capitan."

"Wha 'appen, Cap'n," said Collier, as the men took their seats. The modified chart from the previous day was on the table, weighted with candles. Morgan pulled up two of the candles when Cyrus Jones entered the room. The chart rolled up into a cylinder in an instant.

"I am 'ere, Sirs, to attend to your breakfast," said Cyrus stiffly.

"That bacon smelled sublime, Jones," said Morgan.

"I am sorry, Sir," said Jones. "The ship's surgeon has asked me to look out for you, Sir. Bacon is considered by many to be unfriendly to gout victims, Sir."

"Mister Jones, in future, you will take my orders for breakfast without comment. Please attend to the others."

Jones stung from the rebuke, but he was a survivor and he knew what to do. When he stood next to Collier to take his order, Collier whispered in his ear, "Please instruct Dr. Browne to ease up on my Midshipmen, or *he* will kick the bucket." Jones nodded and left the cabin. The men returned to the chart on the table, freshly unrolled.

"It is clear to me that we need to make an appearance at the Isle of Savona at the appropriate time," said Morgan. "The King was very insistent on that point. If we meet the Plate Fleet, we can easily back down, due to the recent tragedy. Or, perhaps we can take advantage of a twist of fate. But the odds are that we will find nothing, in which case the King will have to reconsider his sources. One way, or the other, he will be placated."

"When is the Plate Fleet supposed to arrive in Savona?" asked Collier.

"That information is somewhat sensitive and it is of no importance, at the present time. What we need to do is set a date for the Maracaibo raid, so that we can create a diversion. I can guarantee the fleet will be there by the middle of March. Are there problems with that date?" The three men shrugged their shoulders and looked at each other, wordlessly. Morgan began scribbling furiously on the border of the chart. He added all the numbers in the date and it came out "seven" on 17, 4, 1669.

"Seventeen April, 1669," said Morgan. "That will give us plenty of time to conduct our business in Savona and re-victualize before the raid." There was a knock at the cabin door and three mates brought in trays with food, coffee and an assortment of Danish-style pastries. The chart on the table convulsed into a cylinder, as Morgan removed the candles. The cabin was silent until the stewards left.

"Captain, I was wondering if we could conduct a few raids during our free time. I have over a hundred men who have never been in battle," said Collier.

"We have over seven-hundred mouths to feed and we have provisions for about ten days. Does that answer your question? We might even pick up a little spending money for all our trouble," said Morgan with a broad smile. The map snapped shut as another mate entered the cabin.

"Shall we discuss the prize crew?" asked Morgan. It was a necessary discussion that would not require him to keep furling and unfurling the poxy chart. He bit into a piece of bacon as Jones cleared away some dishes.

"I was thinking of a crew of thirty six," said Collier. "That would allow us three guards to cover the prisoners around the clock and take care of the deck at the same time." Collier was actually hoping for twenty men, but he made a higher bid, so that he would not come up short.

"How do you propose to transport thirty-men back to the fleet?" asked Morgan, rhetorically. "Captain Velasquez, how many men can you safely transport from Port Royal to Ruba?" Ruba was later to be known as "Aruba".

"It is a five-hundred mile sail and in April, the seas will be more like men, than soft, like women."

"Poetry is soothing for the soul, but it does not tell me what I need to know. How many men can you transport from Port Royal to Ruba?" Morgan demanded.

"Si, Capitan. She is a small sloop. If the seas are fair, we can carry with us, ten men." Velasquez was hoping for fifteen, or less, so he under-bid the competition. In reality, Velasquez knew that he would have to "beat it" all the way south, which is to say that he would be sailing into the wind. It would be an agonizing journey, at least to the English mind. Naturally, Velasquez had an ace up his sleeve. He could sail east approximately eight-hundred miles with the wind on his beam and then cut southwest, for the down-hill run. He was well aware that he could make the eleven-hundred mile journey in less time than it would have taken him to go the five-hundred mile straight shot. Add to that the fact that in an over-loaded boat, tacking is dangerous, especially in a rough sea.

"I will give you twelve men for the prize crew," said Morgan and Collier began to protest. "Hear me out," said Morgan, overriding his Commander. "The *Cor Valant* seemed to get along rather well with a crew of twelve. You have only a three day run to Port Royal, with the wind at your back! Pass me that butter, would you?"

Collier knew better than to protest. Besides, if something went wrong, he was now free of blame.

"Very well, Captain. May I pick the men?"

"Be my guest, Commander," said Morgan, who was serving up his second helping of bacon.

"May I propose wager?" said Velasquez. All eyes were on him. "My sloop will arrive first in Port Royal. I will pay five guineas against your four guineas and two wads," said Velasquez, looking at Collier.

"You have yourself a wager, Captain," said Collier. The *Cor Valant* was very "narrow-waisted", meaning that she was very narrow in her midsection, or beam. Consequently, there was considerably less resistance in the water. She had been built for speed. Sloops were fast boats, there was no question, but the amount of canvas that *Cor Valant* could spread between her two masts was extraordinary, compared to a pitiful lugsail and a jib found on Velasquez's sloop. Collier had no doubt that Owen could win the race. Velasquez, on the other hand, had been experimenting with some new ideas, that he was eager to test.

"Captain, when should I have the prize ready to sail?" asked Collier.

"At the earliest possible time. We need to arrive in Port Royal before the rumors about the *Oxford* begin. I will write a letter of explanation to Modyford and we can try and sell the *Cor Valant* before the next packet departs for England. That way, the King receives twenty-thousand pounds along *with* the news that he has lost one of his frigates."

"May I ask what you intend to tell the Governor about the *Oxford*?" asked Collier.

"I intend to stay as close to the truth as we understand it. We apprehended the officers of the *Cor Valant* on suspicion of piracy involving the *Westin*. The crewmen of the *Cor Valant* were shackled and one escaped and bludgeoned the Buccaneer who was asleep at his post. He also bludgeoned one of his shackled comrades. We are uncertain as to why."

"I believe I may have an answer to that riddle, Captain," said Collier.

"Indeed, Commander?"

"It is my belief, Captain, that the shackled man made a comment about O' Donte's clothing. The French, as you may recall, are exceedingly sensitive about their personal attire." Collier shot the words out of his mouth at bullet speed. Morgan nearly choked on his food as he began laughing.

It was fortunate for Collier that Pulverin had a relatively poor command of English. Pulverin had already killed a man in Port Royal for an offhand comment the man had made about Pulverin's clothing. He was named "Powder Horn" for a very good reason. Morgan regained control and stole a glance at Pulverin, who seemed amused by the whole affair.

"You tread in dangerous waters, Commander," warned Morgan. "The escaped prisoner, who we *assume* was O' Donte, then made his way over to the *Oxford* and released the officers, one of whom fired the magazine. One, or more, of these men survived the explosion and escaped by stealing a bugalet."

"How do you account for the hammer and nail found by the open shackles?" asked Collier.

"I am not sure I follow you," said Morgan.

"The hingepin had been driven out by the hammer and nail. That would have been a noisy proposition and would have awakened the guard."

"Continue," said Morgan, raising an eyebrow.

"It seems possible that the officers escaped on their own and then went over to the *Cor Valant* and rescued O' Donte. It was utter chaos on deck and they would have had the run of the ship," said Collier.

"That sounds reasonable. Anything else?" asked Morgan, looking around the table. "Captain Velasquez would you remain here?"

"Si, Capitan."

Morgan opened a drawer in a corner table and withdrew a slim leather-bound book, which he passed over to Velasquez.

"Un calendario," said Velasquez, opening the book.

"Exactly. This is the bait that you are going to give to Veronica. Here is the way it works," said Morgan, very slowly. "Each letter is shifted forward. So Cuba becomes 'Dvcb'. It is a very simple code. Veronica has been using codes for years. She will have this figured out in minutes. Do you understand, so far?"

"Of course, Capitan," said Velasquez.

"Here is what I want you to do. Go back to the journal you kept during your 'fishing expedition' and write the names of the cities you visited in the appropriate boxes in the calendar. Make a list of who you killed, what you came away with—like a cross, or ring. Put your son's birthday in for good measure. Are you with me?"

"Si, Capitan."

"What I am going to do is give you the date that the Plate Fleet is supposed to be in Savona. This must be kept secret, until *after* it has occurred. Do you understand?"

"I should not give her the calendario until after you go to Savona."

"That is correct, but I do not want you to give her the calendar. Make her work for it. I also want you to write the words 'Incursion de Cartagena' in the 17 April date."

"I understand now, perfectly. This is to make the sheeps go away from Maracaibo. And troops also. This is very good, Capitan." Velasquez sat there smiling, shaking his head in amazement.

"Thank you for your part in this adventure," said Morgan, scribbling rapidly with a wad. "This is the Savona date. Please destroy this paper immediately after you write it in your calendar."

"You may destroy it now, Capitan. I have it here," said Velasquez, pointing to his head.

"As you can see, you have a little over two weeks to wait before Veronica gets the calendar. She is a very cunning woman. I would advise you not to even meet her until the day after Savona." Velasquez nodded his head. "I have arranged to have you stay at the Golden Arrow in Kessenger's apartment. That will give you more credibility."

"Gracias, Capitan!"

"You have earned it. By the way, write the date of the *Oxford*'s destruction in the calendar, along with anything else you can think of. That will be all, Captain."

Velasquez hurried out of the small cabin and went straight for his sloop. He ordered his eight crewmen to careen the boat and scrape her bottom. He meant to win that race.

CHAPTER 15

In the weeks that followed, Collier's green recruits became veteran Buccaneers during a series of raids along the Darien. The fleet arrived at the Isle of Savona on schedule, but, as Morgan had predicted, the Plate Fleet never materialized. Morgan eventually split the fleet in half to make it easier to feed his troops. Raiding small towns rarely produced enough food to feed a hundred men, let alone seven hundred. So Captains Hansel, Collins, Jean and Head went off on their own with nine boats and two-hundred-eighty men. They were to cruise upon the western portion of Central and South America, while Morgan cruised to the east with his nine boats and five-hundred men. Both groups were to meet at the island of Ruba a week before the raid on Maracaibo. Velasquez and his men had been ordered to Ruba, as well. Velasquez arrived on time, but the nine boats in Hansel's group never appeared. Morgan decided the raid would go on without them. Velasquez had succeeded in duping Veronica, so the raid could not be delayed by even a day.

Collier had coughed up the four guineas and two wads to Velasquez, but not with out a protest. It seemed that the rudder had suddenly fallen off the *Cor Valant* a few hours after the race had begun. Owen was suspicious of foul play, but was unable to prove anything. It required the better part of a day to repair the rudder and it cost Owen and Collier the race.

Morgan had taken over Hansel's boat, the *Enchantress,* as his flagship. She was a bark with two masts and fourteen small guns. She was a slow boat, but she only drafted five feet, so she was ideal for the shallow waters in Lake Maracaibo.

Seven boats were now anchored off the coast of Ruba, two having been lost to wood-boring toredo worms. Their shore boats were ferrying wheat, goats and lambs from the island, where they had been produced by the local Indians. Ruba was a harsh, dry island, consisting mostly of white sand, but the Indians were able to eke out a living.

"Go ahead and tell the men we are going on another raid, but don't tell them where. They need to be well-rested," said Morgan, who was afraid that if there were Spanish informants in his ranks they still had time to alert the authorities in Maracaibo.

"Happy to oblige, Captain," said Collier. "Do you think it might be wise to have Velasquez aboard when we go through the channel?"

"I would rather have him ahead of us in his boat. He can take soundings. We sail with the sunset."

"Aye, Captain." Collier found Owen and instructed him to pass the word that the fleet would depart in two hours.

The seaway that the fleet would be entering was shaped like an hourglass with its top removed. The topless half was the Gulf of Venezuela. There were lighthouses on each side of the Gulf, approximately sixty miles apart. That made it possible to enter the mouth of the Gulf and travel unobserved for over fifty miles. At the waist of the hourglass lay the new fort, which would have to be taken before the fleet could enter Lake Maracaibo, the bottom portion of the hourglass.

Assuming that Veronica had alerted her contacts in Caracas, there was a good chance that only a skeleton crew would be manning the fort, the greater part of the Spanish troops having been ordered to Cartagena to protect the city against the up-coming invasion. Morgan decided to sail to within thirty miles of the fort, thus keeping his fleet below the horizon, and rest his men the following day, which was 16 April, 1669. Early the next morning, the boats would weigh anchor, sail the thirty-mile run and attack the fort at sunrise. According to Velasquez, there were large sand dunes in front of the fort that would offer protection.

A Buccaneer celebration was out of the question the night before the raid. The orders had been given when the boats dropped anchor. All fires were to be kept below decks and if any man fired a weapon for any reason he would be put to death. Morgan addressed the men in the pale moonlight, after their supper.

"Lads, tomorrow at sunrise we take the fort guarding the entrance to Lake Maracaibo. The fort will be manned by fourth-rate soldiers, who have never met their fathers. But keep low in the dunes to avoid a lucky shot. Take good aim and show these buggers what a Buccaneer can do with a musket. By tomorrow night, we will have the city of Maracaibo and all of her riches, and pretty ladies! Above all, remember that you may only use torture methods invented by the Holy Inquisitors!" Cheers went up among the crew and when the shouting died down, Morgan continued. "So drink the last of the Bordeaux provided by the *Cor Valant* and join me:

"Our father, who art in heaven…"

It was a magnificent performance. The men felt clean, much the way a Catholic might feel after a laborious confession. They were excited, but having gorged themselves on the last of the goats and chickens, and having drunk the last of the French wine, they were content to find their hammocks and wait for the bell in the early hours of 17 April, 1669.

"Bravo, Captain," said Collier, as he walked aft with Morgan.

"Nothing to it, really. Generals have been doing the same thing for centuries. You have to convince your men that God is on their side. It is utterly absurd, of course, because the other side feels exactly the same way. On the surface, this is a religious war; that much is for certain. Somewhere in the muddy depths lies the true motivation, which is greed. We are going to be stealing from the Spanish King and the Pope so that we can give it to our English King. Some of it, at any rate," both men chuckled. "By the way, I am sorry about the four guineas you lost to Velasquez. I was lucky and bet on his boat."

"I suspect foul play," said Collier.

"Of course! It was my suggestion. Never place a bet you cannot win! Sleep well, Commander."

"Same to you, Admiral." When Morgan opened his cabin door, Collier turned and began walking toward the binnacle to study charts for tomorrow's passage. Owen was there to greet him with a worried look on his face.

"Good evening, Lieutenant," said Collier.

"Evening, Commander."

"What is on your mind, son?" Collier gritted his teeth after he said "son," because it could have been taken as an insult, but it seemed to draw Owen in, rather than push him away.

"What did the Captain mean when he said the things about torture? Will I have to torture people?" The question was so innocent that Collier had an urge to hug Owen, to try and comfort him.

"Lawd, no! All that is required of you is to stay alive. If somebody tries to kill you, make sure that you kill him first! Simple as that. Stay by me and we will do this thing together." Owen was visibly calmer, but still troubled by something.

"What is the business about the 'Holy Inventors'?"

"You mean the 'Holy Inquisitors' and the methods they invented?" Collier had gone full circle from being close to tears, to laughter. Owen nodded his head. "The Inquisition was a group of murderers sanctioned by the church in Rome. It was one of the saddest chapters in English history. Hell, in the history of the entire world, for that matter. I am no expert on the subject, but my uncle *was* a scholar on that very topic and he tutored me for two years at Cambridge."

"You mean the papists?"

"Exactly. The Inquisitors were papists. *Are* papists. They are still around, doing very naughty things. Once we get control of Maracaibo, I will take you to 'The Hall' after it is cleaned up. 'The Hall' is where they torture people. I have been told that there is a 'Hall' in every city in the Darien."

"But why? Why are people being tortured!" Owen was becoming increasingly frustrated.

"For money and power, of course. Let's take a little trip back in history. Do you have any relatives who were put to death for witchcraft?"

"How did you know that, Sir?"

"A lucky guess. Who was she?"

"How did you know it was a she?" asked Owen, incredulously. "She was my great auntie Gwen, on my father's side."

"If you could trace your family line back two more generations, you would find others. My line goes back to eleven-hundred and the church has not been kind to us," said Collier, with a look of disgust on his face.

"I am sorry, Sir, but I must seem like the village idiot. My studies were in mathematics and things nautical. History is not my strong point, but I am eager to learn."

"Very well, Lieutenant, I shall be your tutor until you tire of me. I will leave you with a question: What agent is responsible for the deaths of more people in England than the plague and all of her wars? I do not expect the answer for weeks, or months, or years to come. I suggest a mug of rum for sleep. Good night, Lieutenant." It seemed to Owen that Commander Collier had aged ten years in the last five minutes.

"Good night, Commander." Owen remained on deck after Collier went below. His mind was racing and he suddenly realized that he too, had aged in some mysterious way. He knew that he would not get a wink of sleep, so he followed Collier's advice and went below to find a keg of rum.

At midnight the small ships hoisted their anchors and began the six-hour sail to the channel. The wind was at their backs and the sailing was effortless; a strange calm before the violence that was sure to come. The fleet arrived an hour before dawn and the fort could be seen clearly in the darkness. There was light coming from the windows, but none of the officers who were gathered on the deck of the *Enchantress* could see any sentries. In fact, there was no activity whatsoever. The consensus was that the military had been transferred to another location. Evidently, the fort had been manned by civilians, who had neglected to post sentries. Morgan was amazed by the deductive powers of his officers and wanted to tell them what had actually happened with Veronica, but it would have to wait. She was much too valuable to waste in idle talk.

Morgan positioned his fleet just out of range of the fort's guns. Before dawn he ordered boats lowered over the side and then began ferrying men to the dunes in front of the fort. When dawn broke, over three-hundred men were on shore and the ferrying process continued. An alarm was finally raised in the fort and men began scurrying about. The first shots were from the smaller caliber long guns, which missed the fleet by over a hundred yards. A prudent Commander would have used less powder and made the balls drop short, in the hopes of drawing the fleet closer in, thought Morgan.

When the sun began its magnificent rise in the east, the fort was blinded for two hours. Morgan took advantage of this and landed another hundred men on the dunes without loss, despite the incessant fire from the long guns. The Buccaneers in the dunes took their time and, one by one, they picked off seven men who were manning the gun placements. Morgan had been timing the rates of fire from the fort, and the four guns that were being fired had gone from a cycle time of four minutes, to over seven minutes. So far, the Buccaneers had not suffered a loss.

The breeze that had carried the fleet to the channel now began to harden. Sand was flying in the dunes and eyes were becoming gritty. Worse yet, flintlocks were beginning to jam. By noon, only one-in-ten Buccaneers could fire their muskets. Still, the Buccaneers who could fire, did fire, and the cycle time of the cannons was now greater than ten minutes. For the most part, the Buccaneers wrapped their faces and muskets with whatever cloth they could find and hunkered down in the dunes. The sixty-foot walls above them supported sixteen huge cannons, which could not be pointed downwards toward the Buccaneers. The Spanish defenders continued to fire their cannons, even though every shot came up a hundred yards short.

The Buccaneer fleet was straining at anchor in the strong wind, with their aft ends toward the fortress. Morgan stood on the aft deck of the *Enchantress* with Commander Collier and Lieutenant Owen, watching the insane battle with their telescopes trained on the fort.

"They are beginning to tire, Captain. Shall we go ashore?" asked Collier.

"What are your thoughts, Lieutenant?" asked Morgan. The seventeen-year-old officer hesitated and then cleared his throat.

"I agree with the Commander, Captain. The Dons are tired. They are either behaving irrationally, or they are untrained and they think that, by keeping up their fire, they will prevent our boats from approaching. In any case, they have apparently received no reinforcements and they have lost several men. There are sixteen gun placements in that fort and they are only using four of them. It is almost embarrassing, Sir."

Morgan looked over at Collier and smiled contentedly. "What would you have us do, Lieutenant? Go ashore, or remain here?" It was an awkward question and Owen knew he was being tested. He looked at Collier for direction. Collier nodded his head, giving Owen the freedom to speak his mind.

"Well, Captain, the wind is stiffening. Our men are blind, at the moment, and if we land more men, the situation will not change. It appears that there are only sixteen men in the fort and in another hour, or two they will be utterly exhausted. There is also the possibility that this is all a ruse."

"What do you mean, Lieutenant?" asked Morgan, with a raised eyebrow.

"What we see here, Captain, is utter incompetence!" said Owen, forgetting who he was talking to and just letting his recent stream of thoughts flow. "The Dons have fired over a ton and a half of twenty-four pounders into this bay without a single hit, or even the hope of a hit. They have been given no assistance from Maracaibo. Why build a fort of this size and then not defend it? Maybe they are trying to lure us in with our guard down. They could have a thousand men in there." Morgan smiled again.

"That is a possibility and we cannot prove otherwise until we actually take the fort. Once you get to know the Dons, you will learn to expect incompetence. They are horribly over-extended in the Caribbean and that is why we continue to earn a living here. We go in at dusk. By then, the land breeze will be up and it should temper the blow. I think that you will find the town totally deserted, by the time we get there. In the meantime, we have a few hours to relax and enjoy what may be the last decent meal we see in weeks."

Morgan found the bosun and requested a meal consisting of fruit and cheese, be sent to his cabin. He had to behave himself now. It simply would not do to have a painful toe at the beginning of a raid. When the meal came, he ate it rapidly and then took a nap, having given instructions to be awakened at dusk with a pot of fresh coffee.

For the next two hours, the cannon fire from the fort came to a virtual standstill. The wind was forceful enough to pepper the gunners with sand and force them to retreat from the parapets. As the afternoon sun dipped deeper in the sky, the wind slacked off and the shore birds returned to the lush-green island.

Morgan downed three cups of coffee and went on deck, his heart pounding wildly. Browne, Collier and Owen were already aboard his gaff-rigged gig, raising the sail. Ten other launches were loaded with heavily armed men, chomping at the bit. Morgan patted the pulpers in his jacket one last time before he lowered himself into the gig. The small boats cast off and almost immediately the cannons began firing again. The shots fell short at first, but as the boats moved closer to shore, they were surrounded by violent splashes. Owen raised his telescope and saw two men running from the fort.

"Over there, Sir! The men are deserting the fort!" Owen pointed to the south side of the island, where three men could now be seen wading in the shallows to the mainland. The cannon fire was diminishing, but a little past the halfway point, a launch took a direct hit amidships and exploded. Two men were killed outright and eight others were left to fend for themselves. Musket fire from the parapets kept the men on the dunes from moving.

Morgan's gig was the first to land and by that time, the fort was silent. The Buccaneers in the sand began to rise one by one and shake out their clothes. After twelve hours in the sun they were parched and every bodily orifice they possessed was filled with sand.

"Evening ladies," said Morgan as he ran past a group of men in the dunes. Browne, Collier and Owen were close behind with pistols drawn. Morgan saw another group of Spaniards wading to the mainland, but they were out of range. The hundred-yard sprint to the south side of the fort seemed like an eternity. When the four men finally arrived, they were winded, but they forced themselves forward into the dark building, walking with their weapons drawn and cocked. The clicking of their boots on the stone floor made them sitting ducks for any marksmen who had stayed behind. One by one, the other Buccaneers filed in behind them. Soon there were a hundred men in the fort and one of them farted with a resonant echo. The men laughed and Morgan hushed them to silence.

"Bugger me!" whispered Morgan. He began to sprint to the far side of the fort. He had spotted a dull glow on the floor and took it to be a "match", which consisted of a piece of string that had been embedded with wax. It was burning slowly toward a powder train that would lead to a barrel of powder, or more.

Morgan ran like a demon. Brown and Collier were puzzled and stayed put, but Owen had also seen the dim glow and ran behind Morgan. The closer he got to the glow, the more convinced Morgan became that it was indeed a slow match. Morgan was close now and he could see the outlines of an opened door. There was a small flame just inside, beyond the threshold. The fools left the door open!

In the light-speed thoughts that flood a near-death brain, Gbessay suddenly appeared to Morgan and whispered, "You will cheat death two times," and then she threw her head back and laughed. The *Oxford*, he thought, ah! Suddenly he realized that he was going to make it to the match before it reached the powder train.

Morgan crossed the threshold and put the heel of his boot on the match. He began to laugh hysterically and Owen joined in with him. The room was pitch black now that the match was extinguished, but within seconds, a Buccaneer appeared with a torch. Morgan and Owen were still belly laughing, but suddenly the room lit up and the men froze. Directly behind them were forty barrels of powder. Two thick powder trains led to barrels that had had their lids removed and had been tipped over.

"I don't think they like us, Captain," said Owen. Morgan shook his head and started laughing again.

"Could you bring that torch in here so that we can get a better look at this powder?" said Morgan, who was belly laughing with

Owen again. The laughter was contagious and the entire fort echoed with joy for the first time in its history.

Captain Velasquez joined the throng of men who were rotating past the doorway to see the fort's magazine and the crazy Englishmen inside. He crossed himself involuntarily as he walked by and suddenly started laughing too. He had no doubt that if Morgan had failed to spot the slow match, they all would have been blown to hell, along with the fort itself.

To the crew, this was further evidence that Morgan had supernatural powers. Some felt that the "Obeah Woman" in Port Royal had conjured up powers from the spirit world for him, while others believed what the Spanish did; that Morgan was a demon and simply could not *be* killed.

"Three cheers for the Captain!" The noise was deafening as the cheers went up and echoed against the limestone walls. Morgan covered his ears, and with a broad smile plastered on his face, he began to walk through his men toward the exit as the cheering continued. He looked at the stationary men and studied their clothes. Bandanas on their heads, mostly, knee-length pants, some with shirts, but most without. But each man, with the exception of Pulverin, had a cutlass attached to his belt. All in all, a very frightening group of men. They are going to scare the hell out of the people of Maracaibo, he thought.

Collier linked up with Morgan just outside the fort. The men *inside* the fort had discovered a keg of rum and had opened the bung, helping themselves to large helpings in whatever containers they could find.

"Find fifty sober men and load as much powder as you can into the boats, then find me in the town," said Morgan. "We can spike the guns tomorrow and destroy as much of the fort as we can with the powder that is left over. Belay that order. Just shut the door to the magazine and place a guard."

"Aye, Captain. God bless your eyes," said Collier.

"I was expecting it, so don't give me too much credit. Everybody else was looking up to find snipers. Hired guns do not sacrifice their lives in hopeless causes."

"Point taken, Captain. How many men will you require to take the town?"

"None, I should think, but we should probably make some noise. Say, thirty men who can walk. Find Velasquez and have him arrange to have the men put aboard my gig and the two small sloops. Leave the rest in the fort to sleep it off." Morgan let the hammer down on one of his pulpers, then placed it in his coat.

"Captain, you seem so nonchalant about the possibility of the Dons re-grouping. You act as though the city is already ours."

"It *is* ours, Commander. The men firing on us today were not Spaniards. They were probably Italian mercenaries. All of the Dons are currently in Cartagena bracing for a Buccaneer attack."

"Forgive me Captain, but how do you know that?"

"Because *I* sent them there!" said Morgan, exasperated.

"*You* sent them there, Captain?" said Collier, in a state of total disbelief.

"Correct, Commander and that gives us a fair amount of time to ransack Maracaibo. Then we can proceed along the coast to Gibraltar, just as L' Ollonais did. The difficulty will be forthcoming, when we try to leave the lake." Lake Maracaibo was, in fact, the largest lake in South America and it would take the Buccaneers weeks to raid the two large towns along its banks. By that time, there would be a substantial force at the mouth of the lake.

Collier was dumbfounded and stood there silently as Morgan pulled a white clay pipe out of a leather satchel attached to his rear waistband. Secretly enjoying Collier's utter confusion, Morgan slowly loaded his pipe and felt much the same as a menstruating woman would feel entering a chocolate shop. He had outwitted the Dons—again. Lieutenant Owen walked up to the two men with a smile on his face.

"You are a brave man," said Morgan. Owen flushed and looked down at the ground.

"Thank you, Sir."

"Lieutenant, if you would be so kind, assemble an attachment of thirty men, sober if possible, to take the city of Maracaibo."

"Of course, Captain," said Owen, who turned and walked away.

"Lieutenant, please see if you can find me a torch."

"I will, Sir."

Like every man who participated in the landing, Morgan, who seemed completely oblivious to the cannon balls falling around him, had found it necessary to keep his backside pinched-up tight to avoid leakage. Now it was time to relax and the best way to start that process was to light a pipe containing first-cut, rum-cured Virginia tobacco. He had the pipe! He had it loaded with the best tobacco that money could buy, but his matches were wet. Where was the fochin' torch?

CHAPTER 16

It was a half-mile walk from Maracaibo's wharf to the center of the city. The sober men in the group kept a lookout for traps and snipers, but Morgan was not concerned. He knew that there had not been enough time to construct any elaborate traps, and the mercenaries would have gone deeply into the bush by now. Morgan was at the front of the procession, telling stories to the officers that walked beside him. Just behind him were Owen, Kessenger, Balfor, Browne, Collier and Thacther.

"Can any of you define the word 'city'?" asked Morgan. The implication was obvious: was Maracaibo a city, or a town, with its ten-thousand inhabitants? Kessenger, who had consumed every psychoactive substance available at that stage of their deployment, was the first to reply.

"A 'city' is a place where there are two brothels, or more." There was laughter and Morgan encouraged it. The more noise, the better. The procession moved rapidly along the coastal road with their torches lighting the way. There was an eerie darkness over the city that was coming into view.

"A 'city' is place with at least one Hall of Inquisition," ventured Collier.

"No, that would be a 'Spanish' city," said Balfor. Again, there was laughter. Owen was beginning to cringe about the thought of entering the "Hall" in Maracaibo. The stories he had been told were the stuff of nightmares, but he also had a perverse curiosity that would eventually force him to enter the building.

"According to the King's lexicon, a 'city' is a large 'town,'" said Morgan.

"So that would make a 'town' a small 'city,'" offered Owen.

"Precisely," said Morgan. "Even though Maracaibo is much smaller than Panama, or Caracas, I think we should refer to it as a 'city,' because it sounds so much more impressive. Well, well. What have we here?" Directly ahead was a black slave walking toward them. He was wearing a pair of short brown pants and nothing else. The group of Buccaneers halted and became silent as Morgan grabbed a torch and went forward to greet the man. The slave stood silently with his head downcast and eyes riveted to the ground. Morgan raised the torch to get a better look at the man. He had several missing fingers and tribal markings on his temples, that Morgan recognized.

"Kinny, boo wah?" said Morgan. The slave raised his head in disbelief and smiled. Morgan was speaking the man's dialect! Morgan had mastered the basics of greeting and asking very simple questions, but he would soon have to make the switch to Spanish.

"Boo wah, beseah! Kahunyehna?" Within a few minutes the slave, whose name was Conteh, agreed to help the Buccaneers in exchange for his freedom. As Morgan suspected, Conteh told him in broken Spanish that the town was virtually deserted.

Conteh guided the Buccaneers through the center of the lifeless City. He pointed out the "Hall" to Velasquez, who then split off from the group, taking Collier with him. Owen volunteered to go with them, but Collier ordered him to stay with Morgan; tomorrow would be soon enough to view the grizzly horrors of the Inquisitors. Morgan bivouacked the bulk of the men in the large cathedral in the center of town, while he and the officers headed toward the Governor's mansion that was situated on a small hill just ahead. Their boot heels clicked on the cobblestone street and the sound echoed through the silent city.

A musket shot rang out and the men froze. They looked back at the cathedral and saw a cow in the middle of the road take a step and then fall to the ground dead.

"Lieutenant Thatcher, would you be kind enough to secure the Sirloin from that unfortunate animal?"

"Gladly, Sir."

The Governor's mansion was a classic Spanish design, two stories high, with a beautiful central courtyard. There were lamps burning in some of the rooms, but the house seemed deserted. Morgan put his finger into a horse turd near the front gate. It was warm. There was a loud metallic gong when Balfor kicked a silver serving tray that lay in the shadows on the brick path. A young hundred-pound mastiff was barking on the porch and the men halted. Morgan pulled out a pulper and cocked it. Browne patted him on the shoulder.

"Let me see what I can do with this beast," said Browne. He walked toward the porch and the dog backed up a few steps and barked louder. The dog's gargoyle-like face was flinging spit out of his mouth with each bark. His bared teeth accentuated the wrinkles in his snout. Browne sat on the steps and waited. The barking stopped and Browne patted his thigh. The mastiff's tail dropped and he walked over to Browne and began licking him on the face.

Once inside the mansion, the first order of business was the wine cellar. Morgan walked down the narrow staircase with a lamp in his hand, while the others fanned out to search the house. The door to the cellar was open and Morgan was delighted to see three massive wine racks, each about half full. There was a broken bottle on the floor. Morgan lowered the lamp to read the label; it was a '61 Bordeaux.

"Pity," said Morgan. Most of the wines that had been left behind were Spanish, but they were of high quality and there were a few dozen French and Italian bottles, as well. Ironically, there were also several bottles of excellent Jamaican rum. Morgan selected a bottle of Chianti and a cote du Rhone for tonight and went upstairs to the kitchen.

"Excellent! They have left us some stemware," said Morgan rummaging through the cupboards. Owen heard Morgan's voice and appeared in the kitchen.

"Beg pardon, Sir?"

"Stop calling me 'Sir', will you? I was just thanking the Governor for leaving us some stemware." Morgan began opening drawers, searching in vain for a corkscrew. "Probably made of silver, so they took the damned thing."

"Sir?"

"There you go again," said Morgan absently, as he pulled a pulper from his belt. Owen reflexively took a step backward.

"Relax, will you? Calling me Sir is not a capital offense," said Morgan who turned the pulper barrel downward and put it on top of the bottle of cote du Rhone. "I may be inclined toward a nasty flogging, however." Morgan clasped the palm of his hand on the butt of the pulper and pushed downward. The cork gave way and went into the bottle. Morgan picked a dishcloth off the counter and wiped off the end of the barrel. "Best damn gun ever made."

Morgan placed the pulper back in his waistband and picked up a wineglass. He held it up to the lamp and found a smudge, which he wiped off with the dishcloth. He repeated the process with the second glass and then poured each glass half full.

"The Riches of Maracaibo," said Morgan raising his glass. Owen reached for his glass, but fumbled it, nearly tipping it over.

"Maracaibo," said Owen.

"Starting the party without us?" said Collier walking into the kitchen. "I like your new house."

"The Governor was late on his mortgage. That cupboard over there," said Morgan to Collier, who was trying to find a glass.

"What are we drinking?" said Collier, picking up the bottle. "Oh, very nice." Thatcher walked in next, carrying two banana leaves filled with Sirloin, dripping blood all over the kitchen floor.

"Over there, you little savage. In the sink," said Collier. "We need a cook. Where is Browne?"

"Upstairs trying on clothes, last I saw," said Owen.

"Men's, or women's?" asked Morgan.

Collier walked through the kitchen door and hollered into the living room, "Browne! Are you in here?"

"Upstairs, Governor! Be right down!" Browne hollered back. Collier walked back into the kitchen.

"How was the Hall?" asked Morgan.

"I have no yardstick by which to judge it, but it was the most godawful place I've ever seen. We found a couple of Indian boys locked in a cell. Turns out their parents were murdered by the Dons and they were forced to service the clergy, beginning about six months ago. Velasquez wants to take them back to Port Royal," said Collier.

"Fine by me," said Morgan.

"There was a chair in there that was covered with spikes. The back, the seat, and the leg rests. All covered with spikes. It was dripping with blood," said Collier.

"I have never been one for Spanish furniture," said Morgan.

Browne walked into the kitchen dressed in a Spanish officer's uniform.

"I see we have begun the celebration."

"Where is Jones?" asked Collier.

"He just arrived. I sent him back to the sloop to get some herb," said Browne

"Are you planning to share? Love your jacket." said Morgan.

"Certainly, if you will spot me a glass of wine. You seem to be doing just fine, so it appears that they didn't bother with poison."

"Captain, should we go after the Dons tonight? They cannot be far," said Owen, earnestly.

"Do as you please, Lieutenant, but I am staying here. We will have an excellent meal followed by a sound sleep. The Dons are up to their bung holes in mosquitoes and they will not sleep a wink. By midday tomorrow, they will be ripe for the plucking. Have another glass of wine. Where *is* Jones?"

"'Ere, Sir," said Jones walking into the kitchen with two other Buccaneers, who were carrying a bushel basket full of tropical fruit. "We managed a few eggs too, Sir." Jones headed out to the stove kitchen, which was an out-building, separate from the main house. Another Buccaneer appeared and walked through the kitchen with a young sow in toe.

Jones reappeared in the kitchen and placed a small satchel and a long stem pipe on the counter.

"Gents, this is for medicinal purposes only," said Jones with a wink.

CHAPTER 17

The Buccaneers who had spent the night in the fort awakened feeling better than they had any right to. They had started drinking at sundown and without any dinner in their bellies, most of them were passed out by nine o' clock. Awakening at six o' clock had given their livers nine hours to detoxify their bodies. The bulk of them headed back to the boats anchored in front of the fort to search for food and especially water.

By ten o'clock, the boats had been filled to capacity with powder, shot and an assortment of muskets. Collier had ordered the Buccaneers to charge the cannons in the fort and put wedges in front of the balls, so that when they were ignited they would rip apart. He never wanted to face those guns again. The usual method of "spiking" a cannon was to drive an iron spike into the ignition port on the backside of the cannon. Sometimes an enterprising blacksmith could either drive the spike all the way through into the barrel, or pry the spike out.

Collier ordered Velasquez to lead the boats through the channel into the lake. It was nearly high tide and if the larger boats were going to make it past the sandbars, it would have to be now. Velasquez had a man on the beam of his boat casting a lead weight over the side and then pulling it up to check for depth as they entered the channel.

"Two fathoms!" the man called out. Then as they began the approach over the sandbars he switched from fathoms to feet. "Three feet and sandy! Large rocks to windward!" It was a laborious task because the ships were only moving one knot per hour, but finally, they made it through into the lake. Velasquez spent the next several hours with his crew and the two Indian boys sailing back and forth through the channel always searching for the best route.

Collier decided it was time to blow the castle, so he ordered all non-essential Buccaneers back to the city. Fifteen barrels of powder remained in the fort and they had been placed in strategic locations in the front of the fort, where it was hoped that some of the walls would collapse. The cannons were set to go off first, because the fuses leading to them might be destroyed during the main explosion. Fuses had been cut to exact lengths and placed in the cannons. They needed to explode as close to simultaneously as was possible, because, once again, flying metal might destroy the fuses. It required sixteen men to light the guns simultaneously. The fuses were cut for two minutes and it was a sixty foot run to get out of the fort. It would be close. All of the men were barefoot to lessen the chances of tripping. The black powder in the barrels were each given a three-minute fuse.

"On the count of one!" said the gunnery Sergeant. "Five, four..." Each of the sixteen men held glowing punks in one of their trembling hands, just above the fuses. One lad of perhaps fifteen years, was trembling so badly that he had to steady his punk hand with the other. "Three, two, one!" There was a resonant sizzle as fifteen of the fuses began to burn. The fifteen-year-old hit the glowing end of his punk on the side of the fuse and knocked off the cherry. He bent down to try and re-light the punk and succeeded after a few seconds. He raised up and struck his head on the butt-end of the cannon and was out cold.

Jenkins, who was the last man in the throng running toward the door, heard the thud of the fifteen-year-old's forehead hit the ground and the subsequent egg-shell-crack of his nose being crushed. He stopped and looked back. "Thousand fifty five, thousand fifty six he mouthed with his lips. He was already winded, but he ran back to where the boy had fallen and scooped him up and threw him over his right shoulder. With the extra weight, he had a difficult time walking. He had passed sixty and was now up to "thousand fifteen" on the next minute with forty feet to go.

Jenkins pushed forward toward the door. Each step was a new agony in his thighs as he struggled with the extra weight. Thousand twenty six…he knew he could make it with a few seconds to spare. The fuses continued to sizzle in the distance. There was an irregularity in the floor and Jenkins' right foot was snagged for an instant and then the leg gave out; both men went to the floor, ten feet from the door. Jenkins had a searing pain in his right knee. Thousand thirty eight. He struggled to straighten his knee out, while trying to figure out how to get out of the building. Finally, there was a pop and the knee went straight and the pain was diminished, but he was afraid to bend the knee again, fearing that it would lock. Thousand forty five…

Jenkins figured he had about fifteen seconds left before the cannons blew. If he could make his injured leg work, he should be able to get the boy and himself out of the building in time. If the knee locked-up again, at least *he* could escape. He grabbed the boy's arms and began scooting along the floor. Pull with left leg and scoot. Pull boy forward. Pull with left leg and scoot. The left leg bore the burden and he did not have to use the injured right leg. Jenkins pulled the lifeless body over the threshold and to his immediate left, behind the vertical post of the door. He lay the boy on the sandstone entryway and pulled him out of harm's way. Jenkins then held his ears, bracing himself for the explosion that was about to come. He realized that he had lost track of his "thousand count", but started again with one thousand one, when the first cannon exploded. That meant that in sixty seconds, the fort was going to blow. They had to move quickly.

There was a brief roar of hot gas that blew through the door and sound of serial explosions inside the fort, followed by the sound of metallic clanks at random intervals. A large chunk of metal hit the transom of the door and ricocheted back into the fort. Jenkins looked down at his forearm and saw that he was bleeding. It was a trivial wound and he concentrated on getting the boy to safety. With fifty seconds remaining, he had few options left. With an injured knee, he had fewer still. Jenkins had participated in placing the explosives and he knew that they were directed outward, toward the channel. It made sense to go to the back of the fort to seek refuge. Mercifully, the boy's eyes opened, but he was dazed with blood trickling out of his nose.

"Wake up lad! We need to move now!" screamed Jenkins. Thousand twenty eight... The boy's eyes darted around, as he tried to make sense of where he was and what had happened. Jenkins bent down to pull the boy to his feet and the searing pain returned to his knee. He went down with his right knee half bent and locked in position. Thousand thirty six. The boy rose to his feet, unsure whether to run, or help Jenkins.

"Help me straighten this leg out!" screamed Jenkins. The boy took Jenkins' heel in his right hand and leveraged the upper shin with his left. Jenkins let out a scream when the knee popped back into place. He continued to count; thousand-forty-five... Jenkins struggled to his feet with the boy's help. The boy placed Jenkins' right arm over his shoulder and they began to negotiate the six sandstone steps.

"Only ten seconds left! You better go on ahead, lad!"

The boy did not respond. They were moving together well now, less than a second per step. Thousand fifty five... Finally, they reached the landing and the boy pivoted on his heel and directed Jenkins into the space beneath the stairs.

"Thousand fifty nine," said Jenkins and they both held their ears, but there was no explosion. They looked at each other and shrugged their shoulders. Suddenly, the earth moved with a massive convulsion and a shock wave came that rained debris down on them from the stairs above. They were both temporarily deafened by the blast. Huge chunks of limestone began falling around them and then everything was calm. They took the handkerchiefs off their heads and held them up to their mouths. They were completely enveloped by a dense cloud of smoke and dust.

The Buccaneers on the mainland cheered as the smoke cleared and the damage to the fort became evident. The roof had collapsed and two of the parapets along with it. A portion of the front wall of the magazine had blown out into the channel. It would take six months to repair the damage with the forced-labor of the local Indians.

Morgan and the officers were the first to wade in the shallows on their way to inspect the fort. The cloud of dust had cleared, but there was still smoke rising from the fort. Morgan assumed that the wooden gun carriages were on fire, and if one or more of the cannons had not blown, there could still be more explosions.

Jenkins and the boy were standing on the shore, cleaning their faces with seawater when the officers arrived. Communication proved impossible, because of their deafness, but it was clear that something had gone terribly wrong. Jenkins and the boy were completely white, except for their freshly-washed faces.

The officers were eager to enter the fort, but Morgan ordered everyone to stay away until tomorrow. Morgan studied the undamaged rear portion of the fort. He noticed that there were parapets for cannons there also and he wondered why they would have taken the time to build them. Perhaps they had a contingency plan for an attack from the mainland. "Interesting," he whispered.

CHAPTER 18

During the walk back to town, Morgan told Collier to locate the "Turk" and order him to assemble a group of a hundred men to scour the countryside. The "Turk" was well over six feet tall and weighed in at two hundred fifty pounds. When he was a young child, he had had a high fever and there was not a hair on his body because of it. He had tattoos done with India ink covering his trunk and face, even the top of his head. He was easily the most menacing man Morgan had ever seen. Despite his demonic appearance, he was actually quite gentle unless provoked. He had two wives and six children between them back in Port Royal. In addition, he was one of the most intelligent people Morgan had ever known. He had, in fact, read every book in Morgan's substantial library. Because he was a natural leader, Morgan had tried to promote him to an officer's rank, but he had always refused.

The slave Conteh was certain that he could lead the Buccaneers to where the bulk of the City's inhabitants were hiding. Conteh described a natural spring on a cattle ranch in the foothills, about four miles out of town. He assured Morgan that his men would return with treasure and prisoners.

The Turk assembled the team of Buccaneers and gave Conteh a cutlass, which made him beam with joy. Little did he know that within a short time the Buccaneers would force him to use the cutlass to prove his loyalty.

The party departed and the officers went back to the Governor's Mansion for lunch and naps. Jones had the table set and the food ready when the men arrived. The Buccaneers had found a huge green back turtle laying eggs on the beach last night. They allowed her to complete her task before they slaughtered her.

"Take your seats, Sirs. We have turtle steak today for lunch and a pig roast for dinner. The service life can be rough," said Jones.

"Thank you, Mr. Jones," said Morgan. "Did anybody figure out what happened to Jenkins?"

"One of the men said that Jenkins went back in the fort to rescue the boy and in the process, tore his knee to pieces," said Balfor.

"His knee wasn't that badly damaged," said Browne. "He just tore some cartilage and it locked his knee. He'll be fine. Both of my knees do the same thing." He fired up the clay pipe and passed it around the table. "Captain, what do you make of that Conteh fellow?"

"He is an import from the Gold Coast—been here about two seasons, badly treated, by the looks of him."

"Are you really going to set him free?" asked Owen.

"Absolutely, if he lives up to his end of the bargain. I have been thinking about turning him into an archer," said Morgan.

"What ever for?" asked Collier.

"I have a little wager to propose, Commander." Collier's eyes lighted up. "I will wager five guineas against your three, that after proper training, Conteh can deliver eight arrows into a target twenty feet away, before you can hit it with a pistol shot two times. You may use only one pistol." Collier thought it over for about five seconds.

"You have yourself a bet, Captain," said Collier, with a big smile on his face. Then it occurred to him what Morgan had said; "Never place a bet you cannot win."

"Count me in for three guineas, at the same odds," said Balfor, the handsome mulatto-heartthrob of Port Royal. He had already figured out how to win the bet; place two balls in the first shot and then fire a blank, which could be done in three seconds by just adding a little powder to the barrel and cocking the hammer. Morgan already had something similar up his sleeve.

"Done. Imagine what we could accomplish if we could unleash a torrent of arrows immediately before a boarding. Say we hit our targets half of the time. We would not kill them outright, but they would be in no condition to repel a boarding-party if they knew they were mortally wounded. Add to that the fact that if the archers fired from the shadows, the Dons would have no idea where to return fire." The room was silent as Morgan took a deep draw on the pipe. He passed it along to Owen.

The officers were impressed with the turtle steaks. The meat had been coated with coarse black pepper and butter, with a hint of cayenne and fresh basil from the garden. For some inexplicable reason their appetites had risen to protean proportions.

"What do you suppose caused the scarring on Conteh's back. Wait! Before you answer, I realize it was some sort of whipping, but what could leave such scars?" asked Owen.

"Maybe the Dons flogged him in the Hall," ventured Collier.

"Possibly, but he has been behaving himself for the last six months," said Browne.

"How can you say that?" asked Balfor.

"God almighty, man, you are half Negro yourself. Haven't you ever had a deep wound? It takes up to six months to fully re-pigment."

"Now that you mention it, I did have a bad burn on my hand when I was a child. It was a sickly white color--sort of like you--for about three months. I prayed every night it would not spread," said Balfor, who leaned his head back and began to laugh. There was a palpable tension at the table until Browne picked up a dinner roll and hurled it at Balfor, striking him on the forehead, then everybody began to laugh.

"Browne is actually right, for once," chuckled Morgan. "Conteh came over on a British slaver. The first night on the boat he was chained below decks and got hold of one of the mates' ankles. He bit him down to the bone! When the mate got loose he kicked Conteh in the groin so hard that he lost one of his balls. The following morning, Conteh received fifty lashes with a cat. The mate he had bitten eventually lost his leg due to infection. Conteh said it was a fair trade."

"It is amazing they didn't kill him," said Kessenger.

"And loose a hundred pounds at auction?" asked Balfor.

"In my opinion, if Conteh had lost a hundred pounds, he would be worth nothing at auction," said Browne. Balfor retrieved the dinner roll and threw it back at Browne. The roll knocked over a glass of red wine, which ended up in Browne's lap. Balfor held his mouth in mock horror. Browne stood up and clenched his fists in the air.

"See what you have done! My dress uniform! I shan't be able to attend the Ball tonight!" cried Browne. Serious laughter erupted around the table. Owen sprayed half-chewed turtle steak into his napkin. Morgan choked on his wine. Jones, who had come in from the out-kitchen with a three-layered chocolate cake on a platter, was laughing with such intensity that he tripped on the threshold and the cake pitched forward off the platter, directly onto the tile floor. Jones ended up on the floor with the officers watching him. Every time that he tried to come out of the laughing fit, he glanced up at the table and the whole thing started over again. He realized he might be flogged for insubordination, but even *that* seemed funny.

Browne was the first to make a move. He packed the pipe and picked up the lamp on the table, along with a fork. He walked over and sat down on the tile floor close to the cake, cross-legged. He fired up the pipe and took a deep draw. Browne blasted the smoke out of his lungs, as Jones began another fit of laughter. Browne took a swipe with his fork and brought back a mouth-full of cake.

"Um good. Eat many before tribe come!" said Browne to Jones, who convulsed with renewed laughter. Morgan was quick to see an opportunity and he joined Browne on the floor next to him. Morgan took a spoon full of cake and savored the flavor as he reached for the pipe. He took a long draw and then started laughing. He took some frosting from the cake and coated his front teeth and looked over at Browne, smiling broadly.

"Hey sailor! You wan' blow job?" said Morgan in a high-pitched voice. Browne had just taken a huge bite of cake and he choked on it.

Owen went over and sat down next to Browne and began devouring the cake. It was his first experience with the strange herb and hunger was the natural outcome. Next came Balfor and Kessenger.

"This is incredibly good," said Owen.

"Thank you, Sir," said Jones, during a brief respite from the laughter. "It's me latest invention! I calls it me 'chocolate upside-down cake'!" The laughter resumed.

While the others took their siestas, Collier and Owen walked down to the Hall. There was a strange silence in the city. Although neither man could read nor write Spanish, it was somehow obvious when they passed a bakery, or a dry goods store. Owen had never seen a rabid dog before, but he had paid attention to the stories that he had heard from long ago. When he saw the dog in the distance, he suspected that the animal was rabid. It was the strange way the dog walked and the spit that issued from his mouth that made Owen cock the hammer on his pistol. He looked at Collier and saw that his superior was unaware of the danger that confronted them. Owen drew the cutlass from his belt as a back up plan, in case his pistol misfired. The dog moved closer and Owen was now convinced that the animal was rabid. He raised his pistol on the dog and let a ball fly at thirty feet. He had aimed at the dog's head, but the ball hit the dog in his neck and dropped him cold.

Collier was puzzled by Owen's behavior. The pistol report drew several Buccaneers out of shops they were looting.

"I take it you don't like dogs."

"It's not that, Sir! That animal was rabid!" said Owen defensively.

"How could you tell? By the way, stop calling me Sir."

"It was the way he walked. It is hard for me to say exactly what was different about it, but I've been around dogs my entire life and I have never seen a dog walk that way. When he got closer, I could see him drooling gobs of spit out of his mouth." They walked over to where the dead dog lay in the road. There was a pool of blood forming under the dog's neck and white foam filled his mouth.

"It seems you were right, Lieutenant. A fitting start for a tour of the Hall. Keep a sharp eye out, lads," said Collier to the small group of curious on-lookers. "If there is one rabid dog, there will be others."

Collier looked around to get his bearings. The cathedral was just ahead and the Hall was a block beyond it. In the smaller Spanish towns, the Hall was generally located in the basement of the largest church. In Maracaibo, however, the Hall was in a separate building altogether.

"This is it," said Collier. Owen was relieved to see an ordinary appearing one story building, with the usual red tile roof. They walked inside and found papers scattered everywhere, bookcases turned over and several piles of human waste located strategically, in order to provide the greatest possible insult.

"Terrible housekeepers," said Owen as they moved farther into the building. "Why didn't the men burn the place to the ground?"

"They will in due course, but we will be using the building ourselves in just a few hours."

"Please do not include me in your plans," said Owen.

"Rest easy, Lieutenant. We will both be miles away enjoying a pork roast."

"What about Morgan and the others?"

"Velasquez is the only Officer I know of that has a taste for blood. The others stay completely away from it. I imagine you have heard a thing or two about Velasquez?"

"Only about the string of ears he used to wear around his neck. Where did he get them?" asked Owen.

"People were just dying to give them to him," said Collier, laughing. "He went on a killing spree about a year ago. Five priests and a Bishop, give or take."

"But why?"

"It seems that a particular priest took a liking to Velasquez's son. Velasquez was away at sea when the whole thing happened. Apparently the priest tried to convince Velasquez's wife to let the boy come and live in the monastery, but she refused and was then accused of witchcraft. They burned her *alive*, Lieutenant."

"My God! That is the most horrible story I have ever heard! How did they get away with that? Who *allowed* them to do that?"

"The Church in Rome, of course. But what you need to understand is that this has been going on for centuries! Absolute power." Collier stopped abruptly in front of a wide wooden door. "Here we are, the door to hell. Grab that torch. Here, take these leaves and crush them up. Make two plugs for your nostrils." Collier handed Owen two large basil leaves that he had picked in the Governor's garden right before their departure.

"Why, Commander?" said Owen, genuinely perplexed.

"The smells are unpleasant. Trust me on this point. Pack your nose," said Commander Collier, firmly.

The stairs were carved out of limestone. In fact the entire under-story of the building had been quarried from limestone. The giant pillars that supported the structure above were limestone that had simply not been chiseled away. It was a chilly sixty degrees down in the dungeon, a temperature that kept the Inquisitors from breaking a sweat during their lengthy interrogations.

They were on level ground now, walking slowly through a wide hallway. Owen had an urge to pee, but he fought it down. They came to a room on the left and Collier took the torch from Owen and entered the room. The first thing that caught Owen's attention were the shackles that were fastened to the wall at about head-high and another row that were ankle-high. There must have been twenty pair in all. Suddenly, Owen was slapped in the face by the most revolting odor he had ever experienced. Collier studied him carefully and realized that the smell was about to make him vomit.

"Breathe through your mouth," said Collier. "Any time that you want to leave, just say the word."

"I will be fine. For some strange reason, I need to see this. Better now," said Owen, nasally. Owen pushed the basil plugs deeper into his nostrils. Collier instructed him to turn around.

"Welcome to the rack." said Collier. "If you have ever heard the term 'stretching the truth,' this may have special significance for you." It was a ghastly contraption, twelve feet long, solid oak construction. There was a large drum on one end that had thick ropes wound around it, with long poles inserted into one end of the drum; very much like a capstan on a boat.

"What is that ropy thing on the table?" asked Owen.

"Yesterday, it looked like a piece of intestine. Do you see that stain on the floor over there?" asked Collier.

"Yes," said Owen.

"That is where I lost my lunch. It seems that after they dislocated the shoulders and the hips, they disemboweled the poor sod. I am absolutely certain that they thought they were doing the Lord's work, but see if you can explain to me why a group of learned men would spend time inventing torments that were worse that those inflicted on the Christ?" Owen bit his lip as tears began to well up in his eyes. In the torchlight, Collier could see Owen struggling for control. "It gets worse. You have nothing to prove and I will think no less of you as a man if you decide to leave."

"Let's move on," said Owen stoically.

In the next room stood the "spiked chair" that Collier had described to Morgan. Owen moved in for a closer look. Again, solid oak construction, with two inch spikes coming out of the seat, back, leg rests and arm rests. Heavy leather straps dangled beside the chair. There was a mound of dried blood beneath the chair. Suddenly, Owen began to laugh. Collier was concerned that Owen had lost his grip.

"Lieutenant?"

"It's nothing, Sir. I was just thinking about Morgan's comment about Spanish furniture. That's how you get through this, isn't it? It is so horrible that you have to laugh."

"Exactly!" said Collier, who moved over to a wooden cabinet. He opened a drawer and pulled out a metal object. "Ladies and gents, this 'ers the latest creation from Seville. This is an 'and-forged beauty of a thumbscrew, made of the finest materials and guaranteed to last a lifetime. You'll want to pass this gem on to your children. And it's yours for only five bob, but you'll 'ave to act quickly! We 'ave a very limited supply!" Owen was in pain because of his laughter. Collier continued on in his cockney accent. "And while you 'ave your mother-in-law seated in this finely crafted chair, you won't want to miss an opportunity to use this amazing eye gouge," said Collier, holding up the chisel-like instrument. "Don't be fooled by cheap imitations. This 'ers the real thing, created by the artisans in Vatican City and personally blessed by the Pope! And it's yours for only ten bob!"

"Please stop," said Owen, clutching his stomach. Slowly, he regained control and they moved on to the next room. They had to walk through a narrow corridor past two large cells with grated steel doors.

"This is where Velasquez found the two boys," said Collier. They walked a few more steps and entered a large room with an inclined table in the center.

"I call this the Ben Dover Room," said Collier. Owen studied the table carefully and quickly realized what it was used for. There were leather straps on the front of the contraption to hold the legs of the victim in a kneeling position. At the other end of the table was a winch, similar to the one he had seen on the rack. The winch drum had two ropes with leather cuffs used to bind the wrists. There were a series of iron hooks on the wall that contained an assortment of tubular objects. The one that caught Owen's attention was a jay-shaped metal tube with a funnel on top.

"Oh my God," said Owen, who had just spotted a wood-burning stove in the corner. There was a large cast iron kettle sitting on top of the stove. There was also a charcoal brazier with a large poker on it, hanging from a chain attached to the ceiling. "I have seen enough. I need to get out of here *now!*" Owen's heart was racing and he could barely breathe. He felt like the walls were closing in on him and he began to run. Collier was forced to run along with him, because there was only one torch between them.

Outside of the building, the air was refreshingly warm and the afternoon sun had a healing effect on the two winded Buccaneers. Owen's heart finally began to slow down and the hideous tension that had gripped him in the Hall was released. He let go a powerful sneeze and blew the basil leaf plugs out of his nose.

"I wish I had never gone in that damnable place," said Owen.

"You are a forever-changed man. The only reason I took you in there was so that you could understand the hatred the men feel for the Dons. Several of the men have been guests of the Inquisitors and they know first hand how truly frightening and painful it can be."

"You said that every town in the Darien has its own Hall, correct?"

"I have been told as much, but you have to remember, this is my first raid. Up until yesterday, I could not believe half of what I had heard about the Dons, but seeing *is* believing. Remember also that the Darien is the lifeblood of Spain. Prior to the colonization of the New World, Spain was a third-rate nation that was deeply in debt. Now she is the most powerful nation on earth. It would make sense for the Dons to have a Hall in every town as a way of protecting their income."

"That being the case, I believe that I can answer the riddle you gave me to solve. The answer is 'the Inquisition'. Am I right?"

"According to my uncle, you hit the nail right on the head. It is probably impossible to prove, one way or the other," said Collier.

"But I don't understand it. How can something this monstrous go unmentioned?"

"Because everyone who resisted was killed. The entire population of Europe was terrified. The people writing history were monks! Take the case of Galileo, who was jailed and threatened with death for suggesting that the sun was the center of the solar system. At the time, he was the most preeminent scientist of all time. He was forced to retract his theory, or face death. It was insane. If Henry had not kicked the church out of England, Newton would be in the Tower of London right now for his theory of gravitation," said Collier.

"My mind is spinning. I can't talk about this anymore," said Owen, wiping tears out of his eyes. "What do you say we head back to chateau Morgan and raid his wine cellar?"

"Suits me. There is nothing like a good strong rum after a visit to your local torture chamber."

In the distance, the men could hear the hoof-beats of horses on the cobblestone road.

CHAPTER 19

Word that the Turk had returned with treasure spread like wildfire. Within minutes, over three-hundred Buccaneers had assembled in the town square, along with the officers. The Turk was at the head of the procession, riding a mule that was about half the size of an average horse. It was comical for the Buccaneers to see a two-hundred-fifty pound man on the back of such a small animal, but the Turk rode on, oblivious to the insults being hurled at him.

Behind the Turk was a group of people and mules that stretched over a quarter mile. There were fifty mules laden with the valuables from the houses of the wealthy merchants of Maracaibo. The mules had been divided into two single file trains with the captured prisoners wedged in between them. Of the prisoners, nineteen were women, three were children and eight were men. Morgan noticed that one of the men was a priest. You poor bastard, he thought.

The Turk pulled up in front of the officers and slowly dismounted. He was saddle-sore and had a hard time standing up straight. He walked over to Morgan, rubbing his back.

"You bear a striking resemblance to Sancho Panza," said Morgan.

"As a matter of fact, I have spent the entire day looking for a windmill," the Turk said, "but all that I could find was silver and gold. It was such a disappointment."

Morgan chuckled. "How did we do?"

The Turk bent down close to Morgan's ear. "We kicked their arses, Harry. I make it at ten-thousand guineas. Not bad for a day's work, eh?"

"I am mightily pleased, your Turkishness. A few more days like this and we will be dining at the Golden Arrow!"

"Speak for yourself, Admiral. I 'ave two wives with nasty tempers."

"Quite so, your Turkishness. I only have one wife and she is easy to fool," said Morgan with a huge grin on his face. Morgan turned to Collier, who was standing next to him and issued a series of orders. Collier nodded understanding and began organizing people to carry out the tasks he had been assigned. The prisoners were paraded past the Buccaneers and there were shouts and jeers as they passed by. They were, of course, totally humiliated with their eyes cast down at the ground, except for one woman, who was dressed in peasant garb and laughing.

"Do you have a favorite?" asked Morgan, as the women passed by.

"I do, Captain. It is the one with the big bottom," said the Turk.

"She is yours, if you can handle her," said Morgan, with a sly grin on his face. "Send an escort up to the mansion to retrieve her."

"I will send five men, Harry. That woman is a hell-cat."

"Better you than me," said Morgan.

Commander Collier tasked Lieutenant Owen with the eight male prisoners, ordering him to organize a party and transport the men to the Hall, where they were to be placed in the cell that had earlier housed the two Indian boys. Captain Velasquez, to the astonishment of absolutely no one, eagerly volunteered to go with them, eyeing the priest with anticipation. Velasquez insisted on taking Conteh with him.

Midshipmen Comstock and Thatcher were ordered to form a party and transport the women and three children up to the Governor's Mansion, where they were to wait until the other officers arrived. Thatcher had been instructed to make certain that they had a decent meal.

Collier and Morgan, along with sixty Buccaneers, proceeded to the cathedral with fifty mules in tow. The animals were led up the marble stairs one by one, then into the cathedral, where they were unloaded and then sent back down the stairs without a missed step. It was an impressive haul. Each animal had been loaded with about two-hundred pounds of cargo, mostly silver in the form of serving trays, silverware and the like. When the fourth mule was unloaded the Buccaneers discovered a set of solid gold plates for ten persons, two heavy gold candlesticks, four emerald-encrusted gold crosses and three burlap bags full of silver Reales. Morgan and Collier looked on in amazement.

"Did somebody raid the Vatican?" asked Collier, laughing.

"I think it was the other way around, Commander." Morgan did a quick calculation in his head. "This is going to weigh in at ten-thousand pounds. If we subtract, say ten per cent as wastage, that is still nine-thousand pounds. If this keeps up we are going to have to find some more ships!"

Two guards were placed at each door and they were told to stay sober until they were relieved, or they would loose their heads. Morgan could hear the fiddler playing in the town square.

There was another celebration going on outside the gates of the Mansion. Owen had grown weary of the rude comments and catcalls from the Buccaneers and ordered them outside the gates. There were about a hundred men there, with a raging bonfire and a keg of rum that had been discovered in a merchant's basement. Morgan and Collier wanted desperately to go inside the Mansion and just sit down, but it would have been rude for a Captain and his Commander to refuse a victory drink with his men. So the two officers joined the party long enough to shake hands with the men and exchange congratulations.

Finally inside the Mansion, Morgan and Collier entered the kitchen to find something to drink. Seated at the table were ten of the captured women, feasting on lobster and yams. There were five empty wine bottles on the table. Good sign, thought Morgan.

"Good evening, ladies. My house is your house," said Morgan in heavily accented Spanish. There was no response from the table except from the one dressed in the peasant dress, who was staring at his crotch. Morgan flushed red and turned around, looking for a corkscrew. "Oh that's right! They took the damn thing," he said. "Commander, would you remind me to have the men rummage through the plunder and find a corkscrew?"

"Your wish is my command, Sire," said Collier exhaling smoke. There were six bottles lined up on the counter and Morgan went through each one patiently and finally settled on a pinot noir. He pulled out his pulper and there were gasps from the table. Morgan turned back around to face the table.

"What is it with this damn pistol?" he said to Collier. Collier shrugged his shoulders.

"Listen, this thing for uses of many," said Morgan in his fractured Spanish. The Lady in the peasant dress started laughing and banging her hand on the table. Morgan gave her his best death-stare, but this made her laugh harder. Morgan raised his eyebrows, lowered his head, and began running his tongue deeply into his cheek, in a back and forth motion, staring directly at her. The other women at the table were absolutely terrified, but the peasant lady kept laughing. Finally, Morgan turned around and grabbed the pinot and used his pulper to ram the cork inside the bottle. One person applauded him from the table, laughing. She is actually quite lovely, thought Morgan, looking back at the table. He filled his glass and walked out to the attached prep-kitchen to find Jones.

"Wha' 'appen boss," said Morgan.

"Everee 'ting nice, Captain," said Jones.

"Do you have any of that lobster left?"

"Thirty tails, Sir. The men found a shelf just offshore and laid traps last night."

"My compliments to the men," said Morgan studying an empty wine bottle in the sink. "Jones, there is no cork in this bottle."

"That is correct, Sir."

"How did you get it out?"

"Between you and me, Sir?" whispered Jones, conspiratorially. Morgan nodded his head. "I used a corkscrew, Sir."

"Where did you find it?" said Morgan, exacerbated.

"I brought it with me, Sir," said Jones proudly.

"If you happen to find another one, save it for me."

"You may rely on that, Sir," said Jones passing him a pipe.

Morgan left the prep-kitchen and walked the short distance to the main kitchen. Mercifully, the women had departed for parts unknown. Captain Velasquez was there to greet him and he had a big smile on his face.

"Capitan Morgan, I have good news for you. The priest is big help. He give us location for five-hundred Escudos. They are hiding in the church." Velasquez beamed with happiness.

"I am very pleased, Captain. What became of the priest?"

"Oh, he had accident and is dead. *Carne muerta*," said Velasquez, sliding his index finger across his throat. "Conteh was bad with his cutlass, but he is now with us," said Velasquez, smiling.

"How unfortunate," said Morgan. Another five-thousand Pound Sterling at a mere forty- two pounds of weight. Gold was so much friendlier than silver. "Captain Velasquez, we are going to have to search the women for chain. Could you organize that for me?"

"It would be an honor, Capitan." In the Spanish New World, women wore their wealth around their waists in the form of gold chains. During the Portobello raid, one woman was found with a chain that measured over seventy feet and weighed seven pounds. During Anniversaries the husbands of the Spanish ladies would give them a length of chain, which would then be added to the "wrap" around their waist by the local goldsmith. The wrap was generally worn on top of a finely woven cotton undershirt to avoid chafing.

English women in the Caribbean typically "went native" in a short period of time, say a few months and did away with their traditional temperate costumes. Castilion society was much more severe, however, and the Spanish ladies continued to wear their hideously uncomfortable dresses and their accoutrements, such as corsets and hooped-skirts, until they were either elderly, or dead. Undressing a Spanish Lady was no simple task. Velasques was beginning to realize that when Pulverin walked into the kitchen. The two men began conversing in Basque, virtually oblivious to Morgan's presence. Morgan listened intently, but could not pick up a single word. He wondered if maybe they were having him on, but as the conversation went on, there seemed to be some sort of plan evolving and then they came to some sort of an agreement.

"We are ready for the chains, Capitan," said Velasquez. Morgan could feel the tension in his shoulders ebbing away. The wine buzz had started and he smiled as he realized that he would not have to deal with the laughter aimed at his broken Spanish.

"Is there anything to eat in here?" said Owen, entering the kitchen. Morgan could see the red eyes and knew what Owen had been up to.

"Lieutenant Owen, you forget your manners. You are in the presence of three superior officers. A simple greeting would open many doors for you," said Morgan.

Owen stopped in his tracks. He looked around the room and mumbled under his breath, "Oh shit!"

"Good evening, gentlemen," said Owen, in true aristocratic English, "I trust you all are well?"

"Quite well, thank you," said Morgan, "Jones is preparing our supper as we speak. In the meantime would you assemble the ladies in the library? We are going to search them."

"Of course, Captain," said Owen

CHAPTER 20

The Governor's library was forty feet long and twenty feet wide. The mahogany bookcases stretched about a third of the way to the top of the room's eighteen foot ceiling. Morgan was quite content to let Velasquez conduct the affair at the opposite end of the room. The women were nervous with anticipation, fearing the worst. Velasquez was very gallant and gentle as he addressed the prisoners in crisp Castilian Spanish.

"Ladies, I regret to inform you that we must search you. There are only three Buccaneers in this room with you and we have done this purposely to save your honor and prevent as much embarrassment as possible. Please help us now in return for the courtesy we have shown you and remove everything down to your underclothes. You may assist each other," said Velasquez.

There was no response. The women exchanged nervous glances, but remained motionless otherwise.

"I am afraid I really must insist that you remove your clothing," said Velasquez.

Once again the women remained motionless. Pulverin pulled his foil out of its scabbard and swatted the woman nearest him on her lower back. She let out a yelp and the others began untying each other's dresses frantically. The woman in the peasant dress broke off from the assemblage and walked over and stood in front of Morgan. She smiled and then pulled her dress off over her head. Morgan's jaw dropped open.

"I am not wearing any underclothes. Does that mean that I have to leave the party?" she said in English, supremely confident.

"Who *are* you?"

"I am your next lover, Harry."

"Who decided that?"

"I did." She spun around in front of him gleefully. "Are you satisfied that I am not hiding anything?"

"Quite." She slipped her dress back on and took a seat beside Morgan. "Tell me your name."

"Sara Vaughn," she said, waiting to see if he would recognize her name. She could see his eyes darting from side to side and then finally, upward—then he knew. It all made sense, now. She was a lovely creature and her total lack of inhibition would certainly be a professional asset.

"*The* Sara Vaughn, I presume?"

"Lately His Majesty's Mistress, retired, for the present."

"We need to talk. Shall we say the Governor's balcony in an hour?"

"My social calendar is sparse at the moment. I believe I can make it," she said smiling.

At the far end of the room the ladies were in various stages of undress. Velasquez patiently unwrapped a long gold chain wrapped around a woman's waist, while she stood there in her underwear, sobbing. Pulverin was harassing a young woman with his foil, because she was still almost fully clothed. It required another half hour to complete the task, but it was well worth the effort. The seventy-foot record length of chain recovered on the Portobello raid had been eclipsed by one stretching eighty-four feet. In all, they had unwrapped over sixty pounds of chain from the nineteen women and discovered numerous small bags of emeralds that had been suspended on the hoops of the women's skirts.

"Thank you for your cooperation, ladies. You may come and go as you please," said Velasquez. The women scrambled to get their clothes back on while the officers went off to eat their supper.

The Buccaneers celebrating outside the gates were becoming progressively more obnoxious as the night wore on. At one point they began firing weapons and Morgan ordered them back into town. In the silence that followed, the sound of the tree frogs was intoxicating. The night air was thickly scented with frangipani and jasmine. Morgan ascended the semicircular staircase and then walked down the hall to the Governor's suite. He opened the door and saw the dim lamp on the table in the center of the room. Next to it was a bowl of water with four gardenia flowers in it. The sweet smell was intense, almost like a syrup that coated the inside of his nose. His heart was pounding with anticipation and he forced himself to take a deep breath and let the tension flow out of his body. Sara Vaughn, he thought. What are the odds of this happening? A million to one, at least. So there has to be something other than chance at work here. He decided that the best strategy would be to keep his cards close to his chest. Sara Vaughn was likely to be the most cunning woman he would ever meet. The question is, why is she here? he wondered.

Morgan noticed a flicker of light reflecting off the balcony railing, followed by a hissing sound. His heart began pounding again and he drew in another deep breath. He walked slowly towards the open French doors. He saw her drawing on the long-stemmed clay pipe.

"Lovely night," he said.

"Lovely indeed. I am never going back to England, if I can help it."

"I know the feeling," he said, sitting down next to her on the wicker bench. "If you don't mind me asking, how did you end up here in Maracaibo?"

"It was a game of chance, actually. I was in Cartagena with Don Alonzo when the communiqué came in from the whore in Port Royal. It seemed concocted to me, perhaps a ruse. But the Dons bought into it completely. I suppose the ruse was your doing?"

"I am shocked, Madam!"

"Who are you calling a 'Madam,' sonny boy?"

Morgan chuckled.

"Well, whoever thought it up and carried it through should be awarded a prize. My thinking was that you were actually going to hit Caracas, that is until you had that little problem with Charley's boat. I figured you had probably lost a third of your men and that removed Caracas from the hit list."

"Our losses were actually quite light, considering. But I still do not understand how you ended up here."

"Alonso received word that your convoy had been spotted near Savona a month before the arrival of the communiqué. It was a set up. I was given the information about Savona months before and then I had it sent to Charley. They knew that if Charley found out about it, the information could only have come from me."

"How did you get out alive?"

"Alonso's secretary and I were very close. He was the one that decoded all of the correspondence. He saw the handwriting on the wall and delayed delivering the message to Alonzo for a day. That gave me enough time to hire a boat and get out of town. It was close."

"So why didn't they grab you when they found out about our presence in Savona?" asked Morgan.

"There was no proof that it was anything other than coincidence. After all, you had been there many times before. But they were very suspicious and it raised the hackles on my neck. I had already decided to leave, it was just a question of when. The communiqué forced my hand."

Morgan felt like he was speaking with an old friend. He reminded himself that she was still a conduit for information to King Charles the Second of England and as such, she was in a position to do the Buccaneers a great deal of harm. He noticed that she was now sipping her wine and he began pacing himself with her.

"So tell me, how did you pull off that communiqué?" she said.

Morgan remained silent for a while, weighing the potential harm if what he told her reached the King's ears. She nudged him in the ribs with her elbow.

"All right, all right," said Morgan. "Captain Velasquez was the bait. We created a date book for him with various entries written in a phase-forward substitution code. One of the entries was the Savona date and for that reason, the book was not passed to the whore until the day after Savona. That alone would have given a great deal of credibility to the book, but we added even more tasty tidbits." Morgan took another sip of wine and re-lit the pipe with the candle on the table. Suddenly the frogs stopped singing and Morgan pulled out a pulper and stood up. He moved to the balcony railing and ever so slowly looked over the side. There was a sentry walking in the courtyard below. Morgan slipped the pulper back into his waistband and turned around.

"Sentry," said Morgan sitting down. A brief silence followed.

"Don't be shy, Sailor Boy," she said soothingly. Morgan laughed and then continued his story.

"Velasquez went a little crazy during a reconnaissance trip to the Darien. That was about a year ago and he slaughtered five priests, I think, and possibly a Bishop as well. He is a stealthy little bastard. He came back with a necklace made of human ears."

"Unbelievable! So he's the one. That drove the Inquisitors crazy! They thought it was one of their own!"

"In a way it was. He was a navigator for the Dons and one of the faithful. They really screwed him over." Morgan re-packed the pipe and lit it again. He took a deep draw and passed it to Sara. As they exhaled, the humid trade wind cleared the smoke almost immediately.

"Don't stop now, Sailor Boy, I am getting wet." The two began laughing. Somewhere during the recovery process, they ended up in an embrace and their first kiss followed.

"Finish up so we can go play."

"There is not a great deal more to say. I just had him encode the dates and the places where the killings occurred and, if I remember correctly, he also made notes of the things he made off with—crosses, that sort of thing. Of course, we also inserted the date for the raid of Cartagena."

"Well, it certainly worked. You would not believe the number of man-o-war that are patrolling Cartagena. They are mostly over the horizon waiting for your ships to enter the harbor. They want blood and when they find out about Maracaibo, heads are going to roll."

"It's my turn. When you fled the country with Don Alonzo, was that a ruse?"

"Of course! Charley ordered me to go with the crazy bastard. He happened to have a fascination with me and we exploited it. Initially, Charley had to eat a little crow, but in due course, it cost the Dons over a million pounds. They are well aware of what happened and who did it, so I am a marked woman. Ring any bells, Sailor Boy?"

Morgan laughed. "I was just thinking of the first time the Dons put a price on my head. I was embarrassed!"

"Whatever for?"

"It was a measly five-hundred Reales," said Morgan laughing.

"After they find out about Maracaibo, it will top a half million. I may turn you in myself."

"Lucky me."

"By the way, do you have a plan to get us out of here?"

"I am working on it."

"That's a comfort," she said, filling their glasses. "I just love this 'ball me' weather, Sailor Boy. Would you like to come in and rub my back?" She let her white caftan fall, and Morgan was entranced by the sight of her, naked in the candlelight.

"God, I love my job," he said as he reached out his hand to Sara.

Somehow, Owen had found a fiddler that was still sober enough to play and the party began, hesitantly, at first, but then Velasquez made his move. The women had been assembled in the large foyer with the smooth mahogany floors. It was perfect for dancing and the carpets had been rolled up and set against a wall. A huge chandelier with seventy candles lit the enormous room. Velasquez's voice echoed as he spoke.

"Señoras y Señoritas, I would like to welcome you to the celebration of the century. The Creator has seen fit to provide us with this elegant room and the best wine the planet has to offer. You will find the officers to be charming dance partners and excellent lovers! All that we ask is that you partake of what we offer you and enjoy yourselves." One of the women, who was obviously drunk, got a couple of claps in before the others silenced her.

As ordered, Velasquez walked over to the Señora with the big bottom and stared at her with a smile on his face. The room was silent. She had a look of utter contempt on her face.

"My little dumpling, I have traveled the seven seas to find you. Your beauty astounds me!" She snarled at Velasquez and spat in his face. The other women gasped. Calmly, he took a handkerchief from his pocket and wiped his face. "This is such a disappointment. I assume this means that you are not in the mood to dance?" The officers in the room that could speak Spanish were laughing wildly. Velasquez nodded to the Buccaneer in the kitchen and five men appeared in the room. They attempted to subdue the woman, but she fought back like a demon, swearing and throwing punches. She managed to bloody one Buccaneer's nose before the men tackled her and tied her hands behind her back.

"I shall wait for you my sweetness, a lifetime, if necessary!" screamed Velasquez, as she was led out the front door. Many of the women were exchanging glances and trying to hold back laughter, some more successfully than others.

Captain Balfor approached the young and very beautiful girl who had begun clapping earlier. She smiled back at him as he held out his hand. The fiddler began to play and the couple danced, clumsily at first, but soon they moved in perfect harmony. Others began pairing off and joining them on the dance floor.

Morgan and Sara appeared on the second floor terrace and looked down at the revelers. A strikingly attractive woman in her forties led Lieutenant Owen up the stairs. She was wearing a blue dress that highlighted her small waist and her cannon-ball breasts seemed dangerously close to spilling out.

"I believe he has a woody," said Sara, laughing.

"Me too," said the shirtless Morgan, moving behind Sara, thrusting his hips forward. Sara giggled

CHAPTER 21

The reasoning among the officers was that the wealthy merchants owned the mules that had been carrying the booty the day before. It was unlikely that, as the Buccaneers roamed the county side, they would find any more beasts of burden. Conteh gave Collier a map with twenty locations where he was reasonably certain the Buccaneers would find townspeople gathered. It was decided that this time, the Buccaneers would bring mules with them so that the animals could be used to transport back anything that was recovered. Collier picked a hundred men and divided them into four groups of twenty-five men. Each group was then given ten mules and, shortly after breakfast, the groups departed.

As the day wore on, a curious thing began to happen in town. Women began appearing in the central portion of town, begging for food. They were entering the town in groups of ten, or twenty. Many were nursing children. Some of the women appeared ill and Jones, who happened to be in town looking for vegetables, decided to call Browne in to investigate. All of the women appeared to be either full-blooded Indians, or half-caste. As such, the Buccaneers took pity on them and did the best they could to make them comfortable.

It was an hour before noon when Jones arrived back at the Mansion. Browne was in the kitchen, nursing a cup of coffee, holding his head on the temples, massaging in slow, gentle circles.

"I must say, Sir, I have never seen you in such dreadful shape. If you don't pull through, could I have your instruments? I am particularly fond of your bone saw, Sir." Browne laughed and immediately regretted it.

"Cyrus, don't start with me. I have a musket ball ricocheting in my skull and if you are patient, I am certain that you will see it bursting through one of my eyes in the next few moments."

"There is trouble in town, Sir. I will have you right as rain in a few minutes." Jones went into the attached kitchen, where he had a kettle of hot water ready on the stove. He took a generous pinch of powdered willow bark and placed it on top of a piece of cheesecloth. That would take care of the headache in short order. As a general tonic and appetite stimulant, Jones added a generous helping of indica, then dropped the cheesecloth into a cup of hot water to let it steep. Jones walked back to the other kitchen with a pitcher of water.

"'Ave ya peed yet today, Sir?"

"Nay."

"You'd better 'ave some water. Four glasses should do the trick, Sir." Browne knew that Jones was right, but the thought of putting anything in his stomach was repugnant. Nevertheless, he did manage to down two glasses before Jones returned with the tea.

"I found some orange blossom 'oney in town today, Sir. I think you will find this potion most agreeable." Browne took a few tentative sips and then downed the rest of the cup.

"If all medicine tasted this good Cyrus, nobody would get better."

"I will take that as a compliment, Sir. I will be back in ten minutes and by that time, you should feel almost human, Sir."

"Thank you, Cyrus."

Jones hurried to the outside kitchen and began gathering available ingredients. First, he took the whites of four eggs and put them in a bowl. He added two tablespoons of honey and then squeezed the hearts out of two large lemons, removing the seeds with care. The Buccaneers had rounded up some dairy cows the previous day, so luckily, Jones had a pitcher of milk. He poured a cup-full into a ceramic container and carefully removed the cream on top, then poured what remained into the mixing bowl. He took a wisk and began beating the ingredients until a froth appeared. Next, Jones poured a small ceramic container full of the concoction, then poured the rest into a small baking tray. He garnished each container with cinnamon and placed them in the oven. He began counting, "Thousand one, thousand two…"

Jones opened the oven at five minutes and then closed it again. He began counting, until a minute had passed. He opened the door and saw a nice tan color on top of the foam. He withdrew the containers and set them on the counter top. He took a spoonful from the smaller container, like an expectant father. He blew on it until he was certain that it would not burn his mouth.

"My God, this is good," said Jones, all alone in his kitchen. He picked up his pipe and held a candle to the bowl. "I will 'ave to commit this one to memory, if I can remember," he said to himself, laughing.

"Has your stomach settled some, Sir?" said Jones entering the kitchen.

"I would put my chances of survival at fifty-one percent."

"Try this fat-less concoction, Sir, it should go easy on your innards."

"What is happening in town?" asked Browne. Jones knew that Browne was feeling better now.

"It was most extraordinary, Sir. Indian women are pouring into town and a few Spanish, as well. Several of them appear quite ill. They seem to have no qualms about hoisting their skirts blasting their backsides wherever they happen to be standing."

Browne tried a bite of the meringue and got lost in the flavors for a few seconds.

"So it is some sort of diarrhea?"

"I believe so, Sir. Several of the children appeared close to death's door."

"Just what I needed, a fochin' cholera epidemic. I was involved in one back in sixty four and it was ugly. One of the amazing things about the survivors was that they craved salt for days afterward—I mean they would literally pour gobs of it on their food," said Browne, greedily taking another bite.

"What do you make of it, Sir, I mean the salt business?"

"I am not sure what to make of it, but I think it is safe to say that when your body is low on water you become thirsty. Maybe there is a certain salt content in the body, which becomes depleted and so a craving arises, which is very much like thirst. Originally, I thought that maybe the diarrhea caused the loss of salt, but over the years, I have had diarrhea many times and I have never craved salt. So, there appears to be another agent at work."

"What about laudenum, Sir? It is commonly used to relieve diarrhea."

"Correct, Cyrus. Under normal circumstances, I believe it is effective. But with cholera, it is lethal. One of my friends proved that in sixty four. You have to let them shit it all out and make sure they pee at least every two hours. That was the most effective treatment we found. Coca leaves applied to their bung-holes seemed to ease their suffering."

Jones observed three more bites of the meringue and Browne was no longer rubbing his temples. He smiled.

"Feeling better, Sir?"

"I think so, Cyrus. It is a pity that we are not in Virginia."

"Why is that, Sir?"

"If we were in Virginia, we could heal the sick and then walk on water, a most gratifying experience," said Browne, laughing. Jones sat there, perplexed, but eager to understand the *humor.*

"You have left me behind, Sir!"

"It is *winter*, Cyrus! The lakes are frozen!" Browne laughed.

Cyrus Jones, the master of subtle, understated humor was stumped. He was lost and his face showed the disconnect.

"Cyrus, the lakes are *frozen!* You can walk on the water!"

"I have it now, Sir. Do you have any other material that might actually stimulate laughter?"

"Feeling a little pissy, are we?"

"Just worried, Sir. Me mum died of cholera."

"Sorry, Cyrus. We should probably get to town and see what we can do. I just had a thought, Cyrus. What if we loaded them with salt while they had diarrhea? We could do two groups, one with salt, the other without?

"It sounds reasonable to me, Sir, but where are we going to get the salt?

"The same place we have always gotten it—the ocean! We can give them diluted sea water!"

Maracaibo had gone from a ghost town to a beehive of activity in the space of three hours. Along with another fifty Indians in various states of ill health, the Turk had just arrived with a mule train fully loaded and twenty hogs in tow. He also brought back another fifteen female prisoners, who were mostly poor, judging from their clothes and teeth.

The Turk was at the head of the party on his mule. He greeted Browne and Jones.

"I am sorry about the Indians, but their babies were dying, so I told them to come into town. They were on the outskirts of a pig farm and I think pig shit was going into the well they were using." Browne waited until the Turk dismounted and then pulled him aside, out of hearing range of the others.

"One-hundred people with cholera, give or take. Hell, I had nothing better to do. But let me tell you something. You have jeopardized this entire mission. I appreciate your good intentions, but we could lose hundreds of men because of this. Find your interpreter and get these people to the other side of town," said Browne exasperated.

"A few of the Spanish women are also sick. What should I do with them?"

"Better lump them all together and tell the men to stay away from that part of town. This could get really ugly." It was clear to Browne that the Turk felt badly about what he had done, but Browne was in no mood to console him. Jones came up beside Browne.

"The Turk seems a little out of sorts."

"He should be. He just exposed the entire town to cholera," said Browne.

A twenty-year old half-caste woman held a crying three-year old. The woman's eyes were sunken and hopeless. Watery diarrhea coated the undersides of her arms, which attracted a hoard of flies. It was a very depressing scene for everyone present. The woman walked away slowly, with a tenacious grip on her dying child as the Turk's interpreter began herding people across the square.

"This is going to be a shitty day," said Browne.

In the next few hours, the Buccaneers delivered two thirty-gallon barrels of seawater to the far side of town using a mule cart. Browne and Jones began experimenting with the seawater and found that they could tolerate a one to five dilution, but it was still not pleasant. Fortunately, there were several orchards nearby and the trees were loaded with oranges. Squeezing the juice from ten oranges into a gallon of the diluted seawater transformed it into a refreshing drink and the Indians began drinking gallons of it. Ten Indians were given plain water with ten oranges per gallon, as a control group.

The ship's carpenters took regular wooden chairs and cut out circles in the seats. The chairs were placed at the bedsides of the patients who could stand and a bucket was placed underneath. The Turk volunteered to empty the buckets as penance, but

Browne would not allow it. Cholera "beds" were also constructed for those too ill to sit up, by cutting a hole in the middle of a table and then padding what remained. It was going to be a grueling ordeal, caring for these wretched people.

The other three teams returned to town loaded with plunder and more prisoners, none of whom were sick, much to Browne's relief. There were enough healthy people in the Indian group to do most of the care, thankfully, but by dawn tomorrow, that equation would undoubtedly change. Browne gave very specific instructions to the caregivers about where they could empty their buckets, before he left with Jones.

It was a mob scene at the cathedral. Five-hundred Buccaneers milled around outside while they waited to go in, single file and view the loot collected today. Morgan told the men to select an object they desired—limit, one per customer—because tomorrow, all of the silver not selected was going to the forge to be melted into bars. There were some beautiful pieces, but most of the Buccaneers went for chains and smaller items that could be slipped into a pocket. Lieutenant Owen had a small scale and a ledger book at the only exit and he weighed each man's selection, then went through the laborious process of locating the Buccaneer's name in the book, which was not alphabetized. Thatcher stood by to relieve Owen, who was worn down after only two hours.

Every Buccaneer who walked into the cathedral was greeted by the sight of silver and gold objects stacked four feet deep around the perimeter of the main entry hall. It was a massive amount of loot that boggled the Buccaneers' minds. In its present form, the loot in the cathedral would never fit in the Buccaneer's ships, but by melting the objects down into ingots, the volume would be reduced by ninety percent, at least. "How much longer do you think this can last?" said Collier, referring to the mules being unloaded.

"I am not sure," said Morgan, "but I think a great deal of wealth poured in here after the construction of the new fort, on the false assumption that it made the city impregnable. Based on what I have seen during the other raids, this could go on for weeks. We are going to have to make a serious effort to look for more boats."

"Evening, Buccos," said Browne as he and Jones walked up the steps of the cathedral.

"Evening, Sirs," said Jones. Morgan and Collier exchanged greetings and then Morgan took Browne aside, out of earshot.

"How bad is it?" asked Morgan.

"You mean the cholera?"

"Of course."

"There have been no deaths, so far, but it is very early in the epidemic to make predictions. It could get very ugly, or it could fizzle out. One thing that should help us is that we were able to isolate the sick ones very early on. Add to that the fact that the town is practically empty and it makes me optimistic."

"Do you think it advisable to evacuate the town? Maybe go further down the coast?"

"I considered that, but if cholera hits one of the boats, you'll lose over half the crew. Besides, cholera is a nightmare to manage on a boat, but on land it is much easier. The times I've seen cholera do the most damage is in situations where people were packed closely together. I saw it hit a boarding school in sixty four and it killed a hundred-forty of the school's two-hundred students."

"Are you suggesting that we disperse the men billeted in the church?"

"That would be prudent. I would suggest a maximum of two men per dwelling."

"Easy enough to accomplish. I would like you to give me a daily briefing on the direction this thing is going," said Morgan. Browne noticed that Morgan was playing with the gold shackle in his left ear lobe, nervously.

"Happy to oblige," said Browne.

CHAPTER 22

Jones was pleased with himself that he had had the foresight to bring three cooks into the mansion to help feed the rapidly growing number of residents there. During his absence, the cooks had slaughtered a pig for tonight's dinner. For those not fond of pig meat, there was an option of el dorado, grilled in garlic butter.

People seemed to gather in the inner kitchen, to drink wine, smoke and talk. It was a constant stream of people all night long. Five different languages were being spoken simultaneously. The Spanish ladies were becoming very relaxed with their captors and it was more like a family reunion than an occupation. In a sense, the Spanish women had been liberated. For perhaps the first time in their adult lives, they were free to disagree and argue with men *in public*. Even their clothing had changed from corsets and hoop skirts to simple house dresses.

As the night wore on and increasingly more wine was consumed, the conversation began to take some strange turns. When necessary, Sara and Captain Velasquez, both fluent in Spanish, would intervene to interpret the finer points of the discussion. Sara had just paid a visit to Jones in the outer kitchen and the hilarity of this situation began to take control of her. She found Morgan and pulled him over to the corner of the room. She was bent over, slapping her thighs. She raised up and put her arm around Morgan's neck and began whispering in his ear.

"This is hilarious! The Governor's wife, the one with her hand on Owen's ass, is trying to convince Velasquez that the church is divinely inspired to 'cleanse' the world of heathen non-believers. She actually believes that the Inquisitors are God's soldiers! Velasquez is being very polite and just slowly picking away at her hypocrisy. He just asked her if she had ever been to the Hall. She said no and then Velasquez offered to take her there tomorrow. She declined, saying that it was no place for a lady. Oh, this is good! Velasquez said it was no place for little boys either. That got her!"

"Lieutenant Owen, you will have the honor of escorting the lovely señora to the Hall tomorrow," said Velasquez. It was an order and Owen began to squirm inside.

The mood in the kitchen became somber and Morgan went to the out-kitchen to find Jones, with Sara in tow. There were four sweaty men there, putting the finishing touches on this evening's meal.

"Evening Captain, Mum," said Jones, putting a finish glaze on the el dorado filets.

"Good evening, Mr. Jones. Would you be kind enough to have our food delivered to my room?"

"What a delightful idea," said Sara.

"It would be a pleasure, Sir. What'll it be, Sir, fish, or pork?"

"Fish for me," said Morgan, turning to look at Sara.

"Same for me," she said, pulling him close. "I can't wait to get these clothes off," she whispered. Morgan smiled and pinched her on the bottom. They made a mad dash back into the kitchen and ran for the stairs, hoping the gloom there would not affect them.

Once inside the room, Sara slipped off her dress and gave Morgan a long kiss. Next, she walked into the adjoining room and began stoking the ashes in the fireplace, adding new kindling and then small logs. Morgan stood and watched her, fascinated by her beauty. Suddenly it occurred to him that it was eighty degrees in the room.

"Why on earth are you lighting a fire?"

"So that we can take a bath after dinner, Sailor Boy."

"I don't follow you." There was a knock on the door. Morgan went to the door and let the cook in and showed him to the table on the veranda. While the cook set up the table, Morgan went back to the other room. Sara had a roaring fire going and seemed proud of herself. She looked back at Morgan.

"Take a peek up the oversized flue, Sailor Boy, but don't injure that beautiful face of yours. You will see a metal tank up there, full of water. There are pipes that run under the wainscoting, there," she said, pointing to the waist-high wooden trim, "and wind their way into the bathroom. Come here, I'll show you," she said walking into the bathroom. Morgan traced the wainscoting and, sure enough, it extended all the way to the bathroom. At the middle of the large white marble tub, the side nearest the wall, Sara pointed to a brass pipe emerging from the wainscoting that made two bends and entered the tub. There was a valve of some sort at the first bend. Why hadn't he noticed this before?

"Once again, you have impressed me. Do you happen to have any sisters?" She spanked him hard on his backside and he howled out. Inside he was a mess. After forty-eight hours with this woman, his entire life seemed to be coming apart. It was impossible for him to imagine life without her. For the first time in his life, Henry Morgan was in love.

"Whoever thought this up needs to be awarded some kind of medal," said Sara.

"It is ingenious, but how do you fill the tank?"

"There is a pump on top of the cistern. Let's eat, Sailor Boy. I'm starving!"

Sara led the way to the veranda and Morgan was hypnotized by the undulations of her bottom. There was a gentle breeze that made the candles flicker and the tree frogs provided the music. Morgan poured the pinot into their glasses and took a tentative bite of el dorado.

"My God, this is good," said Morgan.

"My recipe," said Sara with a mouth full of food. "It is a balsamic reduction. The recipe calls for raspberries and blueberries, but mango seems to work just as well."

"Where did you learn to cook?"

"France, mostly. My father was a financier and we spent our summers on the coast of Marseilles. It was a most amazing childhood. By the time I was sixteen, I had spent time in every capital in Europe. I was an only child and I was spoiled rotten."

"Who would have guessed?" Sara caught the sarcasm and kicked him under the table. "Were you ever married?"

"For two years. I was married at seventeen to one of my father's business associates. He was desperate to have children, but I never got pregnant. I have been to half the doctors in Europe. He eventually arranged an annulment."

"Maybe the problem was with him."

"Nyet. He remarried and now has five children. I have never had a monthly, Harry. You've seen my parts and there is not a hint of hair. Same with my arm pits."

"And nobody could diagnose your problem?"

"There was this old Austrian doctor who had seen one other woman with the same symptoms, but he had no idea what caused it. Don't get me wrong on this. I never particularly wanted to have children and serial monogamy seems to suit me just fine. By the way, I have been meaning to ask you; how can you be sure the Dons won't mount a land assault?"

"Runners. I have four of them and they go out every day at sunrise, each takes a different route. All of them speak fluent Spanish and they pass themselves off as locals. They stay on the main roads and run until the sun is overhead and then run back. They are the ones that feed information to the Turk about where to go the next day."

"So how are things with your wife?"

"She leaves me alone for the most part. We actually get along very well."

"Still no children?"

"Right. How do you know so much about me?"

"Charlie has a file on you that goes halfway to the ceiling. It was interesting reading. You have become a sort of folk hero back in London. Charlie even toasted you when he heard about the Portobello raid."

"Tell him thank you when you see him. Rumor has it that the King went into the heart of London during the fire to help out. True, or false?" asked Morgan.

"Absolutely true. I was with him when he got word. Charlie flew out the front door like a madman, with advisors and the palace guards behind him, urging him to go back home. He was out there for six hours and came back filthy, smelling like a chimney sweep. It was a godawful night. Of course, the city has never fully recovered," said Sara, staring at a candle, in a trance. "Charlie nearly went bankrupt," said Sara, setting her fork down on her plate. She picked up her glass and downed the rest of her wine. Morgan noticed tears welling up in her eyes. "It's time for a bath, Sailor Boy." He had an impulse to reach out to her and comfort her, but something inside told him to hold back. She picked up her wineglass and a candle and left the veranda. Out of habit, Morgan stood and looked up at the night sky and found a few familiar winter constellations. He could hear a fiddler downstairs and he smiled. Life was so rich. He inhaled the sweet gardenia aroma and said a silent thank you to whoever had created this planet.

"Who thought this up?" he said aloud, shaking his head and smiling from ear to ear.

By the time he arrived in the bathroom, her mood had improved considerably. There was an earthy smell in the room and a pipe on the counter. She was in the bathtub smiling at him, her nipples slightly above the water line. The candle on the counter top hissed when he tilted it to light the pipe. He took a generous draw and began pulling off his clothes. He set his pulpers off to one side and covered them with his shirt.

He got into the bathtub slowly, easing himself into the water an inch at a time. Finally, he was all the way in and he got the giggles, for no apparent reason. Sara looked at him and smiled, wondering if there was something she had missed.

"Sorry," he said, and his laughter subsided. A blissful silence followed, while their legs intertwined.

"It is time for truth, or dare, Sailor Boy. Tell me the most embarrassing experience of your life."

Morgan hesitated for a few seconds with dozens of memories streaming through his brain.

"Only if you promise to do the same," said Morgan.

"Done," said Sara, relishing what she was about to hear

Morgan hesitated and began laughing again as he remembered the events from a little over a year ago. Had it really happened?

"Don't be shy, Sailor Boy."

"All right, all right," he said trying to suppress his laughter, "I was aboard La Caracola, which I think means snail, or slug."

"Snail."

"Right. The men re-named her La Caracola, because she was incredibly slow, compared to the rest of the fleet. She was a prize that we captured during the Portobello raid. Anyway, we were returning to Jamaica after the raid and got within spitting-distance of Port Royal, when a Northerly came at us at thirty knots, very unusual for that time of year. La Caracola had a nearly flat bottom, unlike yours, and every time we came about, she would actually slip backwards. We fought like demons to gain a little against the storm, but for three days, we continued to lose ground. I was taking an occasional catnap, but for the most part, I did not sleep for three days. The hallucinations were wild. Finally, the strange wind subsided and we sailed a comfortable reach back to Jamaica. I went below to sleep. I have no idea how long I was out, but I awakened when a violent shudder went through the ship. There were jeers and cheers, and some panicky orders from the officers. I had absolutely no doubt that we were being boarded. I grabbed a pistol and ran up on deck, only to find that we were dockside in Port Royal. There were well over two-hundred people there to greet us and there I stood, naked as a jay bird, with a pistol in my hand."

Sara tried to slap her thighs when she began laughing, but she was too deep in the water. Soon, there was an inch of water on the floor and she still continued to laugh. The candles sputtered as they were hit by droplets of water. Morgan looked over at his pulpers and saw wet spots on the shirt covering them. He leapt out of the tub and pulled the shirt off the guns. He picked up his pulpers and placed them high on a dresser in the next room and returned to the bathroom. His anatomy was expanded because of the hot water and Sara studied him as he loaded the pipe and climbed back in to the tub.

"The ladies must have loved it," said Sara clapping her hands, smiling. Morgan held up the candle and took another draw. His face lit up in the candlelight and he had an expression of …Sara could not find a name for it. Ecstasy, she thought.

"I haven't even gotten to the funny part," he said, blowing out a cloud of smoke. He handed her the pipe and helped her with the candle. Morgan slipped forward into the water, until his chin was at the water's surface. He loved this space, because nobody could touch him here. No officers, no messengers; his ears were below the waterline. God, she has a beautiful rack, he thought, looking at her breasts floating in the water. Her lips began to move and he rose up to hear her voice.

"So, what *was* the funny part?"

Morgan mopped the sweat from his eyebrows with his index fingers.

"One of the ladies on the dock put her hand over her mouth and pointed at my crotch. I looked down and realized I had a raging hard-on. Everybody started applauding!" Sara began slapping the water again, fighting for breath amid the spasms of laughter. "I am surprised it wasn't in my file."

"It will be," she said, slapping the water again. "Charlie will love it!" Her laughter finally subsided and Morgan wanted his due.

"Your turn," he said. She smiled and gave her best naughty look.

"It was my first private meeting with Charlie. The girls and I had eaten lunch at a Lebanese restaurant and I had humus. I crave the stuff, but it always gives me the vapors. I thought that I had gotten most of it out of my system by the time I arrived at the castle, all perfumed and polished. I had to spend about a half-hour with Charlie's secretary and my stomach was rumbling the entire time. I was wearing the most ungodly corset. Charlie finally came to get me and we went to a small drawing room. He stayed close to me the entire time. I actually prayed that he would leave the room so that I could relieve some of the pressure. Finally, he gave me the obligatory first kiss and then he squeezed me so tightly that a little gas slipped out." Morgan was in hysterics. "My ass was pinched so tightly that I actually hit a high note. The King—Charlie, released his grip on me and remained motionless for a second, or two and then his body went into a spasm, then another. He backed up from me, and bent over, holding his stomach. Then *I* got the giggles. Every time I laughed, a little bit more would squeak out. He commanded me to stop and then kept on laughing. He was on the floor, Harry!"

There were waves in the tub coming from Morgan's heaving chest

"I managed to squeeze out, 'I am usually not like this,' but then it happened again, this time louder and longer than those before. Charlie was pounding on the floor as his secretary rushed into the room with a couple of guardsmen. Who knows what was going through their minds, but the guards cocked their pistols and pointed them at me. Then *I* bent over, totally out of control.

I realized, of course, that I might be killed, but that made it even worse. Charlie motioned them out of the room with his arm, but they wouldn't leave. More guards arrived and neither of us had any control. Somehow, Charlie made it to his feet and motioned for the guards to lower their weapons. His secretary had a stern look on his face and Charlie started laughing again. To this day, his secretary will not look me in the eyes."

Morgan held his aching belly as the laughter slowly ebbed away and his breathing returned to normal.

"I haven't laughed like this in ten years," said Morgan.

"That is *exactly* what Charlie said! That's why he decided to keep me, I suppose."

"I am sure there were other reasons, as well," said Morgan in his thick Welsh accent, raising an eyebrow and glancing down at her breasts, then meeting her eyes.

"Jewelry and chocolate would probably be the equivalent in my world, but I confess that I do love the sight of your naked body. I could look at you for hours and then feel deprived if you went away." Suddenly there was another creature in the tub with them, trying desperately to break the surface of the water. She smiled. "Before we get distracted, what is this business about the Inquisitor's rules?"

"I am not sure that they *had* any rules. At the beginning of each raid, I tell the men that they can use *only* the tactics *and devices* that have been used by the Inquisitors, before them. Do you have any idea what that means?"

"At last count, I have read close to seven-hundred books and I have been tutored by the best minds in Europe. The 'Inquisition' has never come up, except in vague references, and even then, it involved only Spain. So, while I have heard the term in passing, I have no earthly idea of what it means." Morgan could not have known that she had the ability to recall every page that she had ever read, but he would find out in due course.

"Why do you suppose that is?"

"Enlighten me, Sailor Boy."

"Enlighten yourself. Go on Owen's tour tomorrow with the Governor's wife."

"Will you be joining me?"

"Absolutely not. I went into the one in Portobello and I still have nightmares about it. No thank you." From the look on his face, she knew that it would be impossible to change his mind. What could have had such a profound effect on him, she wondered.

"At least give me some idea of what I am in for."

"I do not have the right words and even if I did, you would not believe me. Go and see for yourself. We can talk about it tomorrow night, but right now, I would like to think about something else." It was an order, not a suggestion. Sara was an expert at reading powerful men and she immediately changed the subject, trying to collect as much information about a given topic as she possibly could.

"Fine with me," she said. "Let's pick something more uplifting, like cholera. Where do we stand?"

"Thirty cases, more, or less. No deaths, so far. Browne has done a superb job up to this point and I would appreciate it if you would mention him to the King."

His words were bitter-sweet and she recoiled as if he had struck her. It was strange for her, because she knew that this relationship would eventually end, as all the others had, but for the first time, the man she was involved with acknowledged it also. Her ability to extract every pleasure out of the present moment was matched by his. She became transfixed on his lips as he spoke, but she could no longer hear the words. They did not matter. She felt a fullness in her groin and needed to move. She stood up gracefully and raised her arms above her head, stretching. She felt Morgan's hands on her bottom, gently pulling her towards him. She shot her arms forward and caught herself on the wall, standing. She leaned her head back and whispered, "God, I love your lips."

CHAPTER 23

It was noon before Browne and Jones ate breakfast and made it into town to check on the cholera victims. The Turk was on another foray to the interior and he had his interpreter with him, which forced Browne to rely on one of the Spanish women captured yesterday. She was in her mid thirties and smiled incessantly, revealing her one remaining incisor tooth. She communicated effortlessly with the Indians, but spoke no English. Browne kept having to say, "hablar lento", or "speak slow" as she interpreted what the Indians said.

From what Browne could gather, one man had died and they wanted permission to bury him. He had been in the "no salt" group, which had fared poorly over night. All of the men in that group were bed-bound today, too weak to stand up. In contrast, the people who had been given the diluted sea water were mostly up and about, helping their weaker counterparts. In both groups the diarrhea persisted, but it appeared to be improved in the sea water group. Browne had seen enough to convince him that salt improved the outcome of cholera, but he wanted to wait another day and see what happened to the "no salt" group, before he switched them over to sea water.

In his broken Spanish he asked how the man had died. Once again, the woman spoke so rapidly that Browne could not understand a thing she said, but then she tilted her head back and began shaking her arms and legs. It was clear that she was describing a seizure. Browne wasn't sure of the word for seizure, so he began pantomiming one.

"Antes?" he asked. The woman shrugged her shoulders and asked one of the Indians if the man had ever had a seizure before.

"No," she said.

"You have quite a talent, Sir," said Jones smiling. "What do you make of it?"

"It could be coincidental, but I seem to recall several seizures at the boarding school. It would be nice to get a look at his brain."

"Good afternoon, Doctor," said Sara, who was walking with Owen, Collier and the Governor's wife. "The Commander was just telling me about your antics on board the *Oxford*. The 'kick the bucket' routine was wonderful. I wish I had been there to see it."

"Good Morning, Sara. You are too kind. Nobody else appreciates me. Hello Commander, Lieutenant and large-breasted Spanish woman," said Browne, nodding his head with each name. "Off to the Holy House of Horrors are we?"

"Yes. The tickets were all sold out, but we happen to know the new owner," said Sara.

"Let me warn you in advance, the seats are a bit uncomfortable. Sara, I wonder if you could do me a huge favor?" said Browne.

"Of course, Doctor, but you will have to buy me dinner first," said Sara. Browne smiled.

"Consider it done. One of the Indians has died and I want to look at his brain. Could you tell that woman with the tooth what we are going to do?"

"Sure, but what *are* you going to do? Smash his head with a rock?"

"I was thinking about a saw, actually, but if you'd like to take a crack at it, be my guest." Jones began laughing hysterically.

"I have never seen a brain before. Mind if I stay and watch?" asked Owen.

"The more the merrier."

Sara began rapid-fire Spanish with the "tooth," who then went on to explain it to a few older Indian men nearby. They seemed unconcerned, but they did ask that all the parts be returned for the burial. They explained that they were going to go and dig the grave now, if that was all right with Browne. Browne immediately gave his consent.

"Mr. Jones, would you be good enough to fetch my saw?"

"Yes, Masta," said Jones.

"Why bother going all the way to the ship?" asked Collier. "Everything you need is in the Hall."

"Perfect. Why don't you go on your little outing and then bring me back a saw and a sharp knife with at least a six inch blade."

"Would you care to join us?" asked Collier.

"Actually, I am missing a sock. I have put off looking for it for about five years now. Today *is* the day, I am afraid. Mr. Jones, would you like to join them on their family outing to the house of horrors?"

"That would all depend, Sir," said Jones. Browne was getting the rhythm of Jones' humor and he knew that one was coming.

"I'll bite. Depend on what, Mr. Jones?"

"On whether the word started with a 'w' or an 'h', Sir." Sara rolled her eyes and moaned.

"That was quite a stretch, Jones," said Sara. "Speaking of stretching, somebody get a rope!" The men laughed. Sara wore a pair of tight knickers and a thin white cotton shirt, tented in the front by her nipples. She had her hair pulled back into a ponytail and she was beautiful—fit for a King.

"Masta, protect me from this vicious woman!" said Jones, darting behind Browne.

"Remain calm, Jones. I will not allow her to hang you. Madam, may I suggest that, since you are going to the Hall anyway, why not put him on the rack? That would really be a stretch."

"A capital idea, Doctor. Come along Jones, while there is still daylight," said Sara, walking away with the four others in tow.

Browne was happy to be alone, finally. He walked down to the shore and stripped off his clothes. It was a perfect afternoon for a swim. As Browne walked into the water, he saw a small sloop in the distance, coming in through the narrow channel. He rolled on his back in the water and watched a magnificent frigate bird playing in the thermals above him. "Storm's on the way," he said. He rolled back on his belly to check the progress of the sloop, which he could see, was just offshore. He recognized Jenkins and waved. Jenkins waved back and held up a beautiful four-foot el dorado. Browne gave him a thumbs-up sign and then rolled on his back to check on the frigate bird.

CHAPTER 24

That night on the veranda, Morgan and Sara had to shout to hear each other. The rain was hitting the roof above and the shrubbery below, with such force that it was impossible to hear anything else.

"The cistern will be full by morning," shouted Morgan.

"Warning about what?" she shouted back. Morgan smiled and shook his head. He placed his index finger over his lips and then took his last bite of food, rose and motioned her into the room. The temperature dropped below eighty with the afternoon cloud cover and Sara was wearing her caftan. They stepped inside and when Morgan closed the door, it was as if a baby had stopped screaming.

"God it's cold," said Sara. "This is incredible! It is still close to eighty degrees and I am freezing my ass off!"

"Welcome to the tropics."

"Let's get in the tub. I would love a repeat of last night, Sailor Boy."

"I might be up for that," said Morgan with a devilish grin on his face.

"Ooh, I love it when you talk dirty," she said, puling off her caftan. Sara assembled everything they could possibly need on the edge of the tub; pipe, tobacco, herb, wine, candles and water. She put the cork stopper into the tub's drain and cranked the valve. The water streamed out, hot and steamy.

Morgan undressed in the other room, wanting to avoid a repeat of last night's spray-injury to his pulpers. He saw rust spots on the barrels in the morning and had spent a couple of hours polishing them back to perfection. When Morgan entered the bathroom, Sara was holding a candle to the pipe. She was beautiful in the candle light, waist deep in the water. Within seconds he was erect and she saw it and smiled.

"I am so happy that I have finally found a man who will stand up for what he believes in."

"I haven't rolled out of bed once since I met you," he said, getting slowly into the tub. "Tell me about your day."

"Harry, this has been the weirdest day of my fochin' life! It began with breakfast. Do you have any idea of what went on downstairs last night? Let me put it this way; the floor was *sticky* when I walked into the kitchen, bare footed, I might add, but I didn't know what it was until Collier gave me a rough description of the night's highlights. They were all dancing naked! Damn, I wish we had been there! There were over a hundred people. Oh well. Then, as we were walking to the Hall, Collier began relating stories about things that had happened aboard the *Oxford*. Christ, what an adventure!"

"The objective is to have fun. Otherwise, why bother?"

"I will never forget what you said last night: 'I do not have the right words and even if I did, you would not believe me.'"

"I said that? What was I talking about?"

"The Hall!"

"It seems to fit," said Morgan. "You spent some time there today, correct?"

"Correct."

"Would you have believed it possible?"

"No," she said, tears welling in her eyes. Morgan leaned forward and grabbed her upper body. He lifted her up and managed to turn her one-hundred-eighty degrees, so that she was next to him. He held her against his body tightly and let her cry. Morgan was not just comforting her, he was also comforting himself. Her sobs ebbed away and then she began trying to make sense of it all. "Harry, how can the church sanction such…such heinous brutality?"

"To put it simply, the church is a business. In order to make money, it has to control people. I think you would have to agree that any person who got out of the hall alive would probably be reluctant to challenge the church's authority again?"

"Harry, *your* men had a man on the rack when we got there!"

"I am not surprised."

"Did you order it?"

"Of course not," he said lighting the pipe.

"But the very fact that you allow it to happen makes you culpable! Doesn't it then become a sin of omission?" Morgan had an urge to lash out at her verbally, but he checked it. He had been over this same moral landscape himself many times before.

"First of all, the entire concept of *sin* is being defined by an organization that buggers little boys on a regular basis, not to mention their use of torture, enslavement, et cetera. They have absolutely *no* moral authority! So lets keep away from a theological examination of my behavior—it would be worthless. Do you see this scar here?" he said pointing to his shoulder.

"Yes."

"I am fundamentally opposed to cutting people up with swords. And yet I am faced with that on a daily basis! We are at war with the Dons! They try to cut us up and we cut back, faster and deeper. Several of the men have been tortured and so they torture back. The rule is, 'do only what the church has done before.' That has been the Buccaneer way since the time when Mansvelt was Admiral."

"That doesn't make it right!"

"Right and wrong are re-defined on a daily basis. I no longer use the terms." Sara could see that further discussion of the Hall and what went on there was pointless, so she changed tack.

"On our way back from the Hall, we delivered a saw and a knife to Browne who wanted to see the brain of an Indian that died last night. It was the creepiest thing I have ever seen."

"You stayed and watched?" said Morgan, astonished.

"Yes, I *had* to watch it. So did the others. When he pealed the scalp back I nearly passed out! He made a cut just above the eyebrows and then extended it to the back of the head. He worked the blade of the knife up underneath the skin over the guy's forehead, until he could get his fingers in there. Then he yanked the skin backwards and it made a horrible noise as it separated from the guy's skull. The thing that made it all bearable was the humor between Brown and Jones. They had us laughing our asses off."

"They are funny. Was there anything wrong with the brain?" said Morgan, shifting position. "Sorry, I have to change position. My arse is asleep," he said, moving to the other side of the tub.

"You just want to look at my chest."

"You have finally figured me out. So what about the brain?"

"Browne said that it was perfectly normal. While we were cutting the Indian's head open, another Indian had a seizure and Browne thinks it has something to do with salt deficiency. When he started sawing on that skull, I almost got sick. It raised the hackles on my neck. I think Collier knew I was getting sick, so he distracted me by saying, 'This is the new, improved Seville skull saw. If you are like me and enjoy doing craniotomies in your home, I heartily recommend this instrument. For a limited time, we will include, at no extra charge, this beautiful scalp knife, made of the finest materials available and imported directly from Rome. I urge you to act now, while supplies last.' He got me laughing and I managed to keep my lunch."

"A tad bit different from your average day in London, I expect."

"As I said, it has been the strangest day of my life."

"Just out of curiosity, how did the Governor's wife do in the Hall?"

"She is convinced that the entire Hall was a conspiracy. She believes that you placed all of the devices in there. I pointed out a cross carved on the front of the 'Ben Dover' device and she said that the Buccaneers had carved it to confuse her. She really isn't very bright. How did the Turk do today?"

"Things are beginning to thin out a bit. One of the teams came back completely empty-handed. We may have to leave before long."

"I am going to miss this tub," said Sara.

"Me too," said Morgan, sighing heavily.

CHAPTER 25

The Buccaneers ended up staying in Maracaibo for an additional two weeks. The Turk had a few bad days, but there were several very good ones also. The men who ran the forge were kept very busy, melting the recovered silver into one pound ingots. The holds of the boats were filling up fast and Morgan was anxious to get to a place the Buccaneers called Gibraltar, which was actually a small city called La Solita, on the southern portion of the lake. He now had over a hundred prisoners from the most prominent families in Maracaibo and he was desperate for some more boats.

Morgan sent two of his male prisoners ahead in a small sloop. He instructed them to sail to Gibraltar and tell the town to surrender, or he would put them all to the sword. Sara winced as she translated for him.

There is a saying among sailors that you should spend a fortnight with a woman on a sailboat *before* you marry her. Morgan slowly began to understand just how true the saying was. He and Sara began to quarrel on a regular basis. Morgan felt as though she actually wanted to fight. On the fourth night after their departure from Maracaibo, Morgan went over to Kessenger's boat, ostensibly to play cards. He ended up getting drunk and spending the night on the other boat. When he returned to his cabin the following afternoon, she was furious.

When Sara had initially called him Sailor Boy, it had been endearing; now it irritated him. The sex was still great, the best he'd ever had, in fact, but she wanted it constantly and he began to grow tired. He wanted desperately to get this cruise over with and go home—alone.

The fleet arrived at Gibraltar on the fifth morning to the hail of gunfire. Morgan had the boats stay out of range while he figured out what to do. He summoned all the officers aboard his boat. They squeezed into his aft cabin. Even with the windows open, it was stuffy. Sara remained in the cabin and seemed disinclined to leave. The men didn't seem to mind her presence, so he let the matter rest.

"Let's get this over with quickly before we die of heat exhaustion," said Morgan, smiling. "Captain Pulverin, would you by any chance be experiencing déjà vu?"

"Oui, Captain. The town did not have cannon when last I was here. We take it in fifteen minutes," said Pulverin.

"I think a frontal assault would be costly. Any other ideas?" asked Morgan.

"How about a decoy frontal and then going through the woods on the right?" asked Balfor.

"Objections?" asked Morgan, scanning the group. "Very well then, begin ferrying the men ashore, say an hour before dawn. Captain Pulverin, how is the shoreline?"

"Sandy and steep. It will be easy for landing."

"Excellent. Captain Kessenger, please get your piper playing. It's time to make them mess their pants. Commander, please put us in a little closer and see if we can tag them with our long gun."

"It would be a pleasure, Captain." The long gun only fired a nine-pound ball, that could inflict only minimal damage, but Morgan was more interested in the psychological damage it would do.

The following morning, three-hundred well-rested men were quietly moved on shore out of sight of the fort. At dawn, the outlying boats were brought in behind Morgan's ship. A piper could be heard on Kessenger's boat and that was the signal to charge the fort. A deafening roar reverberated through the town as three-hundred Buccaneers began running towards the fort, screaming at the tops of their lungs. The Spaniards in the fort realized they had been duped and ran like hell, along with the townspeople. They had wisely packed their belongings on their mules and headed out, as fast as their legs would carry them. Not a shot was fired.

Morgan was at the front of the procession. He was not a bit surprised when they found the town completely deserted. The Buccaneers set up housekeeping, just like they had in Maracaibo. Sara was quite content with the bathtub in the new mansion, but it didn't have the water heater contraption that the other one did. Once back on land, Sara seemed to loosen up and started to enjoy life again. They spent the next five weeks together and there was scarcely an argument between them, much to Morgan's relief.

Morgan managed to round up two boats during a foray up the Bravo River. One night he and the officers actually sat down and calculated what they had amassed. It was over two-hundred-fifty-thousand Reales, or pieces of eight. They had everything they had come for and it was time to go home.

During the four day cruise back to Maracaibo, Morgan paced the deck incessantly, trying in vain to find a way out of the lake. He figured that there would be four Men o' war protecting the entrance, with at least thirty guns each. They could not come after him because of their draft, but neither could he get past them without his fleet being blown to pieces. Sara wisely left him alone. She knew exactly what he was working on in that brain of his and somehow, she also knew that he would solve the problem.

When they dropped their hooks off the coast of Maracaibo, Morgan ordered the lugger to proceed to the entrance of the lake and report back. The town was still deserted and he ordered his sea chest up to the mansion. Sara was excited about a hot bath and a good meal, and she went on ahead.

Morgan went up to *Enchantress'* chart table and glanced at the chart for the thousandth time. He was missing something—he could feel it, but he could not pull it out of his brain. Absently, he began peeling off his clothes, hoping that a swim might refresh him.

"Summon Richard Moss!" he shouted, hoping somebody was still on the boat.

"Aye, Sir," someone shouted from the cargo hold. Morgan did a shallow dive off the starboard rail into the ten-foot-deep water. He did a duck dive and went underneath the boat, checking out the rudder and the planks. A fire ship is a must, he thought. He decided to let somebody else suggest it and then embrace the idea. That would only take care of one of the Spanish ships. What about the other three? Swimmers to disable their rudders? It had been done before. Even so, his boats would have to endure a broadside as they passed by the Men o' war. "What about storming the fort and using it to fire on the Men o' war?" he said aloud, holding on to the rudder.

"Sounds plausible to me," said Collier. Morgan nearly came out of his skin.

"You scared me half to death! If the water starts turning brown, it's your own damn fault!" The two men laughed.

Suddenly something clicked in his brain. If they mounted a land assault from the rear...then the Dons would move the cannons back to the rear ramparts. Morgan struggled to get a visual image of the building. "It must be sixty feet from the front of the fort to the back."

"Every bit of that. I think maybe closer to eighty," said Collier.

"What would it take to move, say thirty cannons—let's compromise—seventy feet?"

"What kind of cannon?"

"I don't know! Where is that lugger?"

There was a splash of water behind them as Balfor dropped a hook.

"Offer you a spot of tea, Admiral?" said Balfor grinning.

"We were just talking about you, Balfor." There was another splash as Kessenger jumped into the water and swam up beside the lugger. Balfor stripped off his clothes and joined the other three men. "How close did you get?" he said to Kessenger.

"Just around the first point."

"Don't stop now!"

"Three men o' war. A forty, a thirty and a twenty four," said Kessenger.

"Not as bad as I thought. How about the fort?" Morgan leaned his head back in the water to get the hair out of his face.

"The fort has not been completely repaired, but there are cannon back in the ramparts," said Balfor.

"How big?" Balfor glanced over at Kessenger, who shrugged his shoulders.

"I cannot honestly say. We were a long way off and the angle was bad."

"All right, I want you to get close up tomorrow and you will be taking a passenger along with you."

"Who?" asked Balfor.

"One of the prisoners. He is going to deliver a letter to their Admiral. Let's say that those cannon are twenty-four pounders. How long would it take four men to pull a cannon out of a rampart, turn it around and push it seventy feet, *then*, set the elevation, aim and fire the damn thing?" There was silence as the men thought about the situation, hovering near the rudder.

"Are you talking 'en mass', I mean all of the guns at once?" asked Collier.

"Yes."

"I see where you are going with this. It seems to me that the Dons are a fairly excitable group. I see nothing but utter chaos if they attempted to move them all at once," said Collie

"Assuming they have practiced doing this, I would guess that it would take between four and five minutes to move a single gun that far," said Balfor. "But if you factor in the confusion, the wild ride that those carriages will give them, collisions and the like, I would put it at eight to ten minutes. It would be worse at night.

Morgan looked at Kessenger.

"Sounds about right to me," said Kessenger.

"We are going to have to pay careful attention to the tides," said Morgan. Velasquez and Pulverin swam over from their boats and joined the conversation. "What are we going to do about the men o' war?" All six men were silent.

"Three. A forty, a thirty and a twenty four," said Balfor. There was silence again. "That is a total of ninety-four cannons!"

"Give me twelve men who are good Swimmers and I will destroy the big ship," said Pulverin, confidently.

"How?" asked Collier.

"I will take the ship that we take in the Gibraltar River and make her a brulot," said Pulverin.

"A fire ship?" said Morgan, gasping.

"Oui, Captain. We can take away her guns and put logs in the gunports. We can put mannequins on deck with hats and montera (hunting) caps. If we come straight at them during the ebb, they cannot fire on us!"

"What a brilliant idea, Pulverin!" said Morgan, giving Collier a wink. "We will put it to a vote tomorrow."

"You called for me, Sir?" said Moss, who stood on the dock about fifteen feet away.

"Yes, Mr. Moss. Please join us in the water," called out Morgan.

"Ah can't swim, Sir!" said Moss in his leather apron.

"Just jump in, we'll teach you!" shouted Kessenger.

"Let's swim over to him. I want you to hear this," said Morgan. The men made their way over to the dock, where Moss was standing very nervously.

"Mr. Moss, I want you to make something for me."

"Jus' describe it, Sir, ya know ah kin do it," said Moss in his thick Scottish brogue, relieved that he was not being reprimanded for some unrecognized offense.

"I want you to construct a floating bomb for me. The concept is to take a small keg of powder, say half full, and drill a hole, so that a fuse can be placed. Next, I want you to make a second lid for the barrel that will cover up a coiled fuse. Are you with me Mr. Moss?"

"Ya know I am, Sir."

"Good. Now here comes the tricky part. The barrels you use to float the platform that the powder keg stands on must be partially full of water, maybe even with some fins attached. I want this object to be driven by the current and *not* the wind. Do you have the concept, Mr. Moss."

"Indee' ah do, Sir!"

"Take as many men as you need. I will require three of these devices each night and they need to be completed by mid afternoon."

"Consider it done, Sir," said Moss, excited.

"You may go Mr. Moss. Thank you."

"It is an honor, Sir," said Moss, walking away.

"Harry, what the hell are you up to," said Collier, intrigued.

"Jus' hopin' ta 'ave a bit o' fun," said Morgan in a Scottish accent. "Commander, see if you can find a pry bar to separate Lieutenant Owen from his Spanish whore. He will be working nights for a while, actually earning his money for a change. I want the sail on the sloop he is taking blackened. Midshipman Comstock, who happens to be the only sonavabitch with a watch that still works, will accompany Owen. They are to release a small lantern riding atop a weighted barrel. They are to time how long it takes for the barrel to reach the Don's ships and then report that to the gunnery Sergeant. Make it work so that, just about the time the Dons get back to sleep, another one goes off."

"So you are not trying to kill them?" asked Pulverin.

"No, just drive them nearer the edge. Tired men make serious mistakes. The beauty of the plan is that we won't even hear them going off."

When Sara saw Morgan walk into the mansion, she knew immediately that he had solved the problem of how to get out of Maracaibo. It was the way he walked and the smile on his face. He sought her out and when he found her, he walked up to her and gave her a big hug.

"You figured it out, didn't you," she whispered.

"Not exactly, but now I have at least twenty options, whereas yesterday I had only two and both of those would have gotten us killed," he whispered back. "Let's talk about it tonight. Do you think you might be up for a bath?"

"Don't bother with the hot water, Sailor Boy, I am wet enough to fill the tub. And I guarantee you, the water will be hot!" she whispered into his ear. "Sailor Boy" suddenly felt good, again.

"I need some help with a letter. Can we do that now?" he asked.

"Only if I can have you in my mouth, first," she said. He could feel fullness in his loins, but he resisted it.

"Quit clowning around, will you? I need to write this fochin' letter," he whispered.

"*All right!*" she said, exasperated. "Let's go and write the fochin' letter!" They went upstairs and she locked the door to the bedroom. Sara slipped off her dress and put her breasts in front of Morgan's face, while he sat before the Governor's desk, trying desperately to compose a letter to the Admiral in control of the Spanish fleet, at the mouth of the harbor.

"Sara, I am begging you, put on some clothes! You know I cannot resist you! But look here, this letter may save our asses, so please, put some clothes on and help me out!"

Reluctantly, Sara left Morgan alone for half an hour, while he drafted the one page document. Sara translated it in less than ten minutes and then Morgan began the laborious process of writing the final document in his masculine hand, sipping coffee all the while. He had nearly finished the letter when his quill pen released a huge drop of India ink directly in the center of the letter. Morgan grabbed the blotter and tried to soak it up, but he was too late. He cursed and pulled out a fresh sheet of parchment. After another hour of painstaking work, Morgan finished the letter and put a red wax seal on it.

The letter simply introduced Morgan as the Admiral of the Buccaneers and said, in no uncertain terms, that if they did not deliver fifty-thousand Reales in the next forty-eight hours, the Buccaneers would burn the city of Maracaibo. The letter went on to say that unless the Buccaneers were guaranteed unmolested passage through the narrows, Morgan planned to storm the fort and offer no quarter, or mercy, to any of the Spaniards. It was a bold move, considering he was outgunned two to one.

CHAPTER 26

The following day, Velasquez and Pulverin were chosen to sail the sloop out to the Spanish ships, because of their language skills, which was ironic, because they never exchanged a word with the Spaniards. They placed a white flag near the top of their mast and approached the largest of the Spanish ships. They side-tied to the massive forty-gun *Magdalena* and allowed their Spanish prisoner to climb the rope ladder, letter in-hand. The officers gathered at the rail glared down at them with murder in their eyes. Pulverin focused his attention on the crewmen, particularly their eyes. They were mostly black-haired with blue eyes. He searched in vain for an Italian, or a gypsy.

The sloop pulled away without incident. Velasquez took the helm while Pulverin studied the landscape, looking for a weakness to exploit that might help them when they tried to leave. He studied the sixteen parapets. Only nine had cannons. He judged them to be five twenty-four pounders and four thirty sixes. Although it was not a full compliment, it was more than enough to demolish the Buccaneer fleet. Alternatively, if the Buccaneers could somehow storm the fort and commandeer the guns, they could possibly destroy the Spanish fleet as well. Once out of musket range, Pulverin could not resist the urge to pull down his pants and flash his bare ass at the officers on board the *Magdalena*. Velasquez applauded enthusiastically.

Pulverin glanced back at the fort. Something was wrong, but he couldn't quite put his finger on what it was. Somehow, the fort looked different, but he couldn't say exactly why. Suddenly it dawned on him what it was; the dunes had been flattened! All of the sea oats had been removed, as well. Pulverin pointed it out to Velasquez in Basque. Both men realized that another frontal attack on the fort would now be suicidal.

There was an improvised dockside crane at Maracaibo, which the men had been using to remove cannon from the fire ship. Morgan instructed one of the shipwrights to mark out seventy feet along the dock, using chalk. Then Morgan organized a team of four Buccaneers and instructed them to pull the cannon back from the imaginary rampart, turn it around and push it to the other rampart, seventy feet away. The limestone dock was essentially identical to the floor in the fort. Morgan's watch had stopped working weeks ago, so he began counting, "One thousand one…" as the men tried to manhandle the four-thousand pound gun. One thing was obvious; it was difficult to push the carriage in a straight line because the wooden wheels were warped and they had very little traction. Every time the men tried to speed the carriage up, it went wildly out of control. "Two minutes, give or take. Interesting," said Morgan under his breath.

When Velasquez and Pulverin arrived back in town, they made some inquiries and finally caught up with Morgan at the dock, where he was chatting with Conteh, the freed slave. Morgan was shirtless and wore a pair of knee-length britches. He was sweating profusely. He had recently hired Conteh as a foreman to supervise the crew of one-hundred slaves, who were doing the carpentry and general labor to refit the ship. Conteh's English had improved dramatically in the last eight weeks and as long as Morgan spoke slowly, Conteh always got the job done *correctly.* "It's hard to find decent labor these days," muttered Morgan.

"Captains Velasquez and Pulverin, how nice of you to drop by," said Morgan. Standing close to Morgan, the men could see that he was covered with sawdust. He had apparently been working on one of the gunports. "Gentlemen, how was your cruise?"

"Buenas tardes, Capitan. We had a fair wind and a calm sea. We have much to tell you," said Velasquez.

"Let's talk now. I was about to quit for the day anyway. How about that Banyan tree over there?"

The men sat down with their demijohns in their laps. They were all happy to be drinking water from the Governor's cistern again. Morgan had his back up against the tree and soon he was brushing ants off his shoulders.

"Any time you are ready, gentlemen," said Morgan.

It was fully two days before the Spanish Admiral had a reply delivered to Morgan. In an ironic twist, Admiral Alonso, who was in command of the Spanish fleet stationed at the entrance to Lake Maracaibo, also happened to be the older brother of the Spanish diplomat that Sara had "run away with." She knew the Admiral rather well and Morgan would not hesitate to suck her dry of any information she could recall about the man.

Alonso's letter was fairly straightforward, but Morgan was annoyed by the man's style and by all the references he made to honor, His Catholic Majesty and basically what deep shit the Buccaneers were in. In general, the letter said that if Morgan would be willing to give up everything he had stolen, including silver, slaves and prisoners, Alonso would graciously allow Morgan and his fleet to pass unmolested past the Spanish fleet and the garrison.

Morgan was required by Buccaneer tradition to share the contents of this letter with his men, so he organized a banquet in the town square that night. The Spanish women had developed a certain passion for partying, particularly because all the Spanish men were locked up and hence, could not control their behavior. Naturally, in the scheme of things, they would be able to fall back on the "I was forced," defense, but in the future, when their eyes met in the market, the women knew that they had had the greatest adventure of their lives and, of course, the best sex. They might eat each other's young over matters of infidelity, issues of state, or the way a bitch dressed and distracted one of their husbands at a party. However, on the issue of what had actually happened during their captivity, they would never dream of revealing what someone else had done, glass houses being what they are.

Morgan wanted to get the men a little tipsy before he read the letter, so that he could steer them in the direction he wanted them to go. Strangely enough, the Governor of Gibraltar had a thirty-gallon barrel of rum made from cane juice, rather than molasses. Even more ironic was the fact that the rum had been produced for export on one of *Morgan's* plantations. Once the cork was pulled out of the bung, Morgan filled his cup first and then waited a few minutes before he toasted his men.

"To the bravest men on the planet! To the Governor of Gibraltar for providing us with the rum in our cups!" The men cheered. "Drink hearty, me Buccoes!" The fiddler started up and the dancing began. Morgan worked the group for about twenty minutes, walking around shaking hands and exchanging pleasantries. He was anxious to get back to the mansion, where dinner was waiting, so he had the fiddler silenced and stood on the rock wall around the fountain. There was dead silence.

"Admiral Alonso is waiting for us at the entrance to the lake. I am told that his ships are manned by cowards, mostly Gypsies and Italians. He knows he is in trouble and has offered to let us go free!" The men cheered so loudly that Morgan had to cover his ears. "He asks only one thing in return," he said, pausing for several seconds. "That we surrender to him all the booty, prisoners and slaves that we have worked so hard to collect," he said softly. "*The man is a fool! Our brothers have died for this booty and he wants to take it away from us! Are we going to let him?*" shouted Morgan, at the top of his lungs. The crowd went wild. Even the Spanish women were cheering. The Turk jumped up on the wall next to Morgan. He whispered in Morgan's ear.

"Nice Job, Harry. I will take it from here. They are waiting for you. Save me some of Sara's pesto, will you?" Morgan nodded and stepped down, with his fists raised in the air. By the time he made it through the crowd, his hand was in agony from the multiple crushes it had received from tipsy Buccaneers, and his back was welted from being slapped so many times. There were times when it was a real pain in the ass being a Buccaneer Admiral.

CHAPTER 27

Sara stoked the fire in the Governor's anteroom fireplace. The temperature outside had dropped below seventy and a hot bath seemed the perfect cure for the confusing emotions she had been experiencing the last few days. From her standpoint, it was pretty clear that the Buccaneers were going to have to take a stand against Alonso and it would have to be soon. Alonso's latest letter had made that abundantly clear. She had interpreted it for Morgan today and it left little doubt that Alonso was losing patience with the Buccaneers. The letter demanded that the Buccaneers surrender all of their ill-gained booty within the space of two days, or "He would come and force them to do it." Morgan scoffed at this, but still, it added to the tension.

Then there was the case of the runaway slave, who had escaped from Conteh's work party and stolen a gig today. He had nowhere else to go except back to the Dons. Naturally, he would tell Alonso about the fire ship to curry favor. The question was, would Alonso listen? She began running through every memory she could retrieve about Alonso. Attitudes, prejudices, lusts, hypocrisies—there were far too many to even consider him a human being. "Work on this," she whispered. "Morgan will need to know."

Her focus on the political intrigues was interspersed with potent emotional suffering. They only had a short time left together, after all, so why had he left her alone? Why had he gone out with the sailor boys at the last minute? She would have to spend the night in the Governor's tub alone.

"Focus!" she told herself. She trained her mind on Alonso memories. Family picnics, birthday parties and funerals. The one constant was, that he was unbending. When he decided something, it became law. Interesting, she thought. His opinion about the Buccaneers? She could remember it clearly, one day at a luncheon she had attended. "These men behave like animals! They are as smart as dogs and cannot possibly understand the value of faith and loyalty!" "Work with this one," she said aloud, trying to stack the logs upright with the poker.

At the last moment, Morgan decided that he needed to be on the sloop with Owen and Comstock. He wanted to see the barrel floating out to the Spanish ships, with the lamp on top. Add to that the fact that Owen's lady had given the Lieutenant a substantial bud of some reddish colored herb from Panama. Morgan decided to make a night of it. He loaded a sea bag with warm clothes, a blanket and four bottles of wine. Sara wasn't around, so he left word with Jones to inform her that he was going to spend the night aboard the sloop with Owen and Comstock. Jones had packed them a superlative dinner, complete with cheese, baguette and pesto.

All day long he had been wrestling with the notion of how much water actually flowed through the shallows during a tide change. The tear–drop shaped Lake Maracaibo was roughly fifty miles wide and one hundred long. To make the calculation simpler, Morgan assumed a tidal drop of one foot and the volume of a gallon of water to be one cubic foot. That worked out to over thirteen-billion gallons in a twelve-hour period, or approximately a billion gallons per hour. In the narrowest portion of the channel, the water would be moving at least seven miles per hour, perhaps as many as ten, or even twelve. The guns in the fort, if stretched to their limit, could cover a span of about a half-mile. Once again, he did the calculation in his head. If there were no slippage in the water, it would require between three and possibly eight minutes to pass beneath the guns of the fort. The problem was, boats were designed to *be* slippery. Damn! It might take three, or four times that long to make the passage.

Morgan lay on the bow of the sloop digesting the "slippery" problem, looking up at the stars. Owen had ventured forward twice and offered the Panama bud to Morgan. He knew that he had the solution to the problem somewhere inside his head, but there were times when it was best to think of something else and accept, rather than force the information. Instead, he imagined himself as Alonso, the Admiral in one of the ships that were just now coming into view. If he was in command and his ships were swinging at anchor with a seven to ten knot tidal surge, what would *he* do?

"First thing I would do is lay the helm over in each direction to see how far she would go, in case I had to open the ports," he said to the stars. "Then I would think of my draft and my butt hole would pucker," he began to laugh. The *Oxford*, despite her massive aft cabin and all the other comforts she offered, had been equally as bad as the worst love affair Morgan had ever had. "Alonso must be going through the same thing," said Morgan, laughing. "The poor bastard."

Morgan imagined himself on board the *Magdalena*. She was a hundred-thirty feet long and had a draft of at least fifteen feet. What would he do if a ship came barreling down on him at ten knots? He would not be able to bring his guns to bear until the boat was along side her. "What if I suspected that it was a fire ship?" he said aloud. "The only option would be to weigh anchor and get some canvas up for steerage. But the problem with this option was that the channel was only three-hundred feet wide and the closer you got to shore, the shallower it became. At some point, the *Magdalena* was going to have to turn one-hundred-eighty degrees in order *not to be going backwards!* That would be extremely risky in the "v-shaped" channel. Morgan tried to imagine giving the order to pull up the hook and then let the ship go *backwards* through the channel. "No fochin' way!" he shouted.

"Sorry, Captain?" said Owen, approaching the front of the sloop.

"Lieutenant, I am going to present you with a problem in a few minutes and I want you to solve it. First though, it might be a good idea to drop a hook before we get blasted by those Spaniards up ahead."

"I'm droppin' 'er now," said Owen, running back to the aft locker. He pulled out an anchor and threw it over the side and cleated it home. There was a jerk in the sloop as the anchor dug in. Morgan walked back and sat with the young Buccaneers.

"Would you like me to release the lamp and barrel now?" said Owen.

"No, I want you to wait until the watch changes. Here is the problem and I want both of you to work on it. You are the Captain of the *Magdalena*, which is a hundred-thirty feet long and drafts fifteen feet. You are riding at anchor in a channel that is three-hundred feet wide. At six bells in the morning, you are awakened by your commander, who reports that seven ships are approaching under full sail. What would you do?" Morgan fired up the pipe. "By the way, you have three minutes to make a decision." Morgan began rummaging through the care package that Jones had prepared for them, searching for a corkscrew. He found a silver screw and kissed it. He then held it up and whispered, "Thank you, Mr. Jones. Henceforth, you shall have an officer's share of the booty." Morgan pulled a bottle of wine out of his bag and uncorked it. He poured a cup for each of them. At the two-minute mark, Comstock came alive.

"I have it, Captain! Open ports on both sides, load guns and wait for them to come along side! Then *blast* them to hell!"

"Sorry, Comstock, you are dead, because the lead ship was the fire ship that *we* are building," said Morgan, "Lieutenant Owen?" There was no hesitation.

"Beat to quarters. Have gun crews on deck immediately. Ready a crew to up-anchor. Ready another crew to rig a sea anchor on the bow. Set fore topmast staysail; set the jib and fore staysail. Instruct the gunnery Sergeant to focus cannon on a nearby target—the bow of a ship! Up anchor and release sea anchor. As the ship turns, release broadside and raise sail. Ready stern chaser and fire at will," said Owen.

That *is* the key, thought Morgan, the sea anchor! The parachute-like device was often set during gale-force winds. Splayed out in the slowly moving water, the sea anchor tended to keep a ship near its original location, in spite of high winds. If you happened to be in a narrow channel that had a tidal surge of ten knots, why not take advantage of it? Using a sea anchor reduced slippage to almost zero.

"Lieutenant Owen, it seems that your new lady friend has taught you a trick or two," said Morgan, delighted. How could he have come up with a solution to this totally impossible problem in less than three minutes, when I have been working on it for six days? Morgan asked himself.

"Lieutenant Comstock, would you be kind enough to go forward and train your telescope on the *Magdalena*?"

"Of course, Captain."

Morgan moved closer to Owen and spoke softly. "How were you able to figure that out so fast?"

"It wasn't all that fast. I have been working on it since we first took Maracaibo."

"Pass me that bottle, will you?" said Morgan. "How about the sea anchor? How did you figure that out?"

"You gave it to me! Commander Collier told me about your design for the bombs—designed to follow the current. Well the problem has always been, how do we turn a hundred-foot ship around in the shortest possible time? There is not enough power in the wind to do it quickly, so the only other option was the current. When I heard about your bombs, I immediately thought about the sea anchor."

"Absolutely brilliant…what is your first name?" asked Morgan, filling their glasses.

"Dylan. Could you pass me the lamp? I have a question for you. What are the chances that Alonso has figured this out too?" said Owen.

"This may sound a little cocky, Dylan, but there are only two people in the Caribbean who could have figured this out and they are both on this boat. Alonso is no great intellect, I can assure you. By the way, call me Harry."

"I wonder if Alonso has even considered the possibility of a fire ship, Harry?" said Owen. It felt funny calling him "Harry".

"I seriously doubt it, but even if the slave who escaped today tells him, he won't be able to figure out what to do in time. I mean hell, we have both been working on it in one form, or another, for weeks. There is an element of terror in being the Captain of a Man 'O War, that you cannot imagine. The concept of pulling up a hook in a ten-knot current at the mouth of a narrow passage is positively nauseating. *He will never do it!*"

"There is still another alternative, besides the sea anchor," said Owen, packing the pipe.

"What would that be?"

"A stern anchor," said Owen exhaling smoke. "He could release one and then haul up his forward anchor. It would be risky and he would have to get his sails up in a hurry to get control. Even then, it would take some massive balls. *I* wouldn't want to try it."

"Have you solved the 'how do we get passed the guns, without getting killed' question?" asked Morgan.

"I have seen you working on it and I think I know what you are up to, but no, I haven't solved the problem," said Owen.

"What *am* I up to?"

"You are trying to figure out a way to make the Don's move their cannon to the land side of the fort, so that you can slip past the fort *before* they can get them back in place and blast you to smithereens. But the problem is, if you land the Buccaneers and have them storm the fort on the landward side, how many men will you loose? And how will you get the survivors back to the ships?" There were bells in the distance. "Would you like me to put the barrel in the water now?"

"Let me give you a hand," said Morgan. The two men placed the weighted barrel in the water, lit the lamp and set it free in the rapid current.

"Watch change on the *Magdalena*, Captain!" said Comstock, at the rear of the class.

"Thank you, Lieutenant Comstock. Come and join us for supper. Please mark the time."

Owen looked Morgan in the eye and whispered, "Have *you* figured it out?"

"Aye, Matey," said Morgan with an eyebrow cocked up and a devilish smile on his face.

Comstock came aft and the trio began to eat to excess. The simple fact was that the food was irresistible, especially after The "Panama Blush," in which Comstock had not partaken. Comstock had consumed several glasses of wine, however, and Morgan and Owen seized upon this behavior to get him to sleep early, so that the two of them could talk. They began a series of toasts. Morgan and Owen were drinking water from the Governor's cistern, and Comstock was drinking wine laced with rum. It was only a matter of time until Comstock passed out.

"Grab his watch, I'll go for a blanket," whispered Morgan. Comstock was tucked in for the night and Morgan and Owen moved to the front of the sloop.

"How long do you reckon it's been since we let the barrel go?" asked Owen.

"Right at a half an hour. They should begin firing on the barrel any minute." Owen marked the time on the watch and subtracted a half an hour.

"Do you ever get the feeling that we have done all of this before?"

"On a daily basis. To me, it feels as though my entire life has been mapped out and that I am able to experience only a moment of it at a time. I mean *really*, how the hell did *I* become Admiral of the Buccaneer fleet? When I came to the Caribbean, it was as a mate on a frigate. Did you know that?"

"I have heard many stories, but I have learned to remember them and not consider them factual. Everybody has a Morgan story. For example, there was a rumor that you were the bastard son of King Charles I and that he had sent you to the Caribbean so that Cromwell would not be able to have you slaughtered. It is absurd, of course, because how could the King have known that Cromwell was going to have him beheaded and take over England? Equally absurd was the story about you flying into a rage in Portobello and killing fifty men. What a pity that the creative energy of a nation is pissed away on gossip."

"I happen to agree with you that energy *generally is* pissed away by the majority of people, especially the politicians. We have Esquemeling to thank for the Portobello massacre rumor. That is why he will never set foot on my flagship again. Pass me that pipe, would you?" Morgan checked on the progress of the barrel. From his vantage point, it looked like the light was headed straight toward the largest of the three ships, well within musket range. Why hadn't they fired on it?

"Just out of curiosity, why do you call your pistols 'pulpers'?"

"That is a great story. During the Portobello raid, this huge Spaniard charged me. He already had a hole in his belly and I suppose he knew he was going to die, so he came at me with his cutlass over his head hoping to split my skull. I fired and hit him in the chest, but he still took two more steps and brought the blade down. At the last instant, I saw the life go out of him, but the blade was still coming down on me, so I moved right and the blade caught me in the shoulder. Obviously, I wanted to avoid a repeat of that experience, so I presented the problem to a gunsmith in Port Royal, named Kurtz. Every once in a while I happen to meet someone who is an utter genius in a particular area and Kurtz was one of those people." Musket shots rang out in the distance. Morgan and Owen watched as shot after shot missed the lamp. After about twenty rounds had been fired, the light finally went out.

"Mark the time," said Morgan. "Tomorrow night I want you to release the first barrel forty minutes later than the one we sent tonight. Then wait an hour, or so and release the second one. Then another hour for the third." Owen held the watch up to the lamp.

"I think I can manage that."

"Getting back to Kurtz, I had to wait about two months for him to come up with the first gun and it cost me a small fortune. One day he sent word that I should come to his shop and test-fire the pistol. He had a melon with a face drawn on it set on a tree stump and I fired the gun. It was the most amazing thing! I was about ten paces away and it didn't look like much had happened, but when I walked up to the melon, I realized that it had turned to pulp. Each eye had several tiny holes in it. I put just a little pressure on the top and it collapsed." Morgan filled their glasses. "Kurtz told me that the idea was to slap the person in the face and blind them at the same time. He had a standing arrangement with Esquemeling, the surgeon, to get body parts so that he could test his weapons. A head finally came up and Kurtz unloaded a round at twenty feet. He said the lead shot only penetrated the eyes. The pellets bounced off the forehead and jaw. But the really interesting thing was that the pellets made it through the thin bones behind the eyes and went through the brain and bounced off the back of the skull, thus destroying more brain."

"So basically, he made you a small caliber shot gun."

"Yes and no. Yes in the sense that it delivers 'shot', but no in terms of the delivery system. He encases the pellets in some kind of wax, so that they stay together longer. The really brilliant thing is that the whole mess, including the powder, is wrapped in these paper cartridges. You ram one down the barrel, then puncture the paper with a tiny fuse, which goes in from the side. Then the flint ignites the fuse. It takes a fraction of a second longer to discharge than a regular pistol, but the cycle time is cut by two-thirds and it has never misfired. The damn thing kicks like a mule and Kurtz told me that when the person gets 'slapped' by one of these rounds, it is with the same force that my hand is kicked with. It would definitely ruin your day," said Morgan yawning. "I think I am going to call it a night."

"I think I might sleep a little better if you told me how you plan to get passed the guns."

"Pushy, pushy. Why don't we talk about it tomorrow when we are both sober?"

"Fine. We can discuss it with Comstock over breakfast."

"You have a point, Dylan."

CHAPTER 28

"How was your night out with the boys?" said Sara, slipping a dress over her head.

"Productive. Owen solved a mystery for me that has to do with the *Magdalena* and may actually get us out of here alive. How bright do you think Alonso is?"

"I worked on that most of last night. He is intelligent, but he has absolutely no creativity. He is an aristocrat in the worst sense of the word. Unbending, dogmatic and superior. Which gets us to the issue of the escaped slave."

"I don't think it will actually matter. I figured out that the tidal surge going through the shallows is going to be moving at about ten knots if we hit them with the tide going out. The only way he can escape the fire ship is by hauling up his anchor and making a run for it. But in that case he is going to be moving backward through the channel. Owen figured out a way to turn the *Magdalena* around with a sea anchor, but I seriously doubt that Alonso will be able to figure that one out."

"Agreed."

"So it doesn't really matter if Alonso believes the slave, or not. There simply isn't a damn thing he can do about the fire ship. Well actually, there is one more thing he could do, but I don't think he will have the time."

"What is that?" asked Sara.

"He could send a launch out with an anchor and then drop a hook so that it was a hundred feet away from the other hook, perpendicular to the flow of the current. Then he could winch the stern of the boat up-stream so that his guns could bear on anything approaching him. That would require some creativity on his part and the only way that it could work is if he already had everything in place. Even then, it would take a fair amount of time on the capstan to pull the ship around in that current and the fire ship could simply alter its course to compensate. He is screwed. I just hope that it creates enough confusion so that we can take the other two ships."

"How long before the fire ship is ready?"

"By tomorrow, I think. But I have to figure out a way to stall Alonso for another few days. I want to tire them out before we make our move."

"Is that what your bombs are all about?"

"Exactly. We set a lamp on top of a weighted barrel last night and it went right for the *Magdalena*. When Owen releases those bombs tonight, it is going to put the fear of God into them! I wish I could be on one of their boats to see their expressions!"

"I missed you last night. It suddenly dawned on me that this adventure is about over. God knows where Charlie is going to send me next, but I am definitely going to miss you," she said.

"I will miss you, as well. *All* of you. The bright side to this ending is that we will not have to sit by and watch the relationship crumble over time. Besides, you would probably be bored to tears in Port Royal."

"The wickedest city on earth? I think not."

CHAPTER 29

Two days later a letter was delivered to Morgan while he and Sara were eating breakfast in the kitchen. It was from Alonso and Morgan instructed the Buccaneer who delivered the letter to detain the man who brought the letter into port, so that Morgan could send back a reply.

Morgan broke the wax seal, unfolded the letter and placed it on the table. A crowd was gathering in the kitchen as Sara and Morgan began reading the letter. The letter had been speedily written and there were several mistakes, with one entire word lined out. Before Morgan had translated the first sentence, Sara began to giggle, pounding her hand on the table.

"What a complete ass," said Sara, still laughing and shaking her head from side to side.

"Auntie Sara, will you share with the other children?" said Browne with a grin on his face. Sara looked at Morgan and he nodded his head.

"Letter from Don Alonso del Campo y Espinosa, Admiral of the Spanish Fleet, unto Capitan Morgan, Commander of the Pirates," read Sara in a deep voice. When she said, "Commander of the Pirates," the ten people in the room booed and hissed.

"My men and I have experienced much laughter at your expense, by way of your impotent attacks on our Fleet," Sara continued in a deep voice. "Impotent? Shall we invite Alonso over tonight, Harry?" The room erupted in laughter. "By design I shall put you and all of your men to the sword, each one without mercy. Except that you should come tomorrow and give back all that you have robbed from His Catholic Majesty and from the innocent people in the Lake Maracaibo environs. Otherwise, with the force of my honor, I shall put an end to your lives in a brutal way."

"Stop right there," said Morgan. "Did anybody remember to burn the Hall?" Laughter again. "Fortunately, I had the foresight to have Gbessay make up some suicide pills. Shall we take them now?"

"Me first," said Collier, and the room went crazy. As the laughter died down, Sara began to read again.

"Dated on board The Royal Ship, *Magdalena*, lying at anchor at the entry of Lake Maracaibo, this 26th day of April, 1669."

"All right Sara, take this down. To Don Alonso, from Henry Morgan, the Admiral of the *Buccaneers!*" The room let out a cheer.

"I am very much afraid that I will be unable to satisfy your request. You see, my men vote on the actions the Buccaneers will take and your lovely Spanish ladies are so practiced at the art of fellatio that the men may never want to leave!" Morgan had to wait until the laughter subsided before he could go on "My officers have become fatigued because of the incessant sexual demands your wives have placed on them. But, there is hope on the horizon. Ever since the big orgy we had in Gibraltar, several of the Spanish Ladies under our protection have developed a strange rash on the palms of their hands. You may want to have your physician look them over very carefully after we are gone. Frankly, the rash is making my men very nervous. Our Ship's Surgeon thinks it may be the pox. We have a cure, do you? By the way, Sara, the vixen who was banging your brother, told me that you like to put strange objects in your mouth. If you are looking for a promotion, my men would love to have you on board, during the trip back to Port Royal. Dated inside the Governor's bathtub, this 26th day of April, 1669."

"Harry, do you seriously want me to translate this?" asked Sara. The room was deadly silent.

"Why not? Remember, we still have the suicide pills!" Laughter broke out again.

"I am warning you, it is going to tip Alonso over the edge."

"That is the whole idea, my dear," said Morgan. "The rest of you, pay attention to this. When the runners returned last night, two of them reported spotting patrols scouting the countryside. One about five miles north of here and the other was about ten miles Northwest. So it looks like Alonso is about to make his move. I am guessing that it will be tomorrow. He will be carrying artillery, so there is no possible way he can be here for at least two days. I am hoping that he will split his forces and that should make it easier on us when we hit the *Magdalena*. In any case, I want the boats loaded and ready to sail tomorrow night. Questions?"

"Do you have a plan to get past the guns?" asked Velasquez.

"Actually, I have several and I will discuss them with you at length while they are being implemented. Anything else?" Morgan scanned the room. "Let's begin our day, gentlemen. Please have Richard Moss sent to me." Everyone scattered from the room and Sara and Morgan were alone again.

"You are a devilish man, Sailor Boy. Alonso will be pacing the deck for hours, plotting revenge against you. I would not want to be a sailor on the *Magdalena*, right now! He will seek out a priest and pray with him to smite you because of your heathen ways! I cannot tell you how many times I had to hold my tongue when I was in the same room with that asshole!"

"Did you notice how many mistakes were in the letter?"

"I counted seven and it wasn't a very long letter. He is usually very meticulous."

"One more night with interrupted sleep and he will be ready to pluck. This is a strange way to make a living! I mean really, did you ever in your wildest dreams imagine that you would be doing…what we are doing?"

"Eloquently put, Sailor Boy. I have been in a perpetual state of sustained excitement for the longest period of my life. Damn you! It may well be downhill from here. Oh well, I intend to savor the next few days, even if you are impotent!" Jones walked into the kitchen and began picking up dishes.

"Ah, Mr. Jones. You have been promoted to Midshipman," said Morgan.

"What did I do to deserve that, Sir?"

"You put a smile on my face, Mr. Jones, because you remembered the corkscrew. People who put a smile on my face advance rapidly. Sara here, is already a Vice Admiral and let me emphasize the word 'Vice.'" Sara began to laugh. "You will now receive an officer's share of the booty and that should enable you to get reacquainted with your family and have a comfortable life." Jones began to tear up.

"I am grateful, Sir, truly I am."

"Think nothing of it Jones. You know what, Mr. Jones, I am going to promote you to lieutenant, because then you will no longer have to refer to me as, 'Sir'. As a matter of fact, you say 'Sir' more than anybody I have ever met. Jones, you may keep your rank and prestige as long as you do not slip up and call me Sir. At that point, I will have you demoted to cabin boy. *Do you understand Jones?*" shouted Morgan.

"Perfectly, Sir! I will be leaving now." Sara began slapping her thigh again and then she began sobbing.

"God, I am going to miss you Harry." Morgan took her in his arms and began rocking her gently back and forth. It was silent in the kitchen and there was a strange sound as the tears rolled off of his chin and hit the back of her dress.

CHAPTER 30

"Right now, we have over seven-hundred-fifty mouths to feed and our provisions are abysmally low. The men in town are now eating the mules," said Collier, standing beside Morgan in the kitchen.

"Can you keep us afloat for another two days?"

"Barely, the space of three days we are going to have to take on provisions.

"I will take care of it, Commander. Hello, Mr. Moss! I need to have a word with you

"Sorry it took so long for me to get 'ere, Sir.

"Perfect timing, Mr. Moss. Here is the problem. There is always a possibility that the Spanish Ship *Magdalena* will be able to fend-off the fire ship. I want to reduce that possibility to *zero*."

"How, Sir?

"I want you to construct a harpoon-like device on the bow of the fire ship. At the base of the contraption, I want you to form a ring to which a chain can be attached. Behind the ring, you will need to narrow the metal so that it will break off there if the stresses are too great. The other end of the chain needs to be firmly attached to the fire ship itself, and don't give it too much slack. The idea is, we come racing in at ten knots and the harpoon, with the mass of the fire ship behind it, pierces the *Magdalena*. The fishhook-tip of the harpoon, which you will construct with the time available, will keep the harpoon from being withdrawn. If the harpoon breaks off at the base, the chain will keep the ships together, regardless of whether, or not the men successfully lash the ships together. Is the concept clear?" Collier looked on in amazement.

"Perfectly, Sir. I expect you want it done by today?"

"That would be most rewarding, Mr. Moss. Will the fire ship be ready today?"

"It is ready now, Sir!"

"Have I told you what a pleasure it is to have you with us, Mr. Moss?"

"Yuh 'aven't actually said that, Sir, but 'ah sure as hell wouldna' want to be on the other side!"

"Excellent, Mr. Moss," said Morgan chuckling. "We will need nine more of your bombs. My compliments to the gunnery sergeant on his fuses. If you are running short on time, just make the component parts and assemble them on board."

"We already have ten, fully assembled, Sir. Would you like to send them two at a time?"

"Mr. Moss, you are a treasure. I shall mention you highly in my report to the Governor." Moss flushed, and lowered his head.

"Why, thank ya', Sir."

"Go and create your harpoon, Mr. Moss."

"Aye, Sir." Moss walked out of the room with his head held high, absolutely beaming with delight.

"Damn, Harry! That was good!" said Collier. "Did somebody teach you this stuff, or did you figure it out on your own?"

"I had a very good mentor. A fellow named John Mansvelt. Take the best that you have seen me do and multiply it by four and you would end up with Mansvelt. He told me one day that you needed to give a man a compliment that he could tell his grandchildren about, over a campfire. He was right." There was silence, as both men thought about the teachers that had moved them along the path that had gotten them this far. "By the way, unless I miss my guess, Owen is going to ask you if he can join Pulverin on the fire ship. The answer is *no!*"

"What should I tell him?"

"Every man on this cruise wants to be on that ship! Myself included! But the Swimmers have been training for this, literally for weeks. Alonso is going to have hundreds of men on deck to repel the fire ship, most with pistols, or muskets and there is a good chance Owen is going to get himself killed. He is far too valuable to have his life pissed away in that manner. Think of something…I don't know. How about letting him captain one of the ships?"

"I will think of something," said Collier

CHAPTER 31

By the time Richard Moss reached the lowest step on the marble staircase outside the Governor's mansion, he already had the design of the harpoon figured out. There were several spare anchors among the various boats in the fleet and he planned to take one to the forge and bend the flukes of the anchor in exactly the opposite direction they normally took. This new inverted arch would then hug the bow of the fire ship and the shank would then be sticking straight out. It would then be a simple matter to fashion a hook-like appendage on the front of the shank, while the metal was red hot. The noonday sun was directly overhead, which meant that he had six hours to play with the final design. Suddenly a thought occurred to him; the wake made by the fire ship will cause the *Magdalena* to rise rapidly just before the harpoon strikes home and that could cause the harpoon to sheer upward. Chains would be needed above and below on the shank to prevent that from happening.

Like every other man in Maracaibo that day, Richard Moss began to fantasize about being one of the Swimmers. Everyone on board the fire ship was designated as a Swimmer, because, at some point, they would each have to dive in the water and swim to safety before the ship exploded. He imagined being on the bow of the fire ship as she sped towards the *Magdalena*, firing his pistols at the ship. In that vision, he began to panic as the distance narrowed. There were insanely angry Spaniards shooting back at him! What would *I* do? He wondered. Best to take cover behind the rail of the fire ship. But he would eventually need to rise up and toss his grappling hook on to the *Magdalena*, then pull for all he was worth. Or, would he? Standing up in that scenario would be suicidal. Moss slowed his pace on the journey back to the docks, lost in thought. Then he stopped altogether and put his hand under his chin, sweating in the Venezuelan sun. Minutes passed and he occasionally moved his foot from side to side, as if he were erasing a blackboard, then kicking up dust in frustration. He was totally oblivious to the fact that a crowd of Buccaneers had gathered to watch his antics. When Moss threw his hands into the air and began dancing, one of the Buccaneers ran up to the Mansion to inform Browne that Moss had, evidently, contracted rabies. Moss ran toward the dock with all the speed that his two-hundred-fifty pound body could manage.

For a man who was about to sail a fire ship into the side of a Spanish Man o' war five times her size, Pulverin was remarkably calm. Of course, the white wine at lunch had helped and the herb had added to his overall sense of wellbeing. Everything had been perfectly arranged. The explosive charges below decks had been given a thirty-second fuse. The powder kegs had been placed toward the starboard side of the hull and sandbags, hundreds of them, had been stacked in the center of the hull. In addition to providing stability, the sandbags would direct the main force of the blast to starboard, or directly at the *Magdalena*. Pulverin had tasked two of the Swimmers to light the thirty-second fuses and then run like hell for the stern of the boat. The fore deck of the fire ship was loaded with dry palm fronds coated with tar and brimstone, otherwise known as sulfur. Pulverin had ordered every other dowel on the port side of the fire ship's deck be removed, so that when she went up, the deck would pivot on the intact starboard dowels and dump all of the combustibles over onto *Magdalena*'s deck.

This was Pulverin's third fire ship and he had thought of everything. It was perfect and simply could not be improved upon. As the workmen removed their tools and the wood scraps, Pulverin slowly paced the deck with his arms crossed and head held high. The fire ship was finished and now all that remained was the task of sailing her out to the Spanish fleet and lashing her to the *Magdalena*. Pulverin hoped that Morgan would choose to do it at night, because it would be a spectacular light show.

For now, he was content to pace her deck and honor her for the Lady she was. Like every Captain since the dawn of time, he was in love with his ship, even though she was old and he would have to sacrifice her in a very short time. Finally, there was silence. The workmen had gone and he could hear the creaking of the dock lines, as the ship struggled against them in the light wind. Peace and serenity, for the first time in god knows how long. It was like a slap in the face when Moss came running up the dock yelling, "Captain, Captain, I have it figured out!"

Before Moss had a chance to step over the rail of the fire ship, Pulverin was there to fend him off, with an outstretched arm.

"Ya' do nah understand, Captain!" said Moss, pleadingly. "The Admiral told me ta' come 'ere and make the modifications!" Moss attempted to swing a leg over the rail, but before he could complete the maneuver, Pulverin had his foil at Moss' neck.

"My ship is per-fect," said Pulverin, lowering his foil. Moss knew he was beaten for the moment, so he withdrew.

"Bloody wankah," said Moss, as he walked over to the forge. With the help of two slaves, one loading coal and the other cranking the fan, Moss had one of the flukes on the anchor red-hot in the next five minutes. He skillfully hammered the anchor-arm into position and then heated up the other side and did the same thing. In the space of ten minutes, he had gone from a

"U with a hard on," to a "Y". Next, he flattened the sharp tips of the flukes into plates and then chiseled holes into them, so that they could be riveted onto the bow of the fire ship. Then came the shank itself. He heated the base and then took a chisel and worked the shank in circles, narrowing its diameter by three-quarters. Then he went to the ring at the end of the shank, where a chain, or a line was normally attached, and he heated the ring up to an orange-red glow. He took the chisel and cut the ring in half. He held each half in two-foot long pliers and flattened out the tips of both pieces. He kept those pieces red hot and then went at the base of the shank, above where it had been weakened and put it in the center of the forge. When the shank was red-hot, Moss took the two half-circles and attached them, one high and one low, with his hammer. This is where he would later attach the bracing chains.

Moss could feel eyes on him and he assumed it was the Indians, who frequently came to watch him work. Without looking back, he placed the tip of the shank into the hottest part of the forge. Once it was red, he trimmed off the hole that previously contained the ring and then began forming the tip of the device. He partially formed an arrowhead and then put it back into the forge. Several hits later, he came out with the finished product and jammed it repeatedly into the center of the coals, ensuring that it would have plenty of carbon for surface hardness. Next, he quenched the red-hot spear in oil. A massive plume of white smoke issued from the oil vat and then he repeated the process. The tip of the shank would have been harder if he had quenched it in water, but it would also have increased the brittleness of the spear-tip and it might have broken off when it hit the oak hull of the *Magdalena*.

Moss cooled the contraption he had made in water, after the oil, and his shoulders began rocking back and forth. He placed the "V" part of the "Y" on his hips and began gyrating his pelvis to some music that only he could hear. When he turned around, he was greeted by the sight of Morgan, Collier, Browne and Jones. They applauded and he continued his dance with the three-foot iron penis.

"Not bad for a rabid shipwright," said Browne. Moss set the harpoon on a table and approached the men.

"Afternoon Sirs. Captain, if yuh want me to attach the 'arpoon to the fire ship, yuh'll need to get that French Gentleman off the ship first. He drew 'is foil on me, by God."

"I do not understand you, Mr. Moss," said Morgan.

"Ah tried to get aboard the ship, Sir, buh 'e wudnah allow it! Ah tole 'im you 'ad sent me to add the 'arpoon, buh 'e said the ship was perfect."

"Captain, I believe I have a solution to this problem," said Browne. Morgan nodded his head eagerly. "Mr. Moss, you are excused. We will have Captain Pulverin occupied with other matters shortly." Moss walked away and began searching for short pieces of chain to use on the harpoon. "Mr. Jones, do you have any opium on your person?"

"I do, Sir and by the way, don't call me Mister."

"Right," said Browne, suppressing a laugh. "How many pipes do we have between us?" Each man pulled out a pipe. "Fine. I am going to mark mine with a lump of coal. If you have plans for the rest of the day, I suggest that you not draw on this one. Lieutenant Jones, could you give me some of your opium?" Jones fished around in his pocket. He produced a small cube that had been cut from the original brick.

"This ought to do the trick," said Jones, passing the lump over to Browne. The Ship's Surgeon walked ten paces over to the forge and picked up a flake of coal from the ground. Walking back to the group, he ran the flake down both sides of the white stem of his pipe. He broke off a small piece of opium and placed it in the bowl.

"Be careful, Doctor, we only have forty-seven pounds left!" said Jones. The group laughed and the impromptu party began. Browne placed a small amount of the Panama Red on top of the opium. In the space of twenty minutes, the kitchen in the

Governor's mansion had placed tapas and wine on their table. They talked and smoked and watched as Moss attached another harpoon to a fifty-gallon oak barrel. Pulverin was still pacing the deck of the fire ship and finally, Morgan went over to ask him to join the celebration in the promenade. Reluctantly, Pulverin agreed.

A pipe went around the table as Jones poured Pulverin a glass of cool white wine. Pulverin took a mouthful of wine and swallowed it as the pipe reached him. The contents of the pipe were exhausted and so the "black streak" was passed to him along with a straw. As he fired up the pipe and took a deep draw, three other pipes mysteriously appeared and Pulverin had no one to pass his pipe to. He blew the smoke out of his lungs and re-lit his straw with the lamp on the table. He took another deep hit and held it. By the time he blew the smoke out of his lungs, his eyes were glazed. He set the pipe on the table and then slapped his forearms on the table for balance. His eyelids went to half-mast and he began to giggle softly. Soon, his eyes were closed more than they were open and then they remained closed as his body slumped in the chair. His head was back and his mouth was open.

"Mr. Moss! I believe the ship is yours," shouted Morgan, holding his glass up. Moss turned to the table and waved. Morgan looked down at Pulverin. "We should probably get him down on the floor," he said to Browne. Browne looked over at Jones and they smiled. Both men stood up and walked over to Pulverin's chair, on opposite sides. Supporting Pulverin's head in their hands, the two men leaned the chair backward ninety degrees. Pulverin's head was now on the sandstone floor and his legs were still on the chair, up in the air.

"I say we circumcise the bugger, Sir!" whispered Jones, conspiratorially. "We could put one of those caps on his head and wait for him to wake up!"

"Yarmulke, Jones," said Browne, on one knee.

"Patois, Sir? As in, 'Ya makka we want to poke you, like a baker testin' 'is risin' bread?"

"No, the 'yamikah' is the cap!"

"I have it now, Sir! 'Yamikah de cap, I gonna wear it!" Browne chuckled and shook his head.

The afternoon was shaping up beautifully. Three boats pulled up to the dock and the Buccaneers on board proudly held up their catch of the day, unfortunately from the lake, because their access to the ocean was blocked by the Spanish fleet. The hundred, or so, people gathered there applauded wildly, grateful that they would not have to eat mule again tonight.

Richard Moss had a barrel suspended on two ropes beneath the wooden crane, which stood forty feet high. The barrel was full of water and had the harpoon attached. Moss connected another line to the side of the barrel and one of the Buccaneers began winching it backwards. Two other men undid the docklines of the fire ship and moved it forward a few feet, so that when the barrel was released, it would strike the side of the aft cabin. It would hit well above the water line, so there was no danger of sinking the vessel.

Morgan stood up and walked over to the dock, pushing his way through the crowd assembled there. One of the Buccaneers set down his filleting knife and began drumming on his table. The other five men beside him did the same until the barrel was released. In the dead silence that followed, the four-hundred pound barrel went through its arc and smashed into the side of the fire ship. The harpoon held and Moss had his clenched fists held high in the air, with an ecstatic smile on his face for about two seconds, until the harpoon pulled out of the fire ship and the barrel swung back toward the crane. There was a deep sigh in the crowd and Moss jerked his arms down and stomped his feet. Once he regained control, Moss went over to his foreman and began an animated discussion. The foreman nodded understanding and then Moss went over to the barrel, which had been lowered to the ground, and began detaching the harpoon. Moss walked back to the forge, harpoon in hand, angrily kicking small stones along the way.

In the next five minutes, the foreman organized a group of Buccaneers, who then began positioning two bugalettes next to each other on the dock. The bow of each ship was tied to an anchor fifty yards away in the bay. The stern of each ship was tied to the dock itself, so that the axis of the boats was perpendicular to the dock. There was a six-foot space separating the boats.

Morgan watched as Buccaneers began climbing the rigging of the left boat. Two men appeared to be reinforcing the lines on the top spar of the main mast. Another man ascended with a line and pulley and he attached the pulley to the spar about a foot from the mast. He put the line through the pulley and then fed it down to the deck, where another man attached a block and tackle to it. The block and tackle was hoisted up and attached to the spar.

"Hi sailor boy," Sara whispered in Morgan's ear. "What are they up to," she said pointing aloft.

"I honestly don't know. Nobody tells me anything, anymore." They watched as the Buccaneers reinforced and placed a block and tackle on the top yardarm of the mizzenmast as well. The couple walked back toward the table in the promenade.

"Just out of curiosity, why is Pulverin lying down on a tipped-over chair?"

"That man has never been able to hold his liquor," said Morgan.

"He is with the wrong woman! He shouldn't have to hold her!"

"What?" said Morgan, pulling out a chair for her.

"Never mind," she said.

The sound of Moss reshaping the tip of the anchor-shank on the anvil echoed through the wharf. Sara exchanged greetings with the men at the table and loaded a pipe.

"Not that one," said Morgan, pointing down at Pulverin. Sara nodded her head, knowingly.

The group watched as the Buccaneers on the left boat put rope netting over a barrel and then hoisted it up to the top of the main top yardarm. In the middle of the discussion about what the Buccaneers could possibly be doing, Collier walked over and whispered in Morgan's ear.

"A set of silks has gone missing." Collier was referring to the black silk clothing that the Swimmers would be wearing on the fire ship. The tight-fitting garments were very costly and the loss of one pair would never go unnoticed.

"Owen?" Collier shrugged his shoulder. "Better search his room."

"I have. They weren't there."

CHAPTER 32

Richard Moss set his hammer on the table and took the red-hot shank-tip and quenched it in oil. The wind shifted and the thick white smoke blew into his face. He cursed and changed position. The new tip had four spines on it, instead of the original two and they were half-again as big. As he waited for the shank to cool, he caught a motion out of the corner of his eye and looked up. An Osprey with a stick in her beak was landing on her nest, atop a dead palm tree. Good omen, he thought. He gathered up the two grappling hooks he had attached chains to, picked up the harpoon and walked back to the wharf. His foreman was there to greet him and Moss handed him the hooks.

"I left out one of the ingredients, so they won't be as good as me own," said Jones, passing a basket of fish balls over to Browne. Moss walked up to the table and was grateful for the shade, under the protection of the roof over the promenade, where the market did commerce beginning every day at sunrise.

"Captain, ah was wonderin' if ya could call for the Swimmers. Ah 'ave a little surprise for them aboard the ship."

"I will see to it, Mr. Moss."

"Thank ye, Sir," said Moss tipping his tri-corner hat. He walked away and began attaching the new harpoon to the barrel.

"Could I try one of your fish balls, Lieutenant?" asked Morgan.

"It would be a pleasure, Sir," said Jones picking up the basket and handing it over to Sara.

"By the way, Mr. Jones, you have been demoted to cabin boy for calling me Sir, again."

"Do you mean it, Sir?" said Jones, beaming with pleasure. "You have made my day, Sir! The terrible burden of command was beginning to eat me up inside. To be honest, Sir, I was having thoughts of doin' me'self in!" Everybody at the table was laughing, especially Sara, who was slapping her hands on the table. Everyone reflexively picked up their wineglasses when she got like that.

Drumming was coming from the fish table down by the fire ship and Morgan raced down to the dock. He positioned himself almost underneath where he thought the barrel would strike, so that he could study the impact. The drumming stopped and the barrel swung. A shudder went through the fire ship as the four-hundred pound barrel crashed into it. It was deadly silent while the Buccaneers waited to see if the harpoon would hold. Five seconds passed and somebody clapped. Soon the entire wharf was alive with cheers and clapping as the barrel remained motionless against the side of the ship. Suddenly, the barrel jarred as the weakened portion of the shank gave way and the crowd gasped. Morgan instinctively jumped backwards. The chain that he had put in the design jerked to life and the barrel was motionless, once again. The cheering began again and Moss danced a jig. Once he stopped, Morgan motioned for him to come join them at the table.

As Moss approached the table, everyone stood and raised their glasses.

"To Richard Moss, the rabid shipwright!" said Morgan.

"Rabid, Sir?"

"Yes, Mr. Moss. One of the men saw you behaving strangely in the street and reported that you had rabies. That is how we all came to be here. He said that you were talking to yourself and then started dancing." Moss' face flushed red.

"That was when ah figured out the grapplin' 'ooks, Sir!"

"Come and join us, Mr. Moss," said Morgan.

"No disrespect intended, Sir, but ah am too excited to sit down."

"Very well, Mr. Moss. Tell us what you figured out."

"The thing is, Sir, when the Swimmers throw their 'ooks and begin ta pull 'em in, they are goin' ta be slaughtered by the Dons! The deck of the *Magdalena* is ten foot 'igher than the fire ship's. They will be shootin' down on the Swimmers!"

"You have a point, Mr. Moss," said Morgan, exhaling smoke.

"Duh ya see them barrels hanging from the yards? Thems fed through the block above with a mechanical advantage of two to one! Each barrel weighs four-hundred-fifteen pounds! That means that if you attach the tail end of that assembly to the grapplin' 'ook, there will be eight-hundred-thirty pounds of force on it. Do ya follow me, Sir?"

"Proceed, Mr. Moss."

"Well, Sir, once we stab the side of the *Magdalena* with the 'arpoon, the men can stay below the rail and toss their 'ooks. Then they pop out a belayin' pin, releasin' the barrels and then they crawl to the back of the fire ship. The barrels will come down and pull the ships together!"

"Fochin' brilliant, Mr. Moss. I want to have your babies!" said Sara. Moss' mouth dropped open.

"We'll see about that," said Morgan, smiling. "I take it you are about to give us a demonstration?"

"Aye, Sir. I'll be shovin' off now." Moss went down to the bugalette he had rigged and spoke with the Swimmers on board her. Moss sent two men below to simulate lighting fuses, placed one at the wheel and two more crouched down behind the starboard rail. That left five Swimmers with nothing to do.

"On my mark," screamed Moss. "Now." Morgan began counting, one thousand one. The two men hiding behind the rail threw their grappling hooks blindly toward the other ship, then pulled their pins and began their crawl to the back of the ship. There was a lunge when the grappling hooks grabbed and started pulling the boats together. Within four seconds, the barrels were halfway down their fifty-foot descent. The Ignitors were out of the cabin and on the deck in eight seconds. The boats slammed together in nine seconds. It took fourteen seconds for the Crawlers to make it to the stern of the ship.

Morgan imagined men dropping from the rail of the *Magdalena* on to the deck of the fire ship. Only the foredeck would be on fire, so it was possible that one of the Spaniards could drop on to the aft-deck, go below into the hold and put out the fuses. Thirty seconds was simply too long. If the Dons did drop onto the aft deck, the Crawlers would run right into them.

"Mr. Jones, would you be kind enough to ask Mr. Moss and the Swimmers to join us?"

"It would be an honor, Sir." Moments later the twelve men arrived.

"Congratulations, Gentlemen. You put on a fine show," said Morgan.

"Why thank ye, Sir," said Moss, for the group.

"How can we make this better, men?" asked Morgan. Nobody spoke. "Don't be shy!" Finally one of the Crawlers raised his hand. Morgan said, "Speak."

"Well Sir, I, that is I think we should have knee pads." The other Swimmers quickly agreed.

"Fine. It will be arranged. What else?" Morgan was hoping that someone would suggest a false top on one of the barrels to conceal the fuse, but nobody spoke up. "Very well, Swimmers dismissed. Mr. Moss, please remain behind. Party hearty, me

Buccoes, we depart tomorrow." Morgan sat down at the table. "Mr. Moss, please join us. This time, it is an order!"

"Aye, Captain," said Moss, disheartened.

"I want you to come up with some solid ideas about how we can do better with the fire ship," Morgan said to the table at large. "Mr. Moss, I want you to put a false bottom on the powder barrels in the fire ship. The Ignitors had plenty of time to get out, so lets put some sham fuses in the hold, as well." Moss nodded. "Since no good deed goes unpunished, I want you to cut some narrow notches in the port rail to use as a kind of parapet. Hang a boson's seat below each one so that the gunners will have a platform to sit on. There were five idle bodies on that ship today, so we might as well utilize them as gunners. Why don't you have your carpenters build shelves that can hold, say five pistols each? Ouch! That's twenty-five pistols! I guess we'll have to steal some more," said Morgan, laughing. "By the way, trim the fuses to twenty seconds. See if you can fashion some sort of quick release mechanism for the seats. I don't want anybody getting fouled in one of them. Anybody else?"

"This is going to sound crazy, but it seemed like the bottleneck in your operation was the Crawlers," said Sara.

"Correct," said Morgan, intrigued.

"Why not put them on carts? You could use another barrel to power the carts. That would allow you to trim another five seconds off your fuses." Moss' eyes were darting all over the place, as he worked the plan through his head. Everybody remained silent and let him take his time. Finally, his eyes looked over at Sara, who was smiling at him.

"Lady, you are the fochin' genius around 'ere," he said and immediately looked over at Morgan. "Beggin' your pardon, Sir." Morgan smiled at him. Moss had to stand up and pace. "May I please be excused, Sir?" he pleaded.

"Very well, Mr. Moss, but you'll have to answer a question first."

"What is it, Sir?"

"Captain Pulverin seems to be coming around. How do you plan to get the harpoon out of his cabin."

"Ah 'aven't figured that out yet, Sir. Maybe you could put your lady friend to work on it? Could you 'ave the Crawlers rounded up for me, Sir, before they get drunk? I will need them to test the carts."

"It will be done, Mr. Moss."

"Thank ye, Sir." Moss practically ran back to the dock. Morgan turned to Collier.

"Why don't you have Pulverin thrown on a donkey cart and taken up to the mansion. I want to keep him away from the fire ship until Moss is finished with the refit."

CHAPTER 33

As usual, Sara was running around the Governor's suite naked. She debated whether or not to tell Morgan what she had found, but by the early part of the evening, she had decided that it would not make any difference if he knew.

"Hey Sailor Boy, come in here and see what I have found," she yelled from the bathroom. When Morgan entered the room, she smiled at him and then swung the mirror on the wall open. Inside the space behind the mirror was a leather valise, overloaded with papers.

"Don't touch. I haven't decided what I am going to do with it yet."

"How did you find it?"

"It seemed to be hanging a little crooked, so I tried to straighten it, but it was screwed into the wall. I thought, 'why would anybody do that'. Then I realized that it simply *couldn't* be done, unless there was access from the back. I found a fine spider web seal on top of it, so that they could tell if anybody had gotten into it. Anyway, I found the release mechanism…it's the head of that exposed nail," she said pointing. "You just press on it with a sharp object and the door opens."

"Did you read the documents? There must be a hundred pages stashed in that case."

"Two-hundred-sixteen pages, in all."

"Anything interesting?"

"Two diplomatic code books, twenty-two pieces of correspondence from the King's secretary along with a hand-written letter from the King himself. Various and sundry bills of sale and one *very* erotic line drawing, which gave me some interesting ideas for tonight. Unfortunately, we would need the assistance of three other people and I kind of wanted to keep you all to myself tonight," she said, moving her arms forward and squeezing her breasts together.

"Did you make copies of the documents?" She pointed to her temple. "You have total recall?"

"I do. Why do you think Charlie sent *me* and not one of his other whores?"

"God, I wish I had that ability," said Morgan.

"No you don't, Sailor Boy."

"Were the letters encoded?"

"Yes, they were."

"Have you read them?"

"No, I can't do the decoding in my head. I've only had time to look at the introductions and endings. I have to write it all out to decode it. I promise to share, but you have to give me something first," she said.

"How about the code books? Were they dated?"

"I will tell you everything I know, but only if we are in the bath tub."

"One question first. How did you decide that the spider web was a seal? Is that something you learned in spy school?"

"If there is a 'spy school,' I was never invited. Here was my reasoning, Sailor Boy. This house is run on slave labor. The Governor's wife is probably a slave's worst nightmare," said Sara, lighting candles. "There is no way they are going to miss a web, especially in the head bitch's bathroom. So here is what I did. I went into every room in this house and tried to find a spider web. There *were* none. The only place in the house where there are spider webs is on the front porch and that's only because the place hasn't been cleaned in what, six weeks?"

"I will buy your argument,' said Morgan stepping into the bath tub. "You could work this a bunch of different ways, couldn't you? The thing that impresses me is that the Governor had the presence of mind to think of the spider web, in the first place. And, of course, you have to wonder where he got the web." Morgan chuckled. "I mean think of it, five-hundred blood-thirsty Buccaneers about to enter their town, the head bitch ordering the slaves around, trying to get all their valuables packed up. Total chaos. Then the Governor says, 'I'll be right back, honey, I have to go and find a spider web.'" Sara began slapping the water. "Did I tell you that I stuck my finger in a horse turd that first night? It was still warm. So we must have missed them by a matter of minutes."

"It all adds up, Sailor Boy. And you are right about working the documents. I could seal the cabinet back up and replace the web. Or, I could close it up and not replace the web. Or, I could leave the door open and take the valise. The question is, how can we harm them the most?" She picked up the pipe and took a long draw, then passed it over to Morgan. "I can tell you one thing, I think I have seen every one of Charlie's code books and there is nothing like the ones in that valise. Odds are that Charlie could use them to great advantage. You too."

"I have five documents now that I have been unable to interpret."

"What sorts of documents?"

"Three were found on Spanish ships that we took as prizes. One was copied from a letter the Spanish whore in Port Royal had in her possession. The last one I am not willing to discuss." It was final and she knew it.

"I have the deal of the century, Sailor Boy. I will give you the two code books and translations of all the documents in the valise for the four documents you have, but can't you sweeten the deal and throw in the fifth document?" She sat higher in the water and began playing with her breasts. He smiled.

"Sorry, out of the question. If the King…never mind. Out of the question."

"All right, Harry, but remember, I know all of Charlie's code books from cover to cover. You will never have a better chance to decode that document than now."

"That is probably true, but I am not going to take the risk. I should just burn the damn thing and be done with it."

"Can you at least tell me where you got the document?"

"No."

Sara decided to switch gears.

"Whatever happened with the cholera outbreak?"

"The one here?" She nodded. "Browne told me that there was one more death in the no-salt group. He switched everybody to the salt concoction and nobody else died. Eventually, it just petered out. What brought that up?"

"I've had diarrhea for the last three days."

"Do you want me to have Browne look you over?"

"No, it has been getting better every day, but having said that, I need to leave you for a few minutes." Sara jumped out of the tub and ran to the privy in the next room. Morgan sunk down in the tub until his ears were under water.

"Ah," he said.

CHAPTER 34

There was genuine concern that, when Pulverin finally awakened from his opium coma and saw his boat, he might actually try and kill Moss. So the Buccaneers hid his foil and his pistols. This in no way guaranteed that Moss would survive, but it certainly increased the odds. Pulverin finally awakened and walked into the kitchen at dinner time. Browne managed to sneak a little laudanum into Pulverin's food. An hour later, he was passed-out again. The men carried him to a downstairs bedroom and ordered the Turk to sleep in the same room with him.

"He won't shit for a week," said Browne to Jones, who chuckled.

That night, Morgan left the French doors open so that the roosters would awaken him at dawn. The next morning he made his way down to the kitchen and, mercifully, Jones was there to greet him with a cup of his own Trelawny coffee. Two cups and a croissant later, he was on his way to the dock. The twenty-minute walk was invigorating and Morgan had a huge grin on his face as he thought about what an incredible life he had had, so far. He was getting hot, so he slipped off his white shirt and jammed part of it into the waistband of his knee-length, tan pants. "God these pants are getting tight," he said out loud. He pinched a roll of fat and felt disgusted with himself. He pulled the shirt out of his waistband and threw it into the bag over his shoulder. "Don't eat red meat," he said in his best whinny voice, "drink more water, stop drinking rum," he said shaking his head from side to side. But on balance, he *did* feel better when he obeyed Gbessay's rules. Time to tow the line, he thought.

As he approached the dock, Moss saw him and waved. Something was happening on the deck of the fire ship, but Morgan could not fathom exactly what it was. There was a lot of laughter as a netted barrel was raised upward toward the yardarm.

Morgan stepped onto the fire ship, which had been turned one-hundred-eighty degrees since the last time he had seen it. On the port side, which now faced the lake, two large sections of the rail had been removed. Two sets of track spanned the deck diagonally, leading to the openings in the rail, one in front of the helm, the other behind. Then he noticed one of the trolleys inching backward with each heave on the barrel. As the netted barrel continued to rise, Morgan saw three smaller barrels descending, simultaneously. Moss walked up to him.

"We worked on this contraption most 'ah last night, Sir. It shoots the Swimmers out in less than five seconds! Would ya like a ride, Sir?"

"Yes, Mr. Moss, but I would prefer to wait until the sun is higher in the sky. Can you tell me what the three small barrels do?"

"Of course, Sir. Them act as decelerators. Each barrel kicks in one after the other during the last third of the big barrel's descent. That keeps it from crashin' through the deck."

"Very clever, Mr. Moss. Are you planning on stacking that railing?" asked Morgan, pointing to the two portions of railing that had been cut out of the side of the ship and placed beside the helm.

"Yes, Sir. We can't have anything bad happenin' to Captain Pulverin, now can we?" Morgan chuckled.

"I suppose not, Mr. Moss. Carry on." Moss touched the brim of his hat and walked away. Morgan was curious about the harpoon, so he made his way forward. He peered down below the bowsprit and saw that Moss had placed two harpoons, both of which had further modifications. There were now four chains on each shank. Moss had also placed a single "loose" chain as Morgan had described in the original design, but with the four other chains in place, it was totally useless. Moss had done it to placate Morgan.

Morgan began to wonder whether, or not, there was really a need for the grappling hooks. The harpoon design had been tested and there was redundancy built into the design with the addition of the second unit. But still, the fire ship simply *could not fail!* There would be no second chances. Then there was the matter of the fuses. Could they be trimmed more? As it was, twenty seconds was a short period of time to accomplish what needed to be done after the initial impact. If Moss was right about the five-second trolley ride, then theoretically the two men throwing the hooks should be able to accomplish their tasks and be off the fire ship in eight, or nine seconds. That would mean the Ignitors would become the new bottleneck. How can we get them out of the hold of this ship faster? he wondered. Going up the stairs and then running along the deck would not only be time-consuming, but also very risky with a hundred guns trained on them. Instantly, he had the answer.

"Mr. Moss," he shouted, "where are you?"

"Down below, Sir," came the muffled reply. Morgan entered the companionway and descended the three stairs. Moss and two other Buccaneers were working on dummy barrels, designed to distract any Spaniard who happened to make it down the stairs.

"Mr. Moss, I want you to cut a hole in the side of this ship, right about here," said Morgan, pointing a few feet behind the beam.

"Whatever for, Sir?"

"So that the Ignitors will not have to go up on deck!" Moss hesitated for a few seconds and then got the picture.

"Brilliant, Sir, absolutely brilliant!" said Moss, beaming with delight.

"That forces us to revisit the fuses," said Morgan. "Mr. Moss, assuming that the fire ship was directly beside the *Magdalena*, and say, a dozen men with pikes were fending her off, how far away would the fire ship be in twelve seconds? By the way, factor in a ten knot current." Moss began a calculation in the sawdust with his fingertip.

"I have it, Sir. The fire ship would only be a pike plus an arm's length away from the *Magdalena*, but the current, which is moving seventeen feet per second, let's see. That is two-hundred and four feet, assuming no slippage."

"At ten seconds, that would be one-hundred-seventy feet. Assuming they were able to dislodge the harpoons and hooks in five seconds, that would still be eighty-five feet. Damn, this is going to be a squeeker. Where are the two Swimmers that are going to be riding the trolleys?"

"That would be Dan and Ward, Sir. Up on deck, I expect. Can't miss 'em, Sir, shaved heads and a whale's tail tattooed on their backs."

"Thank you, Mr. Moss. By the way, if you cut a ten-second fuse, how reliable is the 'ten seconds'?"

"We will use a 'fast fuse', which burns almost exactly one inch per second, Sir."

"Thank you, Mr. Moss. Don't assemble those fuses until I have a chance to hash this out with Dan and…"

"Ward, Sir."

"Right." Morgan counted, one thousand one, one thousand two, and kept counting as he dashed up the stairs and over to the port rail. Seven seconds. He walked over to the two men taking turns on the wench being used to haul up the netted barrel. Positive whale tail signs.

"Dan and Ward?"

"Yes, Sir," said Dan, with skinny legs and a massive upper torso.

"I am Captain Morgan," he said, extending his hand.

"We've heard of you, Sir," said Dan, grinning.

"Yes, I expect you have. All good, I trust?"

"So far, Sir," said Ward, who was practically a carbon copy of Dan, including the shaved head. Morgan guessed they were brothers, but he was wrong, at least in the sense that they had been conceived in the same womb.

"I have to make a decision about how long to make the fuses. Do you have a notion of how long it will take you to complete your tasks and get over the side?"

"Between four and five seconds," said Ward.

"We are about to do a wet run, if you'd care to watch, Sir."

"I would be delighted."

The two men finished the monotonous task of cranking the barrel up to the yardarm and walked over to the trolley that was set to go. Dan picked up a grappling hook and began explaining how it worked.

"When I pitch the hook, this cord begins unfurling, until it finally runs out and then it pulls this plug out of the deck. Once that happens, this keeper here flies off and the barrel starts dropping. So, roughly at the same instant that the hook hits the other ship, there is suddenly eight-hundred pounds of pressure pulling on the chain. We were playing with a four-hundred pound pull yesterday and the two of us couldn't budge the hook, so I think it is safe to say that if the hook grabs *anything*, they will not be able to dislodge it."

"That's encouraging," said Morgan.

"The trolley has been a technical nightmare. At first, Moss had the track running from fore to aft, under cover of the rail. I took the first ride and damn near killed myself by slamming into the stern rail. Then I had to stand up and jump over the rail, which put me directly beside the *Magdalena*. So we talked Moss into laying the track diagonally and removing portions of the rail, so we could just fly into the water and be as far away from the *Magdalena* as possible," said Dan. He picked up a belaying pin and inserted it into a hole just in front of the trolley. Ward went over to the wench assembly and backed the barrel down a couple of inches, until the trolley was firmly against the belaying pin. Ward then disengaged the wench.

"This belaying pin has been greased, but it still requires two hands to pull it out. And you have to grab on to the front of the trolley at the same time, otherwise you'll do a summersault and end up on your ass. It takes some getting used to. I just had a thought. What about a set of leather thongs we could put our wrists into?"

"Bad idea! If you got stuck in them, your arms would be torn off on the other side of the ship!" said Ward.

"You have a point," said Dan, laughing. "Whose turn is it?"

"Yours."

"I am going to try something different. We have been riding on our knees, but this time, I am going to try it sitting, with my heels over the front edge." Dan sat the grappling hook in his lap and placed his heels over the edge of the trolley. He picked up the hook and began swinging it on about three feet of chain. Morgan backed up. "Ready!" shouted Dan.

"Go!" shouted Ward. Dan threw the hook and popped the belaying pin out and threw it backwards as he began accelerating. His heels began to give way, so he reached his hands forward and grabbed the trolley. Morgan was watching intently. One thousand three, one thou…in less than four seconds, Dan was airborne.

"Ward, did you time that?"

"Yes, Sir, three and one-half seconds. A new record."

"Why is that, Ward?"

"Because he threw the hook while he was *on* the trolley. You can't do that if you are on your knees."

Dan swam up to the dock and hoisted himself up. He looked absolutely exhilarated. He ran down the dock and stepped back on to the fire ship.

"How did I do?"

"Three and a half," said Ward. "It looked like your heels slipped."

"They did! I damn near lost it!" said Dan, laughing.

"We can have Mr. Moss put some sort of device on the trolley for your heels, but what I need to know is, how much of a safety margin do you need? Can you do it in less than, say, twelve seconds?" asked Morgan.

"I'd say seven seconds," said Dan, "That will give us time to actually get into the water, which is where *I* want to be when she goes up."

"Ward?"

"Sounds fine to me."

"You know, this is so damn much fun that I bet you we could charge admission for it and people would *pay!*" said Dan.

"Let's be clear on this. You are both all right with a seven-second fuse?"

"Yes."

"Count me in."

"Mind if I take a ride on your trolley?"

"That'll be five pence. You are our first customer," said Dan, grinning. "And you have to help us crank the barrel up."

"Done," said Morgan. "By the way, nice art work on your backs. I think I recognize the work. Barbados. Mike Johnston, missing a right arm."

"That *is* amazing, Captain," said Dan. "How could you tell?"

"I used to run around with a French girl who had the same thing tattooed on the right side of her arse. On the left side was the whale's head coming out of the water. Mike swore that it was the first time that he had ever done that type of picture and he swore he would never do it again. I expect you had to hold a gun to his head. It's amazing that the lines are so crisp. His hand must have been shaking terribly," said Morgan, suppressing a laugh. Dan and Ward began laughing hysterically.

"Was he a Buccaneer?" asked Ward. Morgan furrowed his brow, not really understanding the question. "I mean his arm and all."

"Heavens no! I met him in Barbados fifteen…make that, nineteen years ago. I was new to the island and he was a native. A year older than I was. He took me under his wing. I was a poor mate in Venable's fleet and he was from a good family. Anyway, we had known each other for a couple of years and then lost touch. A year later I received an invitation to his wedding and I was stunned. There was absolutely no way I could afford a present, let alone the new clothes I would have to buy. I was too embarrassed to write him and explain my situation, so I just burned the invitation and pretended like I had never received it. It haunts me to this day," said Morgan, staring out at the lake.

"I call that 'lazy Susan', Captain," said Dan, cranking the four-hundred pound barrel slowly up to the yardarm. "As we sit at the table of life, a bountiful harvest is placed on our circular table, but most of us insist on choosing the items that cause us pain. Why is that?"

Morgan searched for a quick retort, but could not find one. He made a mental note to go back and review this exchange, but right now he could not afford to focus on abstractions.

"Dan, I cannot answer your question. Not now anyway. Ward, I can answer yours. Mike's arm was the result of a birth defect. I once met a Muslim carpet weaver who told me that it was an insult to Allah to weave a perfect carpet, so they always produced a carpet with a small defect. Mike *was* perfect, except for his arm."

CHAPTER 35

"How much do you remember," said Browne, in French.

"Just a bunch of strange dreams, really," said Pulverin.

"I am fairly certain that you came down with Malaria. I treated you with Jesuit's bark. How do you feel now?"

"Heavy. My body feels heavy and I feel weak, but there is no pain."

"Then it *was* Malaria. You had a very high fever, which probably put you in to a delirium and that is what caused the dreams. Your color is back, so the bark worked. Have some coffee and you will feel better," said Browne, passing him a cup.

"Where is everybody?" asked Pulverin.

"Packing up. We are leaving in a couple of hours. And by the way, Morgan was very impressed with the changes you made to the fire ship."

"Changes?"

"Yes, that harpoon thing was a stroke of genius."

"Harpoon where?"

"On the bow of the ship. And using the barrels as weights to pull the ships together! You should get sick more often," said Browne, punching him in the arm and laughing. Pulverin's eyes began darting around the room. He patted down his clothes.

"Where are my pistols?"

"I would assume they are on your ship."

Pulverin sipped his coffee tentatively. He struggled to recall what had happened, but could come up with nothing. He began to feel anxious and started to pace. He bolted and walked rapidly toward the front door. He swung the door open and ran down the stairs.

"Oh shit," said Browne. He ran out of the mansion and headed for the stables. With any luck, he might find a horse there.

"This is my lucky day," he said, grabbing a bridle. He slipped the bridle on the horse and jumped on the animal's back. "Yeah," he said, jabbing his heels into the mare's sides. She bolted out of the stable, happy to be out of her confinement. Browne avoided the main street so that he would not run into Pulverin. The gallop continued all the way to the wharf. Browne tied the horse off and ran to the fire ship, hoping that Morgan would be there. As he stepped on to the ship, he saw Morgan seated on a strange cart.

"Would you mind pulling that pin out for me," said Morgan.

"No problem, Sir," said Dan, straddling the cart and yanking the belaying pin out.

"Captain!" shouted Browne, but he was too late. Morgan went flying over the deck of the fire ship, screaming with delight as he headed for the opening on the other side of the ship. Browne sighed deeply.

"Is there a problem, Doctor Browne?" asked Dan.

"You could say that. Pulverin is headed here right now. You better have Mr. Moss stay out of sight for a while."

"He is down in the hold, why don't you tell him yourself?" said Dan.

"Fine, but will you get Morgan back up here?"

"I will take care of it."

Browne went down into the hold of the ship. Moss and his two assistants were napping.

"Mr. Moss," said Browne. There was no response. Browne went over and shook him, gently. Moss came awake with a start. "Sorry to wake you up like this, but Pulverin is on his way here and he is a trifle upset." Moss' eyes widened. "You may want to clear out for a few hours until we see how this thing is going to go."

"Aye, lad, that wanker 'as it in for me. Of that yuh can be sure!" Moss gathered up a few things and left the ship. Morgan was already back on deck when Browne came topside.

"The little bastard is beginning to annoy me," said Morgan. "Why do we keep having to jump through hoops for this guy?"

"He *does* have two fire ships under his belt and he *is* fearless and he *did* help us take Maracaibo and Gibraltar," said Browne. "I asked him what he remembered from last night and he said 'nothing', so I told him that *he* had ordered the changes to the ship and that you were very happy with him. I also told him that he had Malaria and that he was delusional most of the night."

"Nice work, Doctor Browne!" said Morgan sarcastically. "I guess we are going to have to work with it, but so help me, if he gets out of line, I am going to have somebody put a ball in his head! Pass the word," Morgan shouted. "Everybody stand up and applaud when Pulverin comes into town. Honest to God Browne, what part of your anatomy did you pull that story out of? I think you had better lay off the alfalfa for a while, before you become permanently damaged." Dan was trying, in vain, to control his laughter.

"I think that I need to go to confession. Are there any priests left?" said Browne. Morgan cracked a smile and shook his head.

"If we are going to make this work, I suppose I should go down and greet the little bastard. Have a beautiful day, Gentlemen."

The cheering and handshakes threw Pulverin off balance when he entered the wharf area. Morgan was there to greet him and walk him over to the fire ship. The truth was that Pulverin never bought the story about creating the modifications while he was delusional. If the others wanted to believe it, he had no reason to try and convince them otherwise. After all, it made him look like a hero. He also had a small amount of opium left in his blood stream and that helped take the sting out of his first look at his ship. He looked up at the harpoons and thought, well, maybe I *did* design those, but I would never butcher a ship this way.

Pulverin was so calm and collected, that Morgan actually gave him back his pistols. When it came to his foil, however, Morgan kept it "missing," just in case. In another hour, the ships would all up-anchor and the Buccaneers would say good bye to Maracaibo for possibly the last time.

During the twenty-two mile voyage to the Spanish fleet, Sara stayed below in the cabin and produced the two code books she had promised Morgan. Thankfully, she had something to take her mind off the terrible sense of loss she was feeling. Before leaving the Governor's mansion, she had replaced the spider web on top of the mirror.

CHAPTER 36

When the fleet finally dropped anchor at four that afternoon, Morgan assembled his officers and the Swimmers on the deck of the fire ship. The boats were anchored off the coast of San Rafael, approximately twenty miles away from the Spanish fleet, which kept a vigilant watch on the Buccaneers. Morgan kept the fire ship at the back of the pack so that the Dons would not be able glean any valuable information about her. The men were excited because they expected Morgan to issue orders to ram the *Magdalena* tonight.

"Gentlemen, let's bring this meeting into some kind of order," said Morgan and the boat fell silent. "First of all, are there any problems we need to discuss? No? Then let's get down to business. Tonight we are going to get a good night's sleep and try to keep the Dons awake as much as possible," there was a sigh of regret among the men. "We have ten of the floating bombs left and Commander Collier will assume control of them. We are far enough away so that we should only hear a distant rumble. We will up-anchor at eight bells," which is to say, four in the morning. "We should be on top of them right at sunrise. It will be lights out the entire way there. Captain Pulverin will stay behind until we are a mile away, then the rest of you slacken sail and let him pass ahead. The ship nearest the castle is going to be a tough nut to crack because of the shoals in front of her, so go in slowly on that side. We have a much better chance of taking the ship furthest from the castle, so I want four boats on her, marksmen in the rigging, chain in the cannons. Understood? *Chain, not balls!* By the way, if anybody shoots out the stern windows on either ship, *I will have your hides,*" screamed Morgan. A chain moving at three-hundred miles per hour will cut a man in half, but it will do relatively little structural damage to the side of an oak-hulled ship.

"Captain Pulverin, I suggest that you leave your barrels down until the last minute. The Dons will never be able to figure out what they are actually for, but they may think that they are filled with powder and fire on them. Dan, have you timed how long it takes to crank them to the top of the yard?"

"Just shy of four minutes with two men," said Dan, smiling. "But if Ward and I crank up all four barrels, we will be totally spent right before the impact!"

"Figure it out. There are twelve men between you. By the way, I want some of those pistols back. The Shooters are only going to get off two rounds before they have to jettison. I want the Shooters to focus on the rail of the *Magdalena*. I also want you to grease the aft deck to harass any boarders. Only fire on them if they are a threat to Dan and Ward. Otherwise try to pick off their sharpshooters. Questions?" He paused for dramatic effect. "Get some sleep then, because you will need it for the victory party tomorrow night." The Captains were always stealing his lines, so this time he gave them a good one, which he knew would be a comfort to the men on the other ships. Henry Morgan was scared shitless and yet he tried to quell the fear in his men.

As the men began to disperse, Browne yelled, "Captain! If you die, can I have your pulpers?" Everybody froze and eyebrows went up.

"Are we goin' to split 'em, Sir?" yelled Jones.

"Thems mine," said Dan, doing an imitation of the Turk.

"The hell with the pulpers," said Owen, "I want one of your plantations."

"I want your woman," said Balfor, like a gigolo. The men went, "oooh," in unison.

"I don't see you as much of a threat, Balfor. If memory serves, I believe you had a little difficulty keeping wind in your sails that day on the boom, remember?" The deck was filled with laughter. "The rest of you can have what you want, but the woman goes with me. I am going to lash her on to my back, naked, of course," a cheer went up. "And if a round hits me, then I have a companion to travel with, down the River Styx." The men cheered again, although most of them had no idea what Morgan meant by "The River Styx".

"Dan, a word?" said Morgan.

"To me, or from me?" asked Dan with his never-ending grin in place. They walked up to the fo'castle to get some privacy.

"Very pithy, Mr…"

"Bush, Captain." The name did not seem to fit. Dan seemed far too intelligent.

"How was the ride over?"

"Uneventful, in the usual sense of the word. Are you fishing for something in particular?"

"I call those 'bagel questions', because they leave a big hole in the middle and people can fill it with anything they like. They can get you into a lot of trouble. Did you test the boson seats."

"Over and over. There was not a single failure, once we figured out how to do it."

"What did you end up with?"

"Moss' design let one side of the chair go, but we kept getting slapped in the face by the seat, or hit in the arms. You are not going to believe this, but Pulverin was the one who came up with the solution. He made a quick release above the line in the triangle, using a slipknot on the outside of a loop above. When we release the slip not, the line feeds through the loop and we shoot into the water with our arms up and heads bent forward.

The seat shoots to the surface and we swim under water as far as we can, then rise to the surface and grab another breath, then go again."

"Sounds like fun. Do I get to try it on the next fire ship?"

"You would be most welcome, Captain Morgan. We could arrange a sampler right now, if it would suit you."

"I appreciate the offer, Dan, but I still have to visit four more ships for esprit de corps. You realize, of course, that you are… in a risky occupation?"

"Of course! I wouldn't have it any other way!"

"I thought so. Can I ask you a question?"

"Only if I can ask one first," said Dan.

"I am all ears, Mr. Bush."

"Has anyone ever seen Captain Pulverin smile?" said Dan, with a big grin.

"It is funny you would ask that, because *I* was going to ask you why *you* smile all the time!" What forces are at work here, thought Morgan. "The answer to your question is, yes. Kessenger was the one who saw it, at John Starr's brothel in Port Royal."

"What were the circumstances?"

"I am terribly sorry, but you only get one question. My turn. Why *do* you smile all the time?"

"I don't! I get pulled back into the pig pen all the time! But I mean, look around you! Here we are, sticking to this huge round ball, apparently circling a star we call the 'sun'. *Who thought this up?*"

"I think it is safe to say the design was not a product of the Vatican, or the Admiralty," said Morgan, memorizing this conversation, so that he could study it later. Suddenly, he thought of Sara. There was a real possibility that he would die tomorrow. Why did it make Dan smile, while it made him panic?

"I think the key is having fun, doing what you are doing. Based on what I have seen so far, you seem to embrace this notion. Am I wrong?" asked Dan.

"I embrace it part of the time. The other part is what concerns me."

"Think of the last time you felt like there was no hope. Do you have that memory?"

"Yes," said Morgan. It was the memory of Celeste.

"All right, go back in time. Think of a time in your past when you felt like you were going to die, preferably, over a woman."

"Let me count the times. All right, I have a particularly nasty memory in hand," said Morgan.

"What I would ask you to do is look at the duration of the pain. Did the pain clear faster on the second memory?"

"By about six months," said Morgan.

"That is the essence of freedom. Each time the duration of the pain is shortened, if you are growing. The thing that makes me different from you, is that, instead of having six months of utter bliss followed by six months of hellish pain, I go through that every second! When you learn to do it that fast, you never have a chance to frown."

"Are you having me on, Mr. Bush?"

"You are having *yourself* on, Captain. None of this is real," said Dan, smiling, of course. Dan was amused by Morgan's confusion. "If you want to play with this, just say to yourself about a hundred times a day, 'heaven and hell in every moment. What should I pay attention to?'"

"Where did you get a notion like that?"

"I came across it in some Buddhist texts. I guess that was the seed. Newton and I discussed it during the five years I was at Cambridge."

"Isaac?" asked Morgan, astonished. Dan nodded. "So, let me get this right. You were a student at Cambridge and you ended up as a mate on an English Man o' war? How?"

"Not exactly. I was never a 'student' at Cambridge, I was a professor. I went to London Town to go to my nephew's wedding and got hit over the head by a press gang. I woke up on the *Oxford* and have been smiling ever since."

"Dan, do me a favor. Survive tomorrow, so that we can continue this conversation later. But right now, I have things to attend to. Good luck," said Morgan, walking briskly away. Christ, Pulverin is going to feel slighted because I spent so long with Dan, thought Morgan. He fished a packet of Virginia tobacco out of his pouch to give to Pulverin. In the distance, Morgan heard Dan's voice call out to him.

"Captain, *I* still hear the sound of the riggin' singing, *do you?*"

For no particular reason, Morgan stopped in his tracks and stood by the rail of the ship. He took in a deep breath, letting the fear of what was going to happen tomorrow go where it chose. The red sun was playing with the clouds on the horizon and Morgan soaked it all in. How long had it been since he had actually enjoyed a sunset? "Heaven and hell, in every moment. What am I going to pay attention to?" he said aloud. At that moment, there was no force in the universe that could have prevented him from smiling. Who *had* thought this up?

CHAPTER 37

Morgan made the rounds of the other four boats and he thought how puny they were in comparison to the three Men o' war that they would be facing tomorrow morning. A kind of peace settled over him when he finally realized that the die had been cast. At the same time, he knew that he was surrounded by some of the best minds on the planet and he was absolutely certain that there had never been a fire ship in history that was as well prepared as the one he had been on an hour ago.

Morgan was sailing alone in his gig, back to the *Enchantress*, when he realized that, more than anything else in the world, he wanted to drop his sail and gaze up at the stars. The voices inside his head had finally stopped. How peaceful it would be to just lay down and enjoy the warm trade wind and look for constellations that his grandfather had taught him as a child. He lowered the gaff-rigged sail and lay down in the cramped cockpit. His boat was over a hundred yards ahead and the tide had not begun to turn. It was safe to play for a while. The big dipper. "Take the side farthest from the handle. Those two stars point at the North Star, Polaris," said his grandfather. Morgan could smell the riff-cut tobacco in his grandfather's pipe and tears welled up in his eyes. From out of nowhere, another voice whispered, "Heaven and hell, in every moment." For the first time in his adult life, Morgan realized that he had avoided thinking about his grandfather for over thirty years. It was simply too painful, or at least it *had* been. Memorize this and work on it later, he told himself. Memory! Every time the word "memory" comes up, I am going to think of Sara, probably for the rest of my life.

Sara! Oh shit, he thought, she is going to think I have been fochin' one of the Spanish women! He was laying down, very comfortably just a few seconds ago, but now his bent knees were banging against each other, rapidly, as he imagined the accusations that he would have to listen to.

"Oh shit! Maybe I fell asleep and my gig is floating directly under the Spanish Men o' war!" said a voice in Morgan's brain. His heart began to pound in his chest and he sat bolt upright, feeling for his pulpers. He looked around and realized that his position had not changed perceptibly.

I am back in the fochin' pig pen again! He began to laugh and slapped his thigh. Sara! he thought.

Morgan took an inventory of what was in his blood stream. Absolutely nothing! Does this mean that my own brain can do this kind of stuff? he asked himself. "I guess it just did," he said aloud.

He raised the sail on his gig and headed toward his boat. During the ten-minute ride, Morgan played with the voices in his head. He figured out that when he had gotten to the point where he had done all that *could be done* with the fire ship, it somehow made it all right for him to have a few moments of peace. But *how* had that happened? I guess I just let it go, once I had done all that I could, he thought. But there was something more. Some part of him felt comforted. Was that the part that had driven him to make the fire ship perfect? There was a tug inside his belly and he knew what it was. There was *calm* inside. Suddenly, a picture of the fire ship took hold in his mind. He could feel his pulse quicken and his index finger started tapping the tiller. This is amazing! I went from a state of total relaxation to horror in ten seconds. Maybe this is what Dan was talking about! Morgan felt calmer, just paying attention to the dialog inside his own head. The more he focused on it, the more relaxed he felt and the clearer the voices became. He became aware of the tapping on the tiller and he paid attention to it, letting it direct him where *it* wanted to go.

Morgan had a long forgotten memory blaze into his mind. At the time the memory had been created, he was somewhere around the age of five. He was walking with a group of friends and while he was telling a story, he tripped on an irregularity in the pavement, largely because he was not paying attention. His friends laughed at him! As he played with the memory, he realized that it had been a turning point in his life. From that point forward, Morgan had devoted much of his time to making sure that nothing would ever go wrong and that no one would ever laugh at him again. Attention to detail became one of his trademarks. "My God, this is a revelation!" he said, out loud. On some level, he knew that what had just happened was the end of a long process, which had been speeded up at an alarming rate over the last few hours. But how? Why?

"God, I hope he makes it," said Morgan, pulling up beside his boat.

"You really should stop talking to yourself," said Sara, handing him a basket. "It will make your men nervous."

"What is this?" he asked, taking the basket.

"Dinner! I was hoping we could pull up on one of those islands over there and make a night of it."

"An excellent idea. I was dreading getting back on the boat."

Commander Collier, Lieutenant Owen and Browne sat around the small table in Morgan's aft cabin. Jones brought in a tray with four plates on it.

"'Ere we are Gents," said Jones, doling out the plates filled with food. "Eat hearty," said Jones, sitting down in the fourth chair. "This is the last of the chicken. Tomorrow we are down to filet of mule."

"I suppose we will start packing on weight," said Browne. Jones started laughing.

"Unless we rein in our appetites," said Collier,

"It might spur us on to greater things," said Owen, "but we may end up looking like asses."

"Personally, I can't stand being saddled with that kind of responsibility," said Browne.

"Do ya know who it makes me feel like?" asked Jones.

"No, but it had better be good," said Browne.

"That Spanish fellow, Donkey Hote!" Napkins, a spoon and a chicken bone, were suddenly air born and headed straight for Jones, who ducked and covered his head, locked in laughter's embrace. There was a slight twitch in the boat as the slack anchor cable became taught, signaling the new out-going tide.

"Did I ever tell you about the time that the men found a saddle stirrup in a brine barrel of 'beef'?" said Collier.

About a hundred times," said Browne, taking another draw on the white clay pipe. "But tell us again, because Owen and Jones may not have heard it."

"We were about twenty days out of London on a frigate named…well, it doesn't matter. The thing was, the men opened a barrel that was marked 'Beef' and as they began removing the contents, a little at a time, they found this brass stirrup in the brine with a leather strap and they realized that they were eating horsemeat. It was not the thought of eating horsemeat that troubled the men, it was the fact that the company that had been given the contract by the Admiralty to supply the ships with victuals, had lied. Add to that the weevils in the ship's biscuit and the foul water…it was a very angry group of men. When they dropped me off in Port Royal, it was one of the happiest days of my life."

"Speakin' from me own experience, I would say that the average plantation slave has a better life than a seaman," said Jones.

"How can you say that?" said Owen, angrily. "Slaves have no freedom, no right to own property and they are savagely beaten on the slightest whim of the slave driver!"

"Have you ever been on a plantation, Lieutenant?" asked Browne.

"Not personally, but I have talked to people who have been."

"Don't misunderstand me," said Browne. "I am not a proponent of slavery. In fact, I am quite the opposite. But I think Jones is absolutely right. I have spent time on four different plantations, two in Virginia and two in Jamaica. I have never seen a case of scurvy, or malnutrition on a plantation, but I have seen it in droves aboard ships. Even in London there is starvation! People are hanged daily for stealing a loaf of bread! There is disease and filth everywhere. Compare that with life on a plantation. The slaves have plenty to eat, they have good housing, medical care. Hell, they even have families."

"That routinely get separated!" shouted Owen.

"Agreed! It happens, *occasionally*. But is that any worse than a press gang?" screamed back, Browne. Jones caught Collier's eye and winked.

"I say we let 'em hash it out with pikes up on deck! I've got five quid on the lanky doctor!" said Jones. Collier and Jones began to laugh and it infuriated Owen.

"Bugger off, Jones! How can you make jokes about this?" screamed Owen.

"Sorry Sir, I didn't mean nothin' by it."

"Lieutenant, go back to the Hall. Remember the chair?" said Collier, softly. Owen looked stunned, as though he had been slapped in the face. He took a deep breath and looked over at Jones.

"My apologies, Mr. Jones."

"Think nothing of it, Sir. Does this mean we won't be needin' the pikes?" Owen cracked a smile and then started belly laughing, and the rest of the table joined him. Collier stood up and walked toward the door, still chuckling.

"Thank you for a delicious meal, Mr. Jones. Lieutenant Owen, I am going over to the lugger to deliver some presents to the Dons," said Collier. "Tell the Captain that I am going to the half-way point between here and the castle to release the bombs. I will flash a light at two bells to mark our position," which would be five in the morning.

"Good luck, Commander," said Owen.

The deck of the three-masted lugger was crowded with the ten floating bombs that Moss had manufactured. The thumbnail moon was three quarters of the way down in the Western sky and the tide was ripping through the narrows. Closer proximity to the Spanish fleet meant that the fuses would have to be shortened and Moss had already begun that task. Sailing a beam reach in the trade wind, along with the current, would place them at the halfway mark in less than an hour.

Luggers were the fastest boats on the water. They were used extensively in England to outrun the Customs Service boats during smuggling operations. They were so effective that laws regulating their beam dimensions had been enacted. The narrower the beam, the faster the boat would sail, but at the same time, the cargo capacity was also greatly diminished, making them practical only for the transportation of very valuable items, such as gold and opium.

In the distance, Collier could make out a faint light on the horizon, which he took to be the fort. If they arrived at nine that night, they would have about seven hours to release all of the bombs. That would mean releasing a bomb every forty minutes, or so. Collier breathed a sigh of relief that his boat would be about ten miles from the blasts; close enough to hear them, but far enough away to permit sleep, especially with a couple of mugs of rum on board.

Collier's task tomorrow was to sail up to the ship farthest from the castle and tie off, bow to bow. He would have twenty marksmen stationed on the fore deck, along with four grapplers. Even though the ship they were going to board was a hundred feet longer, the Buccaneers would have the advantage, because two other boats would also tie up to the bow of the ship and boarders would come swarming up over the rail. It would be pandemonium on the fore deck of the ship. A shudder ran through Collier's body as he visualized the Spanish ship swinging her stern around far enough to release a broadside. How could Morgan be so confident that it would not happen?

Collier went through Morgan's line of reasoning again. If the ships were tied perpendicular to the flow of the current, their ship-lap sides would leak like mad and Morgan was convinced that the bilge pumps could not keep up with the volume. So the ships would have to swing at anchor. Assuming that the Dons had had the foresight to place an anchor so that they could winch their sterns around, it would take them at least ten minutes to accomplish it and by that time the boarders would already be in place. The reasoning was sound, but it did little to quell the fear that gripped him. A mug of rum would certainly do the trick.

"The bombs 're ready, Captain," said Moss.

"Thank you Mr. Moss. It looks as though we have reached the halfway mark. Why don't we do a sounding and then throw out a hook with a seven to one scope. You may release the first bomb when it is convenient."

"Ah will attend to it now, Captain."

The fifty-man crew dropped the sails and watched as the anchor was thrown overboard. When the lugger's bow snapped toward the oncoming current, they went astern to see the first bomb lighted and placed gently in the water. The moon was just about to touch the horizon. Soon, it was pitch black and the men had to go below to smoke their pipes.

"Captain," called out moss. "Where are ya?"

"Over here, Mr. Moss."

"Captain, do ya suppose we could keep one small lamp on the stern deck? We could keep 'er turned down to almost nothin.'"

"Go right ahead, Mr. Moss. By the way, vary the timing on the bombs. Don't make them explode at exactly forty-minute intervals."

"Understood, Sir. Thank ya, Sir."

"You are welcome, Mr. Moss. Get some sleep."

"Ya can count on it, Sir."

"Mr. Moss, why are we whispering."

"Damned if ah know, Sir," whispered Moss, laughing.

The men were beginning to settle down. The rum flowed freely and small groups formed, telling stories, or singing softly. There would be no bells ringing tonight. Collier stood on the foredeck and looked up at the stars. He wondered if he would ever see the Southern Cross. He would have to survive tomorrow first. He raised his mug and took a generous gulp of rum. It didn't burn his throat and that was the signal that told him to stop for the night. He arranged for a storm sail jib and a blanket from below, which he then made into a bed on the fore deck. Sleep came fast and the next time he opened his eyes it would be two bells, or an hour before sunrise.

CHAPTER 38

It would be an understatement to say that nobody sleeps soundly the night before a surprise attack with the odds stacked two to one against them. But there can be no doubt that the Buccaneers, with the aid of some fairly mediocre Jamaican rum, slept much better that the Spaniards did.

The galleys came alive at seven bells, or three thirty and by eight bells, the anchors had been hauled and the ships were in motion, as the last of the crewmembers came alive. The fire ship and the five boats ahead of her spaced themselves out to a safe distance and managed to keep their positions known to each other by singing short ditties and shouting out the bawdiest limericks the world had ever known.

In Morgan's aft cabin with the windows open, Sara committed the limericks she heard to memory so that she could share them with the King. She would have his full attention for several weeks, in one-hour bursts, of course, the next time she went to London. In private drawing rooms and castles all over England, she would be a sought-after guest.

Just shy of two bells, a Buccaneer spotted a light about a mile ahead and sent word back to Morgan, who ordered the galley stoves quenched. Dawn would break in about fifty minutes, as the boats traversed the remaining ten miles. Morgan was tempted to slow the fleet down a bit, to compensate for the freshened breeze, but it would be better to arrive a little early, rather than late. Morgan hoped that the three Spanish ships waiting for him would have several lamps burning, so that the Buccaneers could make them out in the moonless night.

When Morgan made a decision, there were always parts of him that screamed out against it, but there was some voice inside him that always seemed to take control and make the right decision. He had learned to yield to it in times of crisis and he was poised to do it again, as his fleet pulled to within five miles of the castle.

"Lieutenant Owen, luff the sails, but keep steerage and command the other boats to do the same. Have men ready on the sheets. It won't be long before we have to haul them in again." Morgan looked at the horizon where he could clearly see lights in the three Spanish ships guarding the channel.

"Aye, Sir," said Owen, reverting to his midshipman days. Morgan remained by the helm and tried to estimate how far away the ships were. He guessed between two and three miles. The men had automatically reverted to bird noises to announce their positions. The breeze picked up even more and Morgan was glad that he had slowed the boats down, because there was still not a trace of dawn. The canvas overhead was flapping and snapping and Morgan wondered if that sound would carry to the Spanish Fleet. "Where the hell is the sun?" he muttered.

Then it happened. There was the barest glow above the hills to the East.

"Haul the sheets in, Lieutenant," said Morgan calmly, wanting desperately to scream the order out himself. Morgan looked over at the rest of his fleet and, for the moment, they were still invisible. He felt the boat lurch forward as the sails filled and stopped their sputtering. He instinctively reached for a telescope, but there was not enough light to gain any information.

"Lieutenant Owen," said Morgan walking up to the nervous teenager. "Commander Collier left me a note informing me that one of the black silks, gone missing several days ago, had been returned to the locker. Would you happen to have any information on this matter?"

"Absolutely not, Captain."

"I thought not. It is another unsolved mystery in the Buccaneer Fleet. Would you be kind enough to assemble the pipers on deck? They are to await my orders."

Actually, there were two pipers on board. One was fond of tobacco and other combustibles. He had lately become short-winded and irritable, but for an occasion such as this, he could at least muster some noise. The other piper was fond of food, especially deserts. He played well, but he tended to get over-heated in the tropics, carrying around an extra hundred pounds of fat. Fortunately for him, there was a good breeze this morning and the sun was still below the horizon. Morgan was certain the pipers would put the fear of God into the Spaniards.

There was adequate light now to make out silhouettes on the decks of the Spanish ships and the distance between the Buccaneers and the Spaniards was rapidly narrowing. As previously arranged, the fire ship began overtaking the other boats, as they slackened sail to let her pass. In true Buccaneer fashion, the Swimmers hung their "bare arses" over the side as they passed each boat. When the first cheer went up, Morgan ordered the pipers to play, now less than a mile away from the Spanish Fleet. Morgan went to the port rail and waited for the fire ship to pass. When it finally did pass, Morgan saw a hand rising above the improvised armor covering the helm, then Pulverin poked his head around the wooden wall. Dan, with his shaved head and his irrepressible smile, waved happily from the deck amidships. Was he going to his death? Or, was he going to his life? Did it really matter? Heaven and hell in every moment, thought Morgan, waving back at Dan.

On the foredeck, Morgan trained his telescope on the *Magdalena*. She was opening her gun ports and running out her cannon. Her capstan was not manned, which meant that his fleet would not be facing a broadside from her, because there was no longer enough time for her stern to be winched around into position, even if they *had* thought of it. Morgan took a deep breath and began to relax.

Sharpshooters with muskets began to assemble on the fore deck along with two grapplers. Morgan's boat was going to tie up bow-to-bow with the *Marquesa*, on the starboard side of the boat that Collier was on with Moss. A third boat captained by Balfor would then tie up on the other side of Collier's boat, so that there would be three successive waves of sharpshooters and boarders within the space of a minute, if all went well. Morgan's men were tasked with disabling the guns on the port side, of *Marquesa,* so that the fourth boat could sail by unharmed and attack the aft of the vessel.

The two remaining ships in the Buccaneer fleet were sloops with shallow drafts, which made them ideal for the attack on the third Spanish ship, nearest the fort. Morgan noticed smoke coming from the fore deck of the fire ship. Four barrels were up in the rigging and as the impact of the two ships was seconds away, the sheets on the sails were let go by the Igniters, who ran below decks to light the sham fuses. The Spaniards began firing on the fire ship, and through his telescope, Morgan could see chips of wood flying from the wooden wall that protected Pulverin. Morgan could see puffs of smoke coming from the Buccaneers sitting in the boson seats on the port side of the fire ship. Several Spaniards on the deck of the *Magdalena* dropped.

The masts of the fire ship shuddered when the impact finally occurred. Morgan began counting. A Spanish boarder landed on the aft deck of the fire ship and hit the grease. Pulverin shot out of the helm, took two steps and dove over the port rail. Dan and Ward threw their hooks. Something went wrong. One of the hooks had apparently bounced back on the deck of the fire ship. Two barrels began descending and the fire ship was pulled in close to the *Magdalena* and hit with a shudder. A struggling Spaniard, impaled by one of the grappling hooks, was raised quickly up to the yardarm, where he remained suspended. Morgan could see another barrel descending. "Thousand three," said Morgan. "Oh shit! Get out of there!" Three more boarders jumped on the fire ship and apparently fell because they went out of sight immediately. The fourth barrel, which powered the second trolley, remained motionless. "One-thousand four, one-thousand five." Finally, the barrel came to life and got about halfway down to the deck when the explosion occurred.

Morgan watched as the port side of the deck raised up violently and flung its flaming cargo on to the higher fore deck of the *Magdalena*. Tongues of fire began licking their way up her hemp rigging and when some of the smoke had cleared, he could see a sizable hole in the side of the *Magdalena*. Soon it was obvious that she was on fire below decks. The sandbags that Pulverin had placed to deflect the blast toward the *Magdalena* had performed beautifully. *Magdalena* was done for and there was absolute pandemonium on her decks. He wondered if the second trolley made it to the edge of the fire ship before the explosion occurred. Morgan jumped when the Buccaneers on the bow of his boat began firing on the sailors on the *Marquesa*. Jenkins threw out the stern anchor at the last minute so that the aft end of the *Enchantress* would not be swept forward in the current.

Morgan collapsed his telescope and pulled out his pulpers. His men were streaming on to the *Marquesa* like ants and he decided to join them. Balfor's boat came in too fast and smashed into Collier's boat. The shock wave knocked Morgan to his knees. Heaven and hell in every moment, ran through his brain. "I can scream and yell, or I can enjoy this," he said to himself, laughing. Sara appeared on deck, obviously distressed.

"What the hell was that?" said Sara in an irritated voice.

"I am afraid that was me. Remind me never to eat mule again. The good news is that we are being moved to a larger room with our own head! I'll be home for dinner," said Morgan, running for the bow of his boat, his cocked pulpers held close to his chest, pointed forwards.

"You can play this any way you want to, but if you want it to be enjoyable, you are going to have to relax your body," said Dan, looking over at Ward on his trolley. "Why not try a deep breath, brother?" Ward took a deep breath and for a few seconds, he forgot that he was on a fire ship that was about to impale a Spanish Man o' war. Dan could see that he was coming around. "Nice. Now, let's do that again and this time, hold it as long as you can." Slowly, Ward's hands and feet began to unlock as the carbon dioxide he had blown off with his rapid breathing, began to re-accumulate in his blood stream. Ward opened and closed his fingers several times with a smile on his face.

"Remember, the outcome doesn't matter. *The process does!*" said Dan with a huge smile on his face. Ward smiled back as the Spaniards on the starboard bow of the *Magdalena* began to fire their muskets. Wood chips began flying as their musket balls struck home. The favorite target seemed to be the sections of rail that covered Pulverin at the helm, but many of the balls hit the hastily carved logs adorned with hats on the first portion of the fore deck, even though they were obviously logs at this distance. When the harpoons pierced the side of the *Magdalena*, all of the Spanish marksmen seemed to fire their muskets and pistols at once and then there was silence. Ward had thrown his grappling hook a fraction of a second too early and his hook was struck by a random shot. The ball ricocheted off the hook and hit Ward in the wrist, shattering his radius. There was no way he could pull out his pin, now. His grappling hook and chain were now over top of Dan's track, blocking his way. The first Spanish boarder hit the aft deck just beyond where Dan lay hidden behind the rail. The Spaniard's boots hit the greased deck and shot forward. His head hit the deck and he was out cold, but he had fallen directly over Dan's track, on top of the chain.

Pulverin crouched low behind his two-inch thick oak wall. Over a hundred balls had struck the wall in the last five seconds and it was beginning to weaken. He waited until the impact occurred and then counted to three. By then, the shooting had stopped and he made a run for the side. One of the seasoned marksmen on the deck of the *Magdalena* had saved his musket for something human to shoot at and he reasoned that someone would eventually have to emerge from behind the wall that protected the helm. His patience was rewarded with a glimpse of Pulverin running for the side. He aimed and fired. The ball struck Pulverin as he jumped over the rail of the fire ship. The impact in the fleshy part of his right shoulder, just to the right of his neck, caused him to lurch forward and he ended up with his back slapping the water below.

Dan could see that Ward was in trouble, holding his wrist in agony. Dan left his trolley and ran the four paces over to him, bent-over under the protection of the starboard rail. "Use your good hand to hold the trolley," said Dan, pulling Ward's belaying pin, still with a huge grin on his face. Ward shot forward as Dan raced back to his trolley, crouched low behind the rail of the ship. Dan was thrown off balance as the aft portion of the fire ship lunged toward the *Magdalena* and crashed into her. He heard the harpoons snap off and the chains tighten on the bow of the fire ship. The Spaniards above him were swinging pikes, trying desperately to dislodge the grappling hook from their ship. Dan regained his momentum and took another step toward his trolley, bent-over behind the rail, running like a fiddler crab, with his arms extended forward for balance. The body of the unconscious Spaniard that had been laying across his track, shot upwards on the grappling hook that had missed the *Magdalena*, toward the pulley on the yardarm above. "Wow," said Dan, jumping on his trolley, laughing as he pulled his belaying pin. Three more Spaniards jumped on the aft deck and began sliding uncontrollably when they hit the grease. As the trolley flew forward, Dan waved at the Spaniards lying

CHAPTER 39

When Morgan climbed over the rail and stepped on board the *Marquesa*, he could see that the Spanish crew had gathered on the aft deck to make a last stand. The hundred, or so men had discharged all of their muskets and pistols and were putting up a brave fight with pikes and cutlasses. The deck was covered with blood and lifeless bodies. One Spaniard had a torch in his hand and attempted to catch the hemp rigging on fire, but a dagger caught him in the neck and the torch fell harmlessly onto the deck. There was a bright light in the sky and the battle stopped briefly as the men paused to watch the deck of the *Magdalena* explode skyward. Seconds later, the shock wave from the explosion came as a deafening boom. The birds on shore, already nervous because of the small arms fire, took to the sky by the thousands. Balfor's men began pouring onto the foredeck of the *Marquesa* and the Spaniards knew their cause was hopeless. One by one they began jumping over the aft rail into the water. The Buccaneers began to cheer, but they did not pursue them.

Kessenger's sloop sailed by the silent cannons on the port side of the *Marquesa*. Twenty-five Buccaneers had weapons raised and ready to fire. The scene that greeted Kessenger's men at the stern of the ship was horrifying. The men lowered their weapons. The water was littered with bodies floating at the surface. It looked as though twenty, or thirty had already drowned and most of the living were struggling to stay at the surface. It was obvious that few of them could swim.

The Buccaneers dropped their sail and threw out a hook. They offered help to the drowning men, but the Spaniards stubbornly refused any assistance. One Buccaneer threw out an oar. A young Spaniard grabbed for the oar and tried to get on top of it. His face went into the water and he panicked and took a breath of water. A few seconds later he was motionless in the water. The Buccaneers fished him out and draped his belly over the rail of the sloop. He came to a few seconds later and began coughing. Another exhausted man grabbed the oar and leaned his head back, trying to catch his breath. The Buccaneers began throwing out anything that would float. Stoppered barrels with lines attached began flying into the water from the aft deck of the *Marquesa*. Morgan wondered if the Dons would include this detail in their history books. He was proud of his men.

The smoke had cleared from the smoldering carcass of the *Magdalena* and the men watched as she went bow-first into the water. Morgan trained his telescope on the third ship, which had been nearest the castle. Apparently, her Spanish crew had run her aground in the shallows. The two Buccaneer sloops were almost on her when she went up in flames. The Spaniards made their way to shore and watched her burn. The Buccaneers backed off, anticipating the explosion of her magazine. Just as the birds were returning to their roosts in the trees, they all took flight again when the ship exploded. Morgan gently collapsed his telescope and went below to see his new cabin. In his mind he began composing a letter to Don Alonso.

Morgan stepped over the threshold and entered the cabin, not needing to duck his head. Despite the fact that the *Marquesa* was twenty feet shorter than the *Oxford*, her aft cabin was half again as large the *Oxford*'s. The overhead beams were carved and gilded with gold leaf. The furniture was full-sized and looked like it had come from a Spanish mansion. There was a gun rack with a glass door that had four muskets inlaid with ivory and mother of pearl. Morgan opened the door to the head and was surprised to find a small marble bathtub, along with a sturdy brass stand with a wooden seat on top and a chamber pot below. He smiled.

"I guess this will do for now," he said. He walked over to the desk and lifted up the hinged center portion. There were several letters inside that he studied briefly. He let the top down and began going through the drawers. In the top left drawer he found a leather pouch with lead weights in it and small holes. His pulse quickened as he pulled out several pieces of parchment, obviously in code. Why hadn't the fools thrown this overboard?

"I like your new boat, Harry," said Sara, stepping into the cabin. "My goodness, a weighted pouch? They must have left in a hurry. I wonder where they are getting their training these days?"

"Come here and look at this. This drawer is only about two thirds the length of the top above. Why *is* that?" He opened the next drawer and it was the same length and the next.

"Maybe they were running low on materials," said Sara, on her knees, searching for an access panel. "Got it," she said. The desk was fairly standard. It had two stacks of drawers with space in between them to put your legs. The left tower had raised oak paneling like the rest of the desk, but the innermost panel, right about where your feet would go, had a release at the top and when pulled, it would allow the panel to swing outward on a hinge. Sara began handing Morgan leather-bound portfolios, five in all, followed by four gold ingots, each weighing about twelve pounds. Morgan whistled. "That's it for this side," said Sara backing up on her hand and knees. She sat up on her knees and Morgan smiled down at her.

"My favorite position," he said, and she began to unbutton the front of his pants. There was a loud knock on the door. Morgan stashed the portfolios and the bullion in the top left drawer. "Coming," he shouted, buttoning his pants as he walked to the door. It was Velasquez with a male prisoner who had been pulled out of the water near the *Marquesa*.

"Come in gentlemen. Mi cabana, su cabana." The two men stepped in the cabin.

"I think you will like what he have to say, Capitan. His name is Carlos Medina and he is pilot in this sheep."

"Señor Medina, mucho gusto. Soy el Capitan Morgan." Morgan took an instant liking to Medina, who eagerly shook his hand. Medina stood a few inches short of six feet and was dressed in an Officer's uniform. His eye contact with Morgan displayed confidence, but was not angry, or confrontational.

"El gusto es mio," he said, humbly. Morgan motioned for them to sit down on the chairs in front of the desk. Sara poured the men some brandy in fine snifters and one for herself.

"Decir la verdad," said Morgan, glancing over at Sara to make sure he hadn't screwed it up. She smiled almost imperceptibly. "Speak the truth," Morgan had said.

"Noble Sir, I will tell you the truth as completely as I can, if only you will spare my life, that no evil will come to me." Morgan looked over and shook his head at Sara.

"Better come over here. I am missing way too much." Sara pulled her chair across the cabin and went back for her brandy.

"He basically said he will tell you the complete truth if you will spare his life."

"Consider it done," said Morgan. Sara did the translation and Medina smiled. "Here is what I want to know. Are there any more ships in their party coming this way? How many men were on each ship. What were their orders when they left Spain? What was the most recent port of call?" Sara began the questioning.

"He says that six ships were ordered by the Supreme Council of State in Spain, to cruise the waters of the Spanish holdings in the New World and root out the English pirates there. He says the Catholic King and the Court have sent Ambassadors to the English King many times to complain and his response is always the same; that he never issued any letters of Marque, nor Commissions against the King of Spain, nor any of His holdings." Sara motioned for Medina to stop speaking. "As we go along here," she whispered into Morgan's ear, "I will try to trip him up and see if I can catch him in a lie."

"Continuar, por favor," said Sara. Medina took a big swallow of his brandy and began speaking again.

"He says that the two largest ships were ordered back to Spain, because of their deep drafts. That was the *Nuestra de la Solidad*, with forty-eight great guns and the *La Conception*, with forty-four great guns and eight smaller ones. That is the one that Alonso was on. Don Augusto de Bustos was in charge of the operation, but he sailed back with the two big boats, leaving Alonso in charge of the Caribbean fleet of four ships. They went to Campeche first, but a severe gale came up and they lost one of their ships. It was the *Nuestra Señora del Carmen*, with eighteen guns and two-hundred-fifty men. He says that Alonso recovered the guns and placed them in the castle with two more from his own boat."

"Hold it, right there. Captain Velasquez, how many cannon did you see in the fort?"

"I counted nine."

"Sara, ask Senior Medina to explain the discrepancy." Sara began her rapid-fire Spanish in an angry tone, hoping to catch Medina off guard. Medina fired right back at her, with righteous indignation.

"All right, what he says makes sense. Apparently two of the cannons were in some sort of a depression and they couldn't get to them. So that left sixteen guns. Alonso added two from his own boat and that totals eighteen. Nine were placed in the front of the castle and the other nine were placed in the rear. There is no way he could have made that story up in the time he had available," said Sara.

"Ask him *why* Alonso put nine guns in the back of the fort," said Morgan. Sara spoke rapidly again, but the anger was out of her voice this time. He replied again without hesitation.

"He says that Alonso is convinced that you are going to attack from the rear," she said, pinching Morgan's backside, the desk preventing the others from seeing. "He has had all of the grape and chain transferred from his boats to the rear of the castle. The bulk of the powder is on that side, as well. They have had two days of artillery practice with the grape and chain being fired at palm logs, but they have not fired a single shot from the guns facing the water."

"My day just got better," said Morgan.

Medina began speaking again, this time with a grin on his face. Sara began slapping her thigh.

"He says that two days ago, a Negro appeared on board Alonso's ship and requested a conference with Alonso. The man said that he had been your prisoner and that he had escaped. He warned Alonso that you were building a fire ship. Alonso laughed at him and rebuked him. Alonso said, 'They do not have enough wit to build a fire ship,' then had the Negro escorted from his ship."

"Amazing! I would say that you predicted his behavior perfectly, Sara. What a complete ass!" Medina began speaking again, this time he was very serious and used sweeping hand gestures.

"Very nice! He says the ship that went aground had forty-thousand pieces of eight on board!" The cabin became silent. Morgan downed the last of his brandy.

"Captain Velasquez, could you assemble a team and begin salvaging the wreck today?"

"It would be an honor, Capitan," said Velasquez, smiling.

"Sara, ask Mr. Medina what he would like to do—join us, or go back with the Dons," said Morgan. Sara began a dialog with Medina that lasted several minutes.

"He says that he would like to join the Buccaneers, but he is concerned about his rank. He would like to remain an officer," said Sara.

"Pushy little bugger," said Morgan, smiling. "Offer him a lieutenant's rank and an officer's share of the booty." Sara began speaking like an excited schoolgirl and Medina's face came alive. In the space of five minutes, Medina had gone from prisoner status to that of a wealthy Jamaican gentleman.

"Mil gracias, Capitan," said Medina leaping out of his chair to shake Morgan's hand and seal the deal.

"One last thing," said Morgan. "Does Medina have any idea how much more we can squeeze the Dons? Say, to release the prisoners and not burn the city?" Sara began speaking rapidly, while Medina nodded his head.

"He says Maracaibo's treasury is in the castle and it amounts to about twenty-thousand pieces of eight. He thinks Alonso will jump at the offer, just to be rid of you."

"Ask him about cattle. Do the Dons have a herd hidden somewhere?"

"He says there is a ranch in the foothills with about a thousand head of cattle," said Sara.

"That will be all for now. Please tell Lieutenant Medina that he is assigned to Captain Velasquez's ship and he will not be accompanying us back to Maracaibo. Captain Velasquez, on your way out, could you ask Commander Collier to come to my cabin?"

"Certainly, Capitan." As the cabin cleared out, Morgan began rummaging through the desk, looking for a quill pen and some paper.

"Sara, we need to write Alonso a letter and get it over to him in the next hour. It would speed things up if you could do the writing."

"Happy to oblige Sailor Boy, but why are you in such a rush? Can we play first?"

"It's the tide Sara. It is coming in now and if we leave soon, it will shorten the trip back by several hours." Morgan stood up and began pacing. Sara located a fresh sheet of parchment and dipped the quill into the ink well.

"Fire away, Sailor Boy."

"To Don Alonso, Admiral of the Spanish fleet. Today you have seen what we are capable of doing. We have both lost many men and further losses of men and property can be easily avoided. For the safe return of all of your people, not including slaves, and a guarantee that the city of Maracaibo will not be burned, I am demanding thirty-thousand pieces of eight and five-hundred head of cattle as ransom. The ransom must be delivered tomorrow morning in Maracaibo. Please acknowledge your acceptance of these terms within the next hour. Lying at anchor aboard the lovely *Marquesa*, this first day of May, 1669." Morgan poured himself another brandy and smiled. "What do you think?"

"I think he will capitulate. Nice touch, with the *thirty-thousand* pieces of eight. He gets to save face—as if he had any left to save. Go ahead and sign it," she said handing him the quill. "It amazes me! This poor bastard has demonstrated gross incompetence, but because of his money and connections in Madrid, he will be received as a hero when he returns."

"I have no doubt." There was a knock on the cabin door. "Come!" shouted Morgan. Collier walked into the cabin and removed his tri-corner hat, bowing at Sara.

"Nice cabin," said Collier, studying the woodwork.

"I just might keep her," said Morgan, dripping red wax on the letter, "if she sails as good as she looks. Commander, would you mind having one of the prisoners deliver this to Alonso? Maybe run him over to the castle in one of the sloops? And have them wait for a reply. Then come back here; I want to know the numbers."

"Give me a few minutes," said Collier, putting his hat back on.

"By the way, have the prisoner tell Alonso that if he wants to send a party out to recover the bodies of his men, I guarantee them safe passage."

"I will pass it along, Captain," said Collier, leaving the cabin.

CHAPTER 40

"You want me to *what*, Sir?" said Jones. "Put your thumb over the hole the next time he coughs. Do it when you hear the air coming out. And then just hold it closed," said Browne, on the deck of Morgan's former two-masted flagship, *Enchantress*.

"I don't think I can bring myself to do it, Sir. What if my finger gets stuck in there?"

"Quit clowning around, will you! There he goes! Cover the hole!" Pulverin coughed and air gushed out of the hole in his back. Jones placed his thumb over the hole and sealed it shut. Pulverin was barely conscious and his skin was blue.

"This is the most revoltin' experience of me life!" said Jones.

"Sorry, Mr. Jones, I would like to help you, but I am a trifle busy right now," said Browne, putting another stitch in the stump where an arm had once been. "One of you men there! Cut me a piece of stiff leather, about a two inch square." One of the men grabbed the end of his belt and cut off the end of it. He held it up to Browne. "Perfect! Now take a sharp knife and cut three small holes along one edge," said Browne, tying another stitch. "How is his color, Jones?"

"He's pinkin' up a bit, Sir."

"Good. Keep the tourniquet on for another twenty minutes, or so and then release it slowly," he said to one of the mates. Browne walked over to Jones and studied the wound in Pulverin's shoulder. "Is there an exit wound on the front side?"

"There is, Sir."

"Above the clavicle, I presume."

"I wouldn't know about that, Sir."

"It would have to be above it, otherwise he would be dead," said Browne.

"Of course he would be, Sir. 'Ow long do you reckon I'll need to keep me thumb 'ere?"

"A few more minutes, Jones. Just let me get this patch sewn on. Could one of you men find me a finger's worth of grease?" One of the mates dashed below and returned with the grease. Browne used the string left over from the arm to sew the leather patch on the edge of Pulverin's wound through the three holes the Buccaneer had cut. "I need the grease now," said Browne, holding up his finger. The mate ran his greased-up finger over Browne's finger, depositing most of the grease. Browne applied the grease to the margin of the hole around Jones' thumb. "When I say three, slide your thumb away from the patch. One, two, three!" Jones jerked his thumb away and Browne slapped the leather patch down over the hole. There was a momentary rush of air into the hole and then the leather valve closed. "On to bigger and better things. What do we have left? Was it two legs?"

"Yes, Sir, two legs and a nose. But aren't you goin' to sew the rest of the patch on?" Browne took a big draw on his pipe and passed it over to Jones.

"No! You see it acts as a flap valve. When he coughs, or sneezes, air will leak out the hole and then the flap snaps shut and doesn't let any air back in," said Browne, proudly.

"Amazin', Sir. So we are trying to drain air out of his lung?"

Browne realized that he had forgotten to inspect the exit wound and he hoisted Pulverin's right shoulder off the table.

Pulverin was not happy about the contortion, but he was too weak to do much about it, other than moan.

"Bugger me!" said Browne as he inspected the wound. "Let's roll him on his back. We are not trying to drain air from his lung, we are trying to drain air from his chest cavity. If we can do that, the lung will re-inflate."

"I get it now, Sir, but isn't there an 'ole in his lung?"

"Do you see this purple streak, Jones? It heads out to his deltoid. I can feel the ball under his skin here on the outside of his shoulder. The ball actually tracked under his skin and that is what caused the purple streak. There is no exit wound, it's just a big bruise where the ball struck his collar bone and bounced off. I can't believe he survived this. Was he wearing a shirt?"

"Not when the men pulled him out, Sir."

"Good. Lets get the ball out."

"What about the 'ole, Sir."

"I am going to sew this one up."

"I mean the hole in his lung, Sir."

"I don't think you can sew lungs, at least I never have. Lungs seal up on their own, somehow. We will need some help holding his arms. I wonder if his clavicle is broken?" Browne pushed on it and it moved as one piece. "I am going to sharpen my knife and get some more thread. Is there anything to eat on this boat?"

"I made up a batch of mule balls, Sir," said Jones, laughing.

"I don't think I could fit a mule's ball in my mouth!"

"You just haven't met the right mule, Sir."

CHAPTER 41

Commander Collier returned to Morgan's cabin to give his report along with Lieutenant Owen, who had just returned from the ship that had been grounded and burned.

"Come in, Gentlemen," said Morgan, opening the door. "Make yourselves comfortable. Would either of you care for a bit of brandy? Help yourselves, it's all on the table." Both men poured two fingers in their glasses and sat down at the table. Morgan sat behind his desk.

"Commander, would you care to go first?"

"Of course, Captain. Twenty-one men dead, eighteen wounded, five seriously, two legs and one arm. None of our officers were killed, but Pulverin was shot in the back and has a collapsed lung. Browne expects him to live, but he may have damaged the nerves to his right arm. At last count, the Dons had lost over two-hundred-twenty, mostly due to drowning."

"Provisions?"

"We are better off than we were two hours ago, but with seven-hundred-twenty mouths to feed, I would guess not more than two days worth of food. We are filled to capacity with shot and powder. The water is marginal. There are eight barrels of Barbados rum below, along with sixteen barrels of Burgundy and three small casks of brandy. There are eight fresh el dorado in the galley, along with a huge swordfish. We should be eating well right before we starve to death."

"All of that may change in the next hour," said Morgan. "I have made Alonso an offer he can't refuse and it would give us five-hundred head of cattle."

"That would help out immensely."

"Lieutenant?"

"The ship they ran aground was carrying over twenty-thousand pieces of eight, possibly as much as fifty thousand. Most of it was melted by the fire they set, but some of it is still in coins. The ship went aground on an oyster bar and that is going to hamper the recovery. The coins will be easy, but if you assume that, say twenty-thousand pieces of eight have melted together, that amounts to over twelve-hundred pounds of silver in one block, possibly more."

"We can have Moss evaluate the situation. Velasquez is going to keep his boat behind and his men will be doing the salvage work. I would like to keep the pressure on Alonso, so let's have Moss make up some bombs and Velasquez can release them from his boat."

"I will arrange it," said Collier. "Maybe Alonso will finally figure out that we are using the bombs to interfere with his sleep." The men laughed.

"Don't count on it, Commander," said Sara.

"What happened to the rest of the fire ship's crew?" asked Morgan.

"They all came out alive. When the ship went up, Dan was on his trolley, just about to go over the side. The concussion knocked him out, but Ward kept him afloat until he came to. He also has some flash burns on his back and head. He is currently in the water, which he says takes the pain away. By the way, Ward was struck by a ricocheted ball that broke the big bone in his wrist."

"Do we have enough food for the Swimmers and Mr. Moss to join us for dinner?" asked Morgan.

"We have enough food for the group *and* their ladies!"

"Fine, let's make a night of it, shall we? By the way, I want Dan and Ward transferred to the *Marquesa*." There was a loud knock on the cabin door. "Come," shouted Morgan. It was Comstock, with a letter in his hand.

"This came for you Captain," said Comstock, passing the folded parchment over to Morgan. Comstock wanted to stay in the cabin to see what the letter was all about, but Morgan had other plans.

"Thank you, Lieutenant. Would you please have someone locate Captain Kessenger and have him report to me?"

"Straight away, Captain," said a frustrated Comstock, who left the cabin and closed the door loudly. Morgan glanced at the door and rolled his eyes. He tore the red wax seal and opened the folded parchment.

"Sara, would you care to do the honors and read the latest installment from the Spanish Admiral," said Morgan, handing the paper to her. "I think we can trust these two," he said pointing at the table.

"I would be delighted." She scanned the document once and then passed it back to Morgan. Her eyes went up and to the right. "This document is in Alonso's hand. It consists of one-hundred-nineteen words, five of which are misspelled. He also got the date wrong. If you look at the forth line, you will see a watermark on the left side of the page. If you continue to look, you will see three other similar marks. I believe he was crying when he wrote this. In the introduction, he refers to himself as the 'Admiral of the Garrison.' But if you look carefully at the 'G' in Garrison, or Guarnicion in Spanish, you can easily see that it started off as an 'F.' The 'F' was for 'Flota', or fleet. I think it had just dawned on him that he no longer had any boats to be Admiral *of*." Collier and Owen sat there with their mouths hanging open.

"Harry, where did you find this woman? Does she have any sisters?" said Collier.

"That is my line and you have to stop using it, or I will deduct it from your pay. To answer your question, *she* found *me*. She has seven sisters who are all more beautiful than she is and she refuses to discuss them." She swatted him with the letter.

"You will pay for that," she said, smiling.

"Quick! Somebody hide the cat," said Morgan, referring to the famous whip.

"Shall we finish the letter?" said Sara.

"By all means."

"I will write you out a complete translation later. But basically, he thinks you are the Devil and he knows he cannot defeat you. He agrees with your demands, but guess what? He can only come up with twenty-thousand reales. He would like for you to send word to him if you accept his offer."

"Let's write it now," said Morgan. Kessenger knocked softly on the door and poked his head into the cabin.

"Come in Captain. Join the party! Pour yourself a glass of brandy. I want you to take over my ketch. See if you can round up Jones and get him and the other cooks back to the City before the rest of us. I want you to try and bag a couple of those sheep we saw on the way here. Tell Jones he is cooking for about sixty people."

"Thank you, Captain," said Kessenger.

"Don't thank me, you've earned it," said Morgan. "Let's get the letter finished. You Gentlemen are excused." Morgan began pacing as the room cleared out. "We need to keep this very simple."

"How about 'I accept your offer'?"

"Write it out and let me sign it." In the space of two minutes the letter was finished and sealed. It would be in Alonso's hand within the hour. "I am going for a swim. Would you care to join me?"

"Thank you for the offer, but I would like to devote some time to the pouch you found, with your permission, of course. I promise to share."

"Let me know what you find," said Morgan, closing the cabin door

CHAPTER 42

The Buccaneers were throwing the last of the dead Spaniards off the deck of the *Marquesa* into the water. The tide was carrying the bodies in towards the lake, where Alonso's men retrieved them and stacked them in the two small launches they had. The launches were dangerously overloaded and there were sixty bodies remaining in the water that they would have to come back for.

Collier had ordered a sloop along side the *Marquesa*, where it was side-tied. The boat was loaded with the bodies of the Buccaneers that had fallen during the battle. Collier realized that the bodies could not be buried at sea, because the fort stood between them and the ocean, so he decided to transport them back to Maracaibo and have them buried there.

Several Spanish captives were on their hands and knees, holly-stoning the blood stains off the deck when Morgan walked by in his knee-length pants, his long hair pulled back in a pony tail. He looked up at the top of the foremast and decided to climb it. He walked over to the starboard rail and grabbed the ratlines. He jumped and swung his body on top of the net-like ratlines and began to climb upward, rapidly at first, but after fifty feet, he had to slow down. He managed to climb the full eighty feet without stopping, but he was winded when he got there. "I need to start doing this every day," he said to himself, embarrassed by his poor conditioning. He heard two muskets fire in the distance. About four-hundred yards up the channel, he spotted his former ketch anchored, lowering a boat over the side. Morgan spotted two white objects along the banks of the narrows, which he took to be dead sheep.

Morgan turned his attention to the deck of the *Marquesa*. The ship had three masts and was approximately one-hundred-twenty feet in length. She was narrow-waisted with a beam of twenty-five feet. He needed to get in the water and see how deep her draft was, but first he studied the guns. The gunports were still open with the guns run out. Below decks, there were eight "great guns" on each side capable of firing twenty-four pound balls. Ahead of the great guns were four smaller-bore brass cannon that were angled slightly forward. It was a well thought-out design and he was pleased. He toyed with the idea of climbing out on a yardarm and diving into the water, but too many voices were screaming at him inside his head, so he yielded and climbed back down the ratlines.

Standing on the rail, Morgan noticed Dan at the front of the *Marquesa*, hanging on to the anchor line, still on his back with his eyes closed. Morgan dove into the water and swam forward against the current. He was just about to call out to Dan, so that he wouldn't startle him when he grabbed the anchor line. But, with his eyes closed and his ears below the water, Dan said, "Hello, Captain." Morgan was surprised.

"Hello, Dan, how is your back? I heard you got spanked by the fire ship." Dan raised his head out of the water.

"It is fine as long as I stay in the water," said Dan smiling. "I have been going through all of my near-death memories and I don't think I have ever come this close before. It has been a most enjoyable day," he said, beaming.

"If you had said that to me yesterday, I would not have understood what you meant. But today, right in the middle of the fracas, I actually laughed!" said Morgan, smiling back at Dan.

"Was it the 'heaven and hell' paradigm?" asked Dan.

"It was! How did you ever come up with that?"

"I didn't! It was given to me by an Indian Prince, who was sent to Cambridge to study the sciences. We became fast friends. I tutored him in the fluxions, which is a strange type of mathematics and he tutored me in Indian philosophy. I got the better end of the deal." Dan dipped the back of his head in the cool water to ease the pain. "When did it come up?"

"It has come up probably twenty times. But the first time I noticed it was when Balfor's boat came screaming in to tie up to the *Marquesa*. He slammed into Collier's boat so hard, that he knocked me to the deck. As I got up to my feet, I could feel a powerful emotion about to explode and that is when the 'heaven and hell' ditty flashed in my brain and I started to laugh. Every time that you are in a situation where there is emotion involved, you have a choice about how you are going to respond. It sounds simplistic, but until today I had never realized how important that could be. There *is* a choice! How did I live thirty-three years and never learn that?"

"You are not alone. I met Kamalesh when I was separating from my first wife. I kept getting drawn into these emotional scenes from which there was no escape, or resolution. To be honest, I was suicidal. She was thriving and I was dying. Kamalesh gave me the 'heaven and hell gift' at about that time and all of the hate and fear just went away and the laughter began," said Dan. "She never got the upper hand again. She ended up in Bedlam."

"I could argue that you are *still* suicidal."

"True, but there is a big difference between pushing until you find the edge, then wisely stepping back—as opposed to putting a ball in your brain," said Dan, laughing. "Besides that, my high-risk escapades are pale in comparison to your own."

"What do you mean by that?"

"Oh let's see, storming a garrison with three men? Running toward a slow match, instead of away from it like any rational being would have done. Am I getting warm?" said Dan, laughing with even greater intensity. Morgan began to chuckle.

"You have a point," said Morgan, belly-laughing with Dan, in the water, hanging on to the anchor line of the *Marquesa*, which had been taken as a prize from the Spanish less than an hour ago.

CHAPTER 43

Commander Collier was preparing *himself* to get the *Marquesa* under way. Once again, he was on a fairly large ship with a deep draft, more friendly than the *Oxford* to be sure, but he *was* in a narrow channel that was scarcely wider than three *Marquesa*'s end on end. The *Marquesa* was frozen in position by the in-coming tide, which was moving through the channel at about ten knots. Unfortunately, she was pointed in the wrong direction. He would have to turn her one-hundred-eighty degrees and not strike either shoreline in the process. He knew that when Morgan came out of the water he would tell Collier the exact draft of the *Marquesa*, which was at least some consolation. Dropping the stern hook and releasing the fore anchor seemed like a good alternative, but if the stern anchor didn't grab hold, it could turn into a disaster. The sea anchor really was the only choice. To hasten the process of turning the bow, he would also raise the jib sails and use the force of the wind.

The *Marquesa* was currently headed due north. The current was pushing due south. The trade wind was out of the east, pushing due west at about fourteen knots, about four knots faster than the tide. Think about the forces on the boat! his brain screamed. The danger here is running aground on the western side of the channel, he thought.

"Mr. Jenkins, a word please," said Collier, catching the attention of the tall and energetic first mate. "Lieutenant! Could you join us?" shouted Collier to Owen, who was inspecting the rigging on the fore mast. Owen was trying to stay busy, so that he could avoid the images that were flashing through his brain. In the vision, his two hands were trying desperately to hold the pistol straight and then he squeezed the trigger. The kick jolted his upper body. An instant later, the man that he had been aiming at was thrown backwards, his feet off the ground, with a look of disbelief on his face, clutching the hole in his chest and then realizing that he was going to die. Tears welled up in Owen's eyes. He pretended to sneeze and hoped that no one would notice his watery eyes.

"Mr. Jenkins, I want you at the helm during this maneuver. Your job is quite simple. Just keep the helm hard alee until she has steerage going with the current. Do your best to keep her a bit upwind of the middle of the channel. Once she has turned around completely, you will need to center the helm, then steer into the wind a bit while we haul in the sea anchor and set the sails. You can see it here on this diagram." Owen stood by the other two men and having figured out this maneuver weeks before, he let the images of the Spaniard with the hole in his chest play in his mind, while Collier and Jenkins talked. "Is everything all right, Lieutenant?" asked Collier, sensing the boy's withdrawal.

"Perfectly, Commander," said Owen, temporarily pulling himself out of guilt prison. Collier sensed there was a problem, but there seemed little point in pressing the matter. Morgan pulled himself over the port rail on to the deck and walked over to Collier, leaving a trail of wet footprints behind him.

"Commander, are we ship-shape?" said Morgan.

"We are, Captain."

"Then get us back to the city. G' day, Lieutenant, Mr. Jenkins," said Morgan, walking back to his cabin.

"Captain!" called out Collier. "What does she draft?"

"Twelve feet, Commander," said Morgan coming to a halt outside of his cabin.

God, what a relief, thought Collier.

"We will need to discharge the cannons after we pass the wreck," said Morgan "You may choose the time, but give me a little warning, because I am down to my last pair of pants." All of the crewmembers within ear shot began to laugh.

"Aye, Captain," said Collier, with a grin on his face.

Owen found the Quartermaster and issued orders. Soon the ship was alive with activity. Jenkins swung the helm to leeward and the aft end of the *Marquesa* lunged toward the Eastern shore.

"Let go the sea anchor," shouted the Quartermaster. "Haul in the anchor!" The men on the fore deck began walking in circles, pushing their capstan poles. Slowly the ship inched Northward, into the current. "Ready the Jib!" When the anchor finally let go, the *Marquesa* lurched backward in the current. "Raise the jib!" The bow of the *Marquesa* began to swing around. "Ready the fore topmast staysail!"

Collier watched in silence as the bow came around. Passed the halfway mark, the ship began moving toward the Western shore at a fairly rapid pace. Come on, come on! Collier was thinking, but he held his body perfectly still, imperceptibly tightening his grip on the port rail, the very picture of calm. Beads of sweat formed on Collier's forehead and there was no way to hide that.

"Fly the fore topmast staysul," shouted the Quartermaster, as the bow began the last portion of her turn. The trade wind filled the sail and the *Marquesa* inched closer to the Western shore. Collier could see rocks at the bottom of the narrows and he gripped the rail a little tighter. Finally, the rudder grabbed hold and the bow shot through the remainder of the turn and the *Marquesa* began moving away from the shore, into the center of the channel.

"Nicely done, Mr. Jenkins," said Collier, walking over to the helm. About a hundred yards ahead, Collier could see the men on Velasquez's lugger pulling up her anchor. As previously arranged, Velasquez would guide the *Marquesa* safely through the shallows with the assistance of Medina, the Spanish pilot.

CHAPTER 44

"Harry, come over here and look at this," said Sara, as Morgan stepped over the threshold into the cabin. "The Dons are using a double cipher system. I've never even heard of this before," said Sara, excited.

"That makes two of us," said Morgan, pouring a generous glass of brandy. "Care for some?"

"Two fingers please," she said, without looking up.

"Can't you wait until we get back to the mansion?"

"What?" she said absently, lost in her codes.

"Not important," he said, pouring her a glass of brandy, two fingers deep.

"Do you remember the two code books that I found in the mansion? Have a seat will you?" she said, never taking her eyes off the papers in front of her.

"The ones you made me copies of?"

"Huh? Yes, those are the ones. Look at the top of the first page of this letter. Can you make out the letters, 'OE'?"

Morgan pulled up a chair and looked at the document. "Yes I can see that," he said, not the least bit impressed.

"Well, the two code books were named 'Mayo and Diciembre.' None of the letters of one are found in the other. Are you with me?" she asked.

"I follow you, so far," he said.

"Here is what the letters mean. In a double cipher system, you need two codes and *an order* in which to use them. So, 'O' first means to use the 'Mayo' book first, because 'O' is found only in Mayo. The work then needs to be run through the 'E' cipher, because 'E' is found in 'Diciembre' and not 'Mayo'. Have you fallen asleep yet?" she said.

"Give me an idea of where you are going with this and I promise not to snore," said Morgan, trying to pull off his wet pants.

"Here is what we have. This piece of correspondence is not an arm of the government, talking to another arm. It is an autonomous group that is stealing from the Dons! Last year, if you can believe this, they walked away with over thirteen-hundred ounces of gold! That is more than a hundred pounds!"

"I am wide awake, now. Can we invite them over for dinner?" said Morgan, balancing on one leg, trying to extract his other leg from the wet pants. Just then, the anchor gave way and the *Marquesa* shot backwards, knocking Morgan to the floor, laughing.

"What *was* that?"

"They just hauled in the anchor. You may want to hang on to something for the next few minutes," said Morgan, finally extricating himself from his pants.

"All right, back to the document. If I am reading this correctly, this group has paid off the assayers at each step of the journey, until finally, the galleons reach Spain and then the losses are uncovered. Suspicion has been directed mainly at the last port of call in the New World and at Cadiz, the entry port in Spain. That was, until two of the assayers in the New World went missing with their families and that has caught the attention of the King of Spain, who is out for blood. Are we spinning?" she said, looking out the stern window. "We *are* spinning! *Why* are we spinning?"

"This is a Spanish ship. All Spanish ships spin like this. That is why they keep losing wars." Still half-way lost in her documents, Sara believed Morgan's story.

"Why don't they do something about it?" she said and then Morgan cracked a smile. Then it dawned on her that he was joking and she threw a blotter at him, which he managed to catch in mid air. "I will get you for this, Sailor Boy."

"I have no doubt," said Morgan, slipping on a pair of dry pants.

"Seriously, why was the ship spinning?"

"We had to turn her one-hundred-eighty degrees to go back to the City. Finish telling me about your papers," said Morgan, pulling a shirt over his head. Sara picked up the parchment and felt herself drawn back into a world of deceit and treachery.

"This is big, Harry. This is far more than a governor and a captain could ever pull off by themselves. What do you do with a hundred pounds of gold? How do you pay people off that are a thousand miles away? How would you recruit them in the first place? There would have to be a huge organization behind them. I wonder if Charlie knows about this?"

"Maybe he is behind it."

"I seriously doubt it. There are undoubtedly things he never told me, but this is not one of them. Whoever wrote this document is a confidant of the King himself and I can assure you, Charlie's connections are simply not that good. This paragraph," she said, pointing to a thick section of text, "is a set of instructions aimed at the mines themselves *and* the mints. Next season, they plan to remove several thousand ounces of gold *before* it is ever entered into the books. Apparently they already have their people in place at the smelters and this ship was carrying additional men to complete the 'teams'. All of the operations of the mines and the mint will now be in control of this secret group, which can generate a staggering amount of gold and silver that is untraceable. It is a brilliant scheme, but I still cannot imagine who has the power to actually make this work. Who could write the orders to sack all of the key people at the mines *and* mints, and then replace them with his *own* people?" she said, thinking out loud.

"How about Carlos?" said Morgan.

"Why would the King of Spain steal from himself? Besides, he is only eight years old and rumored to be an idiot."

"What percentage of the yearly take goes to the Vatican?"

"I honestly do not know, but there has been conjecture that it amounts to twenty-five percent," said Sara. Morgan remained silent while she worked on the problem. "All right, I can see where you are headed with this. If Carlos, or his mother could keep their operation secret and skim, say ten-thousand ounces, off the production side of things, then they could keep an additional twenty-five-hundred ounces for themselves, minus payoffs. They certainly have the power to pull it off." Sara became lost in thought. She looked excited, put her hand up to her mouth and then went rummaging through a stack of papers on top of the desk. She found the paper she was looking for and then began tapping it with her index finger. "This is it! Domingo had—he was the Captain of this boat—two sets of orders. One was the usual set of Admiralty orders that instructed him to cruise off the coast and kill English pirates, excuse me, 'Buccaneers.' But the other set of orders was in code and they directed him to pick up shipments in Caracas and Cartagena and then deliver them directly to 'LRNZ' in Cadiz. But the thing is, I think I know who 'LRNZ' is!"

"Make it fast, because we are about to go through the shallows and I want to be on deck for that," said Morgan.

"Very briefly, 'LRNZ' stands for Lorenzo, who was a boyhood protector of Juan Jose de Austria, King Carlos' bastard half brother. When Don Juan needs something done, especially secretly, he calls upon Lorenzo, who just happens to be one of the most feared men in Spain. My guess is that Don Juan and Lorenzo are planning to raise an army to over-throw the Spanish Monarchy."

"Can the rest wait?" said Morgan walking toward the cabin door. Before Sara could reply, there was a violent lurch in the *Marquesa* that sent Morgan to his knees. "I seem to be spending more time lying than standing," said Morgan, who could see that Sara was very anxious. "Don't worry about that jarring, we just skated over a sandbar. I'll be right back," said Morgan, dashing out of the cabin before Sara could respond.

Morgan went on deck and stood next to Collier by the helm. Two-hundred Buccaneers lined the rails, watching for rocks in the shallow water. Morgan was uncomfortable with the slow speed of the *Marquesa*, but he resisted the impulse to order more sail hoisted. After a few nervous moments, it became clear that the *Marquesa's* helm was responding, so Morgan took a deep breath and decided to enjoy the experience, rather than fight it.

"We have a problem, Captain," whispered Collier.

"I am glad we are down to *one!*" said Morgan, laughing.

"Actually there are about fifty, but this one requires your attention," said Collier. "It seems that Lieutenant Owen has developed a strong attachment to his lady and would like to take her back to Port Royal. I assured him that I would discuss the matter with you," said Collier, with a snicker on his face.

"There is really nothing *to* discuss. If Alonso lives up to his end of the bargain, she is simply one of the prisoners that *must* be returned in exchange for the ransom. If he could set his sights on someone of lesser station, perhaps we could accommodate him, but the Governor's wife *must* be returned to the Dons. I suggest that you have him followed after you give him this news. He may try and steal a sloop and carry her away. That is certainly what I would do in similar circumstances."

The helmsman steered the *Marquesa* sharply to port, just as he had seen Velasquez do a few minutes before. In the center of the channel was a group of sandstone boulders that would have torn the *Marquesa* to pieces if she had hit them. When the

Marquesa slipped by unharmed, there was a collective sigh of relief as the ship was steered back to starboard, thus centering her in the channel, just inside the shallows. Collier expanded his telescope and, in the distance, he could see Velasquez holding two children in his arms, both of them waving back at the *Marquesa*. The ship was out of danger now and Morgan ordered a barrel of rum be brought up on deck so the Buccaneers could begin the celebration that they had so valiantly earned today.

CHAPTER 45

The Buccaneer fleet arrived back in Maracaibo with about two hours of sunlight left, thanks to the incoming tide. That gave the Turk some extra time to set up the beach for the daunting task that awaited the Buccaneers at sunrise. "Five-hundred beeves," muttered the Turk, shaking his head in disbelief. He angrily kicked the sand. He had been given five-hundred men and the prisoners to accomplish the task, but he knew that, even with the combined effort, they could only process one-hundred-fifty cattle a day. Included in that estimation was the necessity of perfect days without cloud-cover and absolutely no rain.

The Turk had been chosen for this assignment because he had spent five years on Hispanola perfecting the art of boucan. By the early part of the seventeenth century, Spanish colonial rule the population of the Eastern half of Hispanola decimated and so the cattle had taken over the island. The local Indians, who had somehow managed to survive in spite of the European presence, were able to provide boucan at such a reasonable price, that even the stingy English fleet commonly dumped their pickled-beef barrels over the side and stocked their holds with Caribbean boucan. Soon the demand greatly outstripped the supply and out-of-work English and French sailors flocked to the southeast coast of Hispanola to make their fortunes.

The beauty of working with boucan was that it did not require expensive salt for its curing process. The beef was thinly sliced and then dried on racks in the sun. Once the strips were rubbery, they were then placed on green branches that had been stripped and placed over red-hot coals. The intense heat from the coals liberated oils and steam from the branches, which penetrated the meat. The experienced Buccaneers always chose Mangrove, Gumbo Limbo, or Lignum Vitae branches, because they were naturally oily and non-toxic. The addition of sage in the smoking process added an irresistible flavor.

He paced in the sand, working numbers through his head. Five-hundred beeves, each yielding a hundred-fifty pounds of boucan. "Car-rist! That is seventy-five-thousand pounds of boucan!" he said out loud. The computations continued in his head. Let's assume that we have seven-hundred-fifty Buccaneers and slaves on board the ships…let's see, assuming the average person eats a pound per day…Car-rist! That is enough for over three months! It is only going to take three *days* to get back to Jamaica! He kicked the sand again in frustration. His youngest son's fifth birthday was coming up in seven days and he wanted desperately to be in Port Royal for the party. Once again, he kicked sand high into the air and tears began streaming down his cheeks as he visualized his son kicking sand the same way, a little over five months ago. The Turk told his son that, "Daddy has to go away for a while." He promised his son that he would be back in time for his birthday party and that had seemed to dry up the boy's tears. Now it looked as though he would never make it.

The Turk scanned the shoreline for bamboo that could be fashioned into drying racks. He saw a thick stand about a quarter mile away and walked over to investigate. The bamboo thicket stood on the edge of an immense rice field that had been recently harvested. There were a series of levees that divided the rice field into plots about one-hundred-fifty by fifty feet wide. He caught motion out of the corner of his eye and focused his attention on a porcelain drainpipe that penetrated one of the levee walls. Inside the pipe were hundreds of crayfish and for the first time that day, he smiled broadly. He walked into town and organized a party to cut and prepare the bamboo for tomorrow and then made his way to the Governor's mansion to find Sara and Jones.

Within the space of an hour, the dried-up rice field was teaming with officers carrying gunny sacks, half in the bag themselves, laughing like school kids on an outing. At the intersections of the levees, where there was still some standing water, there were crayfish by the thousands, battling each other for the deepest water.

There were, of course, the perfunctory jokes, most of which had some reference involving "tail," but for the most part, it was simply a group of friends doing something out of the ordinary during a brief armistice. Everyone was still in a state of shock that the Spanish fleet had actually been destroyed and few now doubted that Morgan would somehow get them passed the fort, more or less intact.

Sara filled her gunny sack first. She was bare footed and knee-deep in mud, having the time of her life. She had finally coaxed Morgan into the mud next to her and she laughed when he felt a crayfish scurry over his feet and instinctively reached for his pulpers. In the process, he let go of his bag and lost half his catch. Thanks to the ministrations of Jones and his "Panama Surprise," as it was now known, Sara and Morgan both got the giggles, knee deep in mud, in a rice field off the coast of Maracaibo, where the sun was setting, 1 May, 1669.

When the laughter subsided, Sara pulled Morgan close and whispered in his ear, "The spider web and the documents have disappeared."

"But why? Why would they risk that?" he asked.

"What they *couldn't risk,* was the possibility that the documents onboard the *Marquesa* could be de-coded. It would be a disaster for them. Now that the code books are safely back in their hands, they will assume that they will not be found out and they will be lulled into a sense of infallibility, once again. Charlie is going to love this!"

Now it was Morgan's turn to feel the remorse inherent in their up-coming separation. It was only a matter of days before they were both back in their own worlds. Tears briefly welled up in Morgan's eyes when the realization took hold, but then he ran the "heaven and hell" paradigm and the sadness faded.

The Turk arrived with a donkey cart as the sun touched the Western horizon. Sixteen hemp gunny sacks, filled to the brim with crayfish, were loaded on to the cart for the two-mile trip back to the Governor's mansion. Sara and Morgan joined the Turk on the rough bench seat. Clicking noises came from the gunny sacks as the crayfish jostled for position. The Turk pulled out his demijohn and passed it to Sara, who took a sip of rum and passed it over to Morgan.

"Harry, have you given any thought about the weight the boucan will add to the boats?" asked the Turk.

"To be honest, I have had one or two other things on my mind," said Morgan, smiling. "Tell me what you have come up with."

"If you assume that we can produce one-hundred-fifty pounds of boucan per cow, that works out to about seventy-five-thousand pounds, or the equivalent of over four-hundred-seventy men. Add to that the twenty-thousand Reales that Alonso is going to deliver us tomorrow, plus the thirty-thousand Reales from the wreck and you come up with a total of seventy-nine-thousand pounds." The Turk neglected to mention the fact that the weight of over one-hundred prisoners would be subtracted before the fleet left for Jamaica. "You may have noticed that the boats are riding low in the water *now*, and all of the ballast stones have been thrown overboard." Morgan took a slug from the demijohn and passed it back to the Turk, who downed the remainder. "To simplify the math, if you divide eighty-thousand by six, the number of ships we have, that works out to an additional thirteen-thousand pounds per ship. I honestly don't think we can manage that amount of cargo."

"What would you suggest we do?" asked Morgan, who suspected that the Turk might have ulterior motives for this line of reasoning.

"I think it might be wise to limit the number of beeves to two-hundred-fifty. We could accomplish that in two days and the extra freeboard will make the trip back much safer. By the way, that would give us provisions for about two months," said the Turk, stretching the truth.

"It is hard to argue with your reasoning and it would be nice to get back to Port Royal a few days early. Make it happen, your Turkishness," said Morgan, much to the relief of the Turk.

"The men will be pleased, Captain."

CHAPTER 46

"There is simply nothing I can do for you, except help ease the pain," said Browne. This infuriated Owen, who stood in the center of the kitchen with his pants down. There was a large collection of blood under the skin on the inner aspect of Owen's right thigh and, almost by the minute, it traveled downward toward the knee.

"Can the blood be sucked out?" asked Owen.

"I suppose it could be," said Browne, "but if putrefaction sets in, you are a dead man. So the answer is no."

"What about leeches, Sir?" said Jones, passing the clay pipe.

"That is not a bad idea, but leeches only work on thin skin," said Browne, holding a straw to the pipe and inhaling deeply. Owen was crestfallen. "I remember one time when I was on a cotton plantation in Virginia, there was going to be debutante ball for the planter's daughter, with over two-hundred guests. The planter's wife had a huge black eye two days before the celebration. There were a number of stories about how it came to be, but in any case the planter was horrified that everyone would think that he had beaten her. With his permission, we collected four leeches from a nearby river bank, with the intention of placing them on her face. She was absolutely horrified by the notion, so we sedated her with laudanum. I placed the four leeches on the crescent below her eye and within four hours the leeches had swollen up to the size of a finger and dropped off. Aside from four little red dots, there was no evidence that there had ever been an injury."

"A lot of good that does me," said Owen, sarcastically, pulling up his pants.

"You have gotten off lucky, Lieutenant. You have torn a muscle, but it was only a partial tear and you will be as good as new in six weeks." Owen clinched his fists. "The muscle you tore is the 'gracilis.' We call it the 'virgin's muscle,' because it pulls your legs together," said Browne, chuckling, with Jones joining in. "You may want to re-think your rum consumption before doing the splits on the side of a dock."

Owen fought to keep his rage in check. After all, he was going to need some opium to control the excruciating pain in his groin. "Point taken, Doctor Brown. You mentioned something about getting me out of pain?"

"Mr. Jones, how is our opium supply?" said Browne.

"Dwindling rapidly, Sir. We are down to forty-six pounds."

"Very well. See if you can accommodate our friend here." Owen limped over to the table and sat down. At the other end of the table, Ward was passed out with his head in a pillow. Browne had splinted Ward's injured arm with a padded piece of hardwood that had been laced to the forearm with a piece of sailcloth. An eyehook had been screwed into the wooden splint and through it ran a narrow hemp rope that was looped over a beam in the ceiling above him, thus keeping the arm pointing upward. Browne had gone to this arrangement because, by the time he and Jones had finished with the two legs and the nose, Ward's hand had swollen to twice its normal size. Browne could see that Ward's fingertips were purple and he feared that one of the arteries in the wrist had been ruptured by the ricocheted ball. Luckily, the skin, although crushed, was intact.

Jones set a lamp in front of Owen and produced the white clay pipe with the black smudges on the stem. He broke off a sunflower seed-sized piece of opium and placed it in the pipe. He topped that off with an oily wad of Panama Surprise. He handed Owen a broom straw.

"I would suggest you wait five minutes before you take the second draw, Sir."

"I will, Mr. Jones. Thank you."

"It has been my pleasure, Sir." With that, Jones went in search of a pillow for Owen's face, which would soon be on the table. Owen placed the straw in the lamp and then over top the bowl of the pipe. He took a tentative draw on the pipe and held it as long as he could. One of the cooks began lighting the lamps in the kitchen and Owen decided that it was the most beautiful thing he had ever seen. He smiled contentedly as the pain in his groin slowly ebbed away. In the distance there was a male voice singing, "Anabell's love canal." Owen smiled and his eyelids slowly began to drop. Suddenly there was a great commotion, as the Turk burst into the kitchen singing at the top of his lungs, banging the two bags of crayfish he carried into everything in his way. Owen was startled by the noise and almost came out of his skin when he saw the shirtless tattooed-Turk coming straight for him, with the two bags swinging wildly. Owen jumped to his feet and that was a colossal error. He rose off balance and raised his hands over his head to compensate. He let out a guttural scream, which scared hell out of the Turk, who tried to come to an instant halt. He lost his footing on the tile floor and had to let the two gunny sacks go as he braced himself for the pratt-fall. His hands hit the tile floor first and did manage to take up some of the shock, but his backside hit with such force that it bounced upward, thus shooting his head backward into the floor. He was out cold and the crayfish that had escaped their Hemp prison slowly moved toward him.

Owen sat down slowly, oblivious to the Turk's plight. Owen re-lit the pipe and drew in the smoke for all he was worth. The cooks in the outdoor kitchen heard the scream and came running. There were a series of crunching noises, followed by curses as the injured crayfish pinched the bare feet of the cooks. The cooks could see the Turk in the middle of the floor, but they backed out of the kitchen to find some more lamps. Owen put his head down on the table and went into a pain-free sleep.

CHAPTER 47

"'Ere we are, ladies and gents," said Jones, his hands protected by oven mitts. He and another cook tilted the cast iron cook pot and lunged it toward the table. A red tide of cooked crayfish spilled out on top of the fifteen-foot long table in the dining room. The forty people standing around the table cheered Jones and then began the ritual of snap-sucking the thorax, then pitching it in the nearest bowl and starting to work on the tail. The wine found on board the *Marquesa* had turned out to be surprisingly good. Among the officers and guests staying in the mansion, there were only two that had not consumed a rather substantial quantity of wine. Both of them happened to be in opium comas. Jones removed his mitts and wedged himself between Browne and Lieutenant Comstock, who was still referred to as Mid Shipman Comstock by all of the officers, even after four months together. The Governor's wife was between Comstock on her left and the freckle-faced Thatcher on her right. She had chosen them as escorts during Owen's unfortunate absence. In her brief history of competition with Sara for the title, "Sexiest, Most Desirable," the Governor's wife had changed her wardrobe radically, but had always been a step behind Sara. Tonight she had come out ahead. She wore a finely woven white silk shirt that was obviously designed as underwear. The really sinfully exciting part was that the shirt was very short and it revealed her abdomen! Her pulse rate was over a hundred as she took notice of the hateful looks she received from the other women. Sara would not make eye contact with "The Bitch." The room was getting hot and the men began pulling off their shirts, one by one. The feeding frenzy continued until the chili pepper had finally kicked in. People were hiccuping and sweating uncontrollably. Still their hands worked more crayfish. Sara could feel the Governor's wife trying to catch Morgan's attention. She could also sense that Morgan was ignoring the woman out of respect for her, at least for now. With the passage of time, the thin sleeveless shirt worn by the Governor's wife became more transparent, as the sweat accumulated. Sara noticed that several of the more intoxicated men at the table were openly staring at her chest. Sara stole a glance at the "Bitch's" chest, but the "Bitch" caught her in the act. End of round one. Ten points for the Governor's wife.

Morgan, who sat directly opposite Browne and Jones, raised his glass.

"I propose a toast to the Swimmers who saved the day," said Morgan, with a big smile on his face. "Swimmers please raise your glasses that we may recognize you and salute you."

"Swimmers!" shouted the group. Dan, who stood on Morgan's right side, burst into smile. Behind him stood his native girl, dressed in a flowered lappa, cut short and wrapped around her waist. She had removed her top when the Captains had. Several eyes were on her, including Sara's, from time to time, as she stood behind Dan, fanning his red back with a palm frond, her breasts swaying with the motion.

"I say we give them a twenty-one gun salute," said the tipsy Browne, raising his pistol into the air. Immediately, five other pistols were raised.

"Slow down, Buccos," said Morgan, calmly. "We already have one ricochet victim."

"The Capn's right!" shouted Jones. "If we was to shoot 'oles in the ceiling, we might not get invit'd back next year!" There was laughter around the table, except from the women, who had their attention focused on Balfor's woman-girl, who was fanning herself, intermittently unbuttoning another button on her blouse in between bites of crayfish, supplied by a much more sober Balfor.

Morgan motioned Collier forward and whispered in his ear. Collier left the table for a short time. A few moments later the first Indian girl appeared and began fanning Sara with a palm frond. The girl's top did not stay on long, once she saw her friend fanning Dan's back. The heat was truly oppressive, largely because the land breeze had not yet come. More native girls entered the room and began fanning the people standing in front of the table. Jones and his apprentice spilled another tsunami of crayfish on the table and the crowd cheered, much to the delight of the native girls.

For the first time, Morgan loosened up and looked at Dan's girl. Dan caught him peeking and smiled.

"I like the little brown ones," said Dan, flashing his signature smile.

"I can certainly appreciate…your appreciation!" said Morgan, who instantly recognized that he had had too much to drink. It would be water for the next hour. "Gbessay would be proud of me," he said softly. It became extremely quiet around the table as the crustacean-feeders studied the new arrivals. Sara didn't mind the attention being given to the Indian girls, as long as it was directed away from the Governor's wife. She wondered absently what the Governor's wife's name was, so she asked.

"Mid Shipman Comstock, can you tell me the name of your new lady friend?"

"I am afraid I do not know it," said Comstock, embarrassed.

"How about you, Lieutenant Thatcher?"

"Her first name is Matilda," said Thatcher, beaming with pride. Hearing her name, the Governor's wife, along with all the Spanish women, with the sole exception of Balfor's girl, suddenly directed their attention to Sara, who began slapping her thigh.

"You have to be joking," said Sara, slapping her thigh with great enthusiasm and laughing uncontrollably. "Matilda," she shouted, slapping her thigh more forcefully. The Governor's wife had daggers in her eyes and she wanted to kill Sara, plain and simple. Morgan sensed a calamity in the making and held Sara in his arms, as her laughter continued. Throughout this time, Sara was very much aware that Balfor's woman-girl was trying to unfasten her last button, fanning her chest. Sara stood up straight, pushing free of Morgan's embrace. She pulled her top over her head and said, "God it is hot in here", extending her arms as high as they would go, lifting her ample thirty-four year old breasts up high. Just enough, in fact, to make the Governor's wife grab her midshipmen by their waists and pull them away from the table. All eyes were now on Morgan's lady, who kept her arms high in the air, yawning, as she was being fanned by her Indian attendant.

"Good night *Matilda!*" Sara shouted in her best bitchy Spanish voice. "Be sure and let the boys poke you in the ass!" Morgan didn't understand the sentence completely, but he did get the word "culo" and noticed that the Spanish women gasped. It was clear that this was going to erupt into a fight and Morgan wanted no part of it. He also noticed that Velasquez was laughing hysterically. Matilda clenched her fists and tried to come up with a more powerful insult, but Sara was too fast. "At your age, you could probably fit them both in at the same time!"

The Governor's wife was unable to contain her anger. She focused her eyes on Sara's breasts and lunged toward her, belly first on the table, crunching crayfish with her impact. Her claw-like nails were extended as weapons and she meant to scar Sara's breasts. Sara timed the anticipated move and pulled her left foot backward, her chest out of harm's way, swaying her breasts elegantly in the process. She grabbed Matilda's right wrist and gave a light tug, thus insuring that Matilda would do a belly flop on the floor. Sara cocked back her left arm and shot a blow forward. Sara's timing was a little off because of the wine she had consumed and her left hook caught Matilda on the side of her neck. Even before she hit the floor, Matilda had her hands up to her neck as her vocal cords went into spasm and cut off her air supply. She hit the hardwood floor with a loud thud.

"Would you please pass me a potato?" asked Sara in Spanish, addressing one of the stunned women on the other side of the table. Gurgling noises were coming from Matilda, just before she lost consciousness. "No, that one there," said Sara pointing to the smaller red-skinned potato. The Spanish woman was dumbfounded, but she fished out the potato.

Morgan made eye contact with Browne and motioned his head toward Matilda, who was motionless on the dining room floor of her own house. Browne moved quickly and once beside Matilda, he went down on one knee and rolled her over onto her back. In the dim candle light, Browne could make out Matilda's purple lips.

"I think these potatoes are a little over-cooked," said Sara in Spanish to the woman who had passed her the potato. Again in Spanish, "Doctor Browne, why don't you let the dog-bitch die?" The Spanish women gasped and began fanning themselves rapidly, except for Balfor's Lady, who applauded and then finally succeeded in taking off her top. The Spanish women then applauded also, finally realizing that their least-favorite oppressor had been taken down. Balfor's lady thought they were applauding her and so she took a bow.

Browne lifted up Matilda's skimpy top and saw a slight rise in her chest and then another. He put his ear against her chest wall and then repeated the process on the other side. He looked up at Morgan and gave him a "thumbs up" sign and then began inspecting Matilda's neck.

An obviously intoxicated fiddler appeared in the room and played a few notes. He tilted his head to the side and grimaced. He plucked the strings, one by one and made adjustments at the top of the violin. He shook his head violently side-to-side, slapping himself twice in the face with his ponytail, desperately trying to wake himself up. Then he began to play. Initially, it was a slow funeral march as he learned exactly where to put his fingers on the fretless instrument and then the fun began. The fiddler began playing an impossibly fast sonata and Sara began gyrating her hips to the music. Sara climbed on to the table and danced there, while the spectators clapped in time with the music. Sara grabbed hands with Balfor's lady and helped her up on top of the table and began dancing with her. Both women were swaying their hips and breasts and soon the Governor's wife was forgotten.

Browne tried to get the attention of Thatcher and Comstock, once he had determined that the Governor's wife was out of danger, but they were hypnotized by the dancers on the table. Another Spanish woman removed her top and joined the dancers on the table. The crowd roared their approval.

Jones filled four pipes, careful to avoid anything with a black smudge and sent two in each direction around the table. The cooks filled the ladies' wine glasses and then stood back and enjoyed the show. Another Spanish lady had climbed atop the table and bared her breasts and then she began removing her skirt, until finally, she was naked and there was more applause.

Browne finally snatched Thatcher and Comstock from the far side of the table and dragged them over to where the governor's wife was sitting up, breathing slowly and trying to figure out what had happened. What had at first appeared as a sure thing to them, now became an irritant to the young officers, who had never seen anything even remotely similar to

CHAPTER 48

Owen was awakened by the sound of clapping and fiddle music in the distance. He raised his head off the pillow slowly, not sure where he was. There was a small lamp burning on the counter top and he realized he was in the kitchen, lying beneath the table. A feeble attempt to stand became an exquisitely painful reminder that he had shredded a muscle in his groin. His mind was still in an opium fog and he wanted desperately to be in his upstairs bed. Using the table as a brace, Owen worked his good leg underneath his weight and pushed up to a standing position. He knew that sleep would be impossible without more opium, so he grabbed the pipe on the table and checked to see if there was another hit left.

"Thank you, God," whispered Owen under his breath as he held the pipe up to the lamp. He debated whether, or not to take a puff right now to make it easier going up the stairs, but thought better of it and hobbled out of the kitchen. Collier intercepted him before he made it to the stairs.

"Why don't you come and join the party?" asked Collier.

"Thanks for the offer, but my leg is killing me," said Owen, still in a fog.

"In that case, why don't you use my room downstairs?"

"Thanks just the same, but I want to sleep in my own bed," said Owen, turning away from Collier, heading toward the stairs.

"Come back here Lieutenant. That is an order," said Collier firmly. Even in a fog, Owen could sense that something was terribly wrong. "You will be spending the night in my room and that is final. Here, let me help you," said Collier, walking toward Owen.

"I can do it myself," said Owen. For whatever reason, Collier had not made eye contact with Owen and that had never happened before. "What is going on up there?" demanded Owen. Collier hesitated and then looked Owen in the eyes. Collier recognized the fact that Owen was going to find out about Matilda tomorrow anyway, so he decided to just go ahead and tell him the truth.

"The Governor's wife is not alone," Collier said gently. Owen choked up and fought to restrain tears. Collier was glad that it turned out this way, because now he would not have to be the one who had to endure Owen's wrath.

"Who is she with?" asked Owen, still fighting back tears.

"Comstock and Thatcher," said Collier, who could feel the bite of those words himself. Owen couldn't hold back the tears any longer and Collier took a step forward and gave him a tentative hug. In a few seconds, Collier had tears in his eyes as well. "Let's find a place where we can talk."

Collier led Owen out to the front porch and sat him down slowly into a whicker chair. Collier ran back inside and grabbed his pipe, then ran by the kitchen and filled a demijohn with red wine. He poked his head in through the living room door to check on the progress of the party. Nobody was standing. "That's a good sign," he said, walking back out to the porch.

Owen was sobbing when Collier arrived. Collier pulled a chair next to Owen and loaded his pipe, then took a piece of spaghetti and lit it with the lamp on the table. He lit the pipe, took a long draw and then passed it to Owen, who managed a hit in between sobs.

"I know that this will do absolutely no good," said Collier, blowing smoke out of his lungs, "but let me assure you that we *all* go through this at some point in our lives.

"I feel like killing those bastards," said Owen.

"That is a completely normal reaction. Anger is always driven by pain. Remember that," said Collier, taking a slug of wine out of his demijohn, then passing it over to Owen. "And remember, they did not seduce her, *she* seduced them. They are just a couple of dumb kids trying to get laid. For the first time, I might add, just like you two months ago. Am I right?" said Collier, laughing.

"Well...yes, now that you mention it," said Owen, cracking a smile.

"All right, that's better. Look at how far you have come in the last four months. You've gone from sheltered Midshipman to cunning linguist," said Collier, realizing at once that Owen did not get the joke. "Cunni lingus is what it is called when you lick a woman between the legs." Owen still had a blank look on his face. "Cunning linguist! Do you understand?" Owen finally started laughing, thanks to the Panama Surprise.

"God I feel like such an ass," said Owen, starting to sob again.

"Imagine how much worse it would have been if you had carted the bitch off to Port Royal with you and it had happened there," said Collier.

"You have a point," said Owen, sucking tear-diluted snot back into his nose.

"Think of her as a teacher. Your Spanish has improved tremendously. Not to mention the fact that she introduced you to the world of love. I guess you could say that she gave you first crack at her crack," said Collier, laughing.

"Maybe I can use that tomorrow," said Owen, laughing.

"Be my guest. You might also point out to your comrades that it took two of them to accomplish what you managed solamente for two solid months. You have nothing to be ashamed of, me Bucco. By the way, you missed a fantastic fight tonight," said Collier, reloading the pipe.

"Between who?" said Owen, downing the rest of the demijohn, then belching.

"Between Sara and your former mentor," said Collier, blowing out a cloud of smoke. Owen smiled. "It seems that Matilda was making eyes at Morgan and Sara decided to torture her a little. Sara slipped off her top, which infuriated Matilda, who then decided to leave with her two new consorts. As she was leaving, Sara made some obscene comments in Spanish and the next thing I knew, Matilda *dove* across the table at Sara," said Collier, picking up the demijohn and sprinting to the kitchen, then returning with it filled.

"So, who won the fight?" asked Owen. The frogs stopped singing until Collier sat down.

"Sara, by a knock out. When Matilda flew at her, Sara stepped backwards and hit the bitch on the neck as she slid by. She went down and didn't get back up. There is nothing like a cat fight to liven up a party."

The two men sat silently and took in the evening sky and the fragrances that engulfed them. Two owls were hooting at each other nearby and bats were flying through the porch area, picking off insects that were drawn to the lights. Owen began sobbing again.

"She really isn't worth the tears," said Collier.

"It's not that. I killed a man today and I can't stop thinking about it. It is slowly driving me mad," said Owen, fishing a handkerchief out of his pocket.

"Same for me. It was my first, how about you?"

"Of course it was my first! I am only seventeen," said Owen, indignantly.

"Well, you never know. You seem to be doing everything at an earlier age that I did."

"Like what?"

"Like the first time you got laid," said Collier, firing up the pipe.

"How old *were* you?"

"Me? I am still a virgin," said Collier proudly. Owen began laughing uncontrollably and Collier joined him. The sun was rising in the eastern sky and Collier swore he could hear cows mooing in the distance.

CHAPTER 49

The cattle began arriving about an hour after sunrise that morning. Eight men drove them into the center of town on horseback and the Turk faced his first problem of the day. There was a corral about a quarter of a mile away, but it would only hold about a hundred cattle. The Turk instructed the riders to return half of the cattle to where they had come from and to place a hundred in the corral, but that still left a hundred-fifty cattle to deal with. The Turk decided to leave the cattle in the central portion of the City and simply seal off the streets. That way the animals could drink from the fountain during the oppressive noon-day sun.

A small donkey cart appeared next, guarded by four heavily armed men on horseback. The cart driver explained that this was only half of the twenty-thousand Reales that Alonso had promised. The remainder would be delivered tomorrow. In the back of the cart were thirty-three hemp bags full of silver coins, each bag weighing about twenty-five pounds. That amounted to over eight-hundred pounds of silver. The Turk shook his head, exasperated about where he was going to find room in the cargo holds for this latest addition, with more coming tomorrow. Then there was the boucan to top it off. He began rubbing his temples.

"Unbelievable!" he said to himself. "Jenkins, will you come over here?" The red-haired Jenkins already had his shirt off, exposing the thickened lizard skin on his shoulders. "Will you take a few men and go down to the wharf with this cart? We need to distribute these bags evenly in the boats. You better count the coins and give the driver a receipt. When you get finished there, come and help us on the beach."

"Not a problem," said Jenkins, hoisting one of the bags and whistling. "Mouts Caca is going to be very pleased." Mouts Caca was the Buccaneer Fleet's accountant, whose real name was "Lipshitz". In Patois, there was no word for "lips", so they used the word "mouts", for "mouth", instead.

"No doubt. I just hope we don't sink the damned ships. Velasquez is salvaging an additional twenty-five-hundred pounds and then we have the weight of the boucan. It is going to be tight," said the Turk, with a worried look on his face.

"It's a hard life being a Buccaneer, what with having to haul around tons of gold and silver, surrounded by buxom wenches all the time! I don't know about you, but I need some rest!" The Turk cracked a smile.

"Get to work, Jenkins," said the Turk, chuckling.

The preparations on the beach were nearly completed. There were over a thousand bamboo drying racks set up on the sand and the fire pits were loaded with small pieces of hardwood, with stripped branches beside them. An improvised corral that could hold about ten cows had been erected. There was a shoot at one end that would hold one cow tightly while its throat was cut. A noose was then placed over the cow's neck and it was dragged out of the stall, down toward the surf. As the body was dismembered, the waste products were hurled into the water. Soon the beach was covered with flies and seagulls that were greedily feeding on the body parts. Turkey vultures descended and began working on the discarded heads, tearing at the eyes with their sharp beaks.

After the first hour, the Turk was disappointed with the progress of the Buccaneers. Many of the men were crewmen from the *Oxford* and had never participated in a slaughter like this before. The bottleneck seemed to be the dismembering of the carcasses. The Turk told the men to leave the heads on and the bellies intact. They were to remove the legs and strip the skin off the backs of the cows and remove the sirloin. A team of men then dragged the carcasses out into waist-deep water, while other teams sliced the muscles into thin strips and placed them on the drying racks.

By one in the afternoon the Buccaneers had processed one-hundred-twenty-five cattle. The fires were lit and the strips of meat that had been drying in the sun for almost two hours were placed on stripped gumbo limbo branches. The water off the coast looked like a scene from hell; it was blood-red and littered with thousands of cow parts. What a relief it would be when the tide went out and took the carrion with it.

CHAPTER 50

"We need to draft a letter to Alonzo and have it ready by tomorrow morning. Once we have the second installment of silver I am going to have one of the prisoners deliver the letter and plead our case," said Morgan, shifting his weight in the bathtub.

"What case are we pleading for?" asked Sara, bobbing her breasts in the water.

"We are going to try and convince Alonzo to let us pass by the fort unharmed. Not a terribly likely scenario, given the fact that we promised to release the prisoners after the silver was delivered. First he looses his fleet and now he has given us five hundred—correction, two-hundred-fifty beeves along with twenty-thousand Reales. He has nothing to show for it. Pass me that pipe, will you?"

"So now he is in a real bind," said Sara. "He has to either let us pass unharmed and pray that we will release the prisoners, or he has to take us down, with the prisoners along for the ride. Fairly dicey, I would say, shooting at Matilda. The Governor is almost certainly enraged by Alonzo's incompetence and if his wife gets killed in the process there is going to be hell to pay. What would you do?"

"Put a ball in my brain, probably," said Morgan, laughing. "You are absolutely right, though, he has painted himself into a corner and it is going to be messy."

"Just how good is your 'plan B'?"

"Since I have never used it before, I have no way of knowing, but based on what I've seen so far, I think we are in good shape. In a worst case scenario, we would be running the gauntlet at night and there would only be nine guns firing at us. Let's say that their cycle time on those guns is two minutes, totally impossible, of course, but as I said, worst case. Our time under fire with an outgoing tide and sails hoisted halfway through the run is right at six minutes. That is a total of twenty-seven balls, which is very generous, since the cycle time is going to be more like five minutes in the dark. Factor in the fact that we are moving and there is no moon. What percentage of the balls will actually hit a boat?"

"I haven't the foggiest notion, but I was talking with Medina—the Spanish pilot we picked up. He told me that the Dons have scoured the countryside in Spain for 'pretty boys', as he calls them, meaning classic Castillion types, to put on the Galleons and the three ships that came here. Most of the crewmen are farmers with very little in the way of training. So, I would imagine that they are going to miss the majority of the time," said Sara.

"Interesting. I would be willing to bet that if their cannon were manned by *our* best gunners, at least half the boats would make it out in one piece. But the good news is that if they fall for the ruse, we will make it out Scott free. We wouldn't want anything to happen to Matilda, would we?" Sara splashed water at Morgan, and then began to laugh.

"What a character she is. Why don't you have her deliver the letter?" said Sara.

"Thatcher and Comstock would never forgive me. What do you say we write that letter now?"

"Suits me. I am too sore to do anything else."

The land breeze had picked up and blown the dead cow smell away from the mansion, to be replaced by jasmine. Morgan stood on the porch and paced in his knee-length pants. Sara sat naked in a chair in front of a table, enjoying the feel of the breeze on her skin. She dipped the quill into the ink well and began the introductory part of the letter.

"How do you want to play this? Murdering pirate, or respectful diplomat?" asked Sara, turning up the lamp.

"The idea is to get him to let us through the channel. We should try to appeal to his logical side, assuming he has one. How about a respectful introduction and then an apology for not handing over the prisoners. Tell him the Buccaneers voted on it and there was nothing I could do. Point out that all of the prisoners are alive and well, and we are tired of feeding them. We *want* to get rid of them as badly as he wants them back. All that we ask is that we be given free passage through the channel, then we will send a boat back with *all* the prisoners.

"If our demands are not met, we will put the prisoners to the sword and take the fort, giving no quarter. Tell him that the prisoners will be equally divided among the boats. Can you think of anything else?"

"That pretty well covers it I think. By the way, are they going to slaughter more cows tomorrow?" asked Sara.

"As far as I know, yes. Why do you ask?"

"That smell was getting to me today. What do you say we take a boat out on the lake tomorrow?"

"Let me get some housekeeping done in the first part of the morning and you have yourself a partner," said Morgan.

CHAPTER 51

"It is a pleasure to see the two of you again," said Collier, pouring coffee into his cup.

"Good morning, Commander," said Comstock, with a big grin on his face.

"Hello, Commander," said Thatcher, embarrassed.

"We have a big day ahead of us. Lieutenant Owen is still in a bad way, so the two of you will have to take up the slack. I can only spare about fifty men, until the boucan is finished. You will need to distribute the booty in the boats so that each man's share is on the same boat he is. Is that clear?"

"As crystal," said the cocky Comstock.

"You will need to organize a team to top off the water barrels from the Mansion's cistern. Make sure you leave enough water for the house to run two days. Put a team on the forge and get that block of molten silver broken up and cast into ingots. Leave the coins intact. We don't have time to melt them all down. We may be pulling out of here tomorrow morning, so we have to be ship shape. Are there questions?"

"How do we divide up the shares?" asked Thatcher.

"There is a copy of the 'Articles' on every boat and that spells it out. Basically, you need to go back to the list of men, figure out who is still alive, who is missing parts and who has made withdrawals. One half of the take goes into the Buccaneer coffers, the other half is what you divide up. The officers get three parts and the crewmen get one. Remember that the Swimmers, Sara, Medina and Jones were ranked as officers. The Admiral takes ten shares. Questions?"

"I don't understand why we are doing this," said Comstock.

"Because we were ordered to, for crissakes. Think about it. If all of the booty was on one boat, what would we do if she sank? We would be working for the King again, that's what!"

"I hadn't thought of that," said Comstock.

"That is why you are still a midshipman. Start trying to think ahead. Eat your breakfast and get out of here," said Collier, disgusted. Thatcher pulled a small book from his shirt pocket and began writing furiously with a wad. Collier was in a foul mood and Thatcher didn't want to miss a thing.

CHAPTER 52

"I want you to pack up tonight," said Morgan, stacking his clothes on the bed.

"What is your hurry?" said Sara.

"An intuition, that's all."

"What does your intuition tell you?"

"That we should leave tomorrow! I have this gut feeling that some calamity awaits us if we stay. Maybe ships are on their way from Cartagena. I don't know exactly what it is, but there is something in the air. Maybe a land force is headed our way. Who knows?"

"How often do you get these intuitions?" asked Sara.

"Not often, but when they come, I listen," said Morgan. He wondered if she was probing so that she could add another selection to the "Charlie Stories".

"Are they usually right?"

"I am still alive and I shouldn't be, about a hundred times over," said Morgan, lost in thought. There was a knock on the door. "Who is it," yelled Morgan.

"Jones, Sir."

"Come."

"Sorry for the bother, Sir, but the prisoner you sent out this morning has returned and wishes to speak to you." Jones looked worried.

"Please send him up to me, Mr. Jones. By the way, could you brew me a few doses, just in case?"

"It would be an honor, Sir."

"Thank you, Mr. Jones," said Morgan, closing the door. "This doesn't sound good." A few seconds later there was another knock at the door. "Come," shouted Morgan. The door opened and Jones escorted the terrified Spaniard into the room.

"I'll be shoving off now, Sir," said Jones.

"Thank you again, Mr. Jones," said Morgan, closing the door. The Spaniard, whoever he was, was scared to death and his eyes never left the ground.

"You are safe and welcome here," said Sara in Spanish. "Tell us why you are here."

"I was ordered back here by the Admiral," he said.

"What is your name?"

"Carlos Gonzales de la Vega."

"May I call you Carlos?"

"Si."

"My name is Sara and this is Captain Morgan. Mucho gusto."

"The pleasure is mine, Lady," said Carlos, finally making eye contact with Sara for an instant.

"Did the Admiral give you a letter?"

"No. He slapped me and told me that I was a coward when I asked him to let your ships pass."

"How was he dressed?" asked Sara.

"In a dressing gown and slippers. He looked ill."

"In what way did he look ill?"

"He was very pale and irritable. He kept screaming at people. Maybe he had a headache." Carlos was beginning to loosen up a little and made eye contact with Morgan. Carlos was dressed in clothes that must have been expensive when they were new.

"Ask him if people were yawning," said Morgan.

"He says yes, almost everybody. It sounds like Velasquez is earning his money," said Sara.

"Ask him how many men there were."

"He says he isn't sure, but he thinks there were at lest two hundred."

"Did any of them look sick?" asked Morgan.

"He says they looked miserable. Nobody was smiling, or joking. He was glad to get out of there," said Sara.

"Tell him thank you for the information. He is a free man." As Sara translated this, Carlos' eyes lit up and he began to smile. "Tell him to go and stay in the old part of the city, where the Indians are. I'll walk him down stairs."

Morgan showed Carlos out the front door and then went into the kitchen, searching for Collier.

"Mr. Jones, have you seen Commander Collier?"

"He was here not more than a minute ago, Sir. I told him we was out of water and he became, well, I would have to say 'omicidal, Sir. 'Ave a seat, Sir and let me get you a glass of red."

"Thank you, Mr. Jones. Did you say we were out of water?" said Morgan, the implications sinking in.

"Correct, Sir. The cistern is as dry as a desert goat turd," said Jones, filling the wineglass. "'Ere we are, Sir."

"How can that be, Mr. Jones? It has rained twice since we have been back."

"I am afraid I cannot answer that question, Sir, but I think I hear the Commander's voice." Sure enough, Collier was dragging Comstock down the stairs by the back of his collar.

"Have the bitch taken down to the hall and lock her up with the men," screamed Collier. "As for you, you little bastard," Comstock lost his footing on the hardwood floor and Collier was literally dragging him toward the kitchen. "If I decide to let you live, you will be scrubbing out heads all the way back to Jamaica," said Collier, depositing Comstock in the center of the kitchen floor. Collier was so enraged that he didn't realize Morgan was in the room. "You are finished as a Buccaneer. Maybe mommy and daddy can buy you a spot on another one of the King's ships, but you are definitely finished here. You are going to receive a seaman's portion of the pot and most of it will go to buy a third rate passage on the next ship bound for England. Stand up, asshole and go round up your gear. You have lost your berth on the *Marquesa*, so find accommodations elsewhere." Collier pulled out a pistol and cocked it. "You had better run, boy." Comstock was out of the kitchen and up the stairs before Collier could lower the hammer on his pistol.

"I take it you are a trifle upset with Mr. Comstock," said Morgan. Collier jumped halfway to the ceiling.

"God! You scared me," said Collier, clutching his chest.

"Pull up a chair when the chest pain stops," said Morgan, laughing. Jones entered the kitchen and discretely placed a white pipe and a three-inch bud on the table in front of Morgan. Jones raised an eyebrow and flashed Morgan a "thumbs up sign" and then wisely left the room. Morgan caught motion out of the corner of his eye and looked up just in time to see Comstock sprinting toward the door with a pile of clothes in his arms.

Sara poked her head in the kitchen and noticed Collier bent forward with his hands on his thighs, breathing heavily.

"Is it safe to come in?" she said. Morgan waved her in. There was a woman's scream somewhere in the house and a few moments later, two Buccaneers came down the stairs with the Governor's wife, bound and gagged, between them. When Sara saw that, she ran to the kitchen door and put two fingers in her mouth. She let out a deafening whistle and the trio halted and looked back. Sara lifted up her top and exposed her breasts, fluttering her eyelids. The Governor's wife went insane with rage and started dragging her escorts toward Sara. They finally gained the upper hand and pushed her out the doorway. Sara walked back into the kitchen very pleased with herself.

"Will somebody please tell me what is going on around here?" asked Sara.

"Commander?" said Morgan, loading the pipe. Collier was still too wound up to sit down, so he paced as he told his tale, while Sara and Morgan sat patiently at the table.

"I ordered that little piss ant to top-off the water barrels and divvy up the booty along with Thatcher. I *specifically* told him to leave a two-day supply of water in the cistern! Well, it turns out that he walked down to the dock and issued some orders and then came back here and spent the remainder of the afternoon mounting his bitch! Meanwhile, poor Thatcher is still working on the division of the booty. I ended up sending Owen down to the dock in a cart to help out." Said Collier, pounding his fist into the other palm. "Speaking of which, I should probably get down there myself and see how things are going."

"Before you go," said Morgan, "Can you explain *how* we ran out of water?"

"Oh that. Simple really—somebody left the tap open. But the really irritating part of the whole thing is that the diameter of the pipe is less than an inch! If piss ant Comstock had gone down there just *once* to check on things, there would still be ten-thousand gallons left in that tank."

"On a brighter note, we have a tank full of water in our bathroom that will hold us over night," said Sara. "I think we can forego a bath tonight," she said, looking at Morgan.

"Fine by me," said Morgan. "By the way, we are leaving tomorrow. We need to get to the channel three hours before sunset. I want all of the officers onboard the *Marquesa* after we drop anchor. And make absolutely certain that every boat has a functional sea anchor."

CHAPTER 53

After breakfast the next morning, Browne and Jones held an impromptu clinic in the kitchen. The first item was Owen's leg, which had gotten worse overnight. Browne instructed Owen to drop his pants and things did not look good. The initial bruising that had appeared on the upper portion of the inside of the right thigh had migrated down the leg past the knee. Owen's right calf and ankle were swollen to twice their normal size. Browne felt the inside portion of Owen's thigh and came across a ropy vein full of clotted blood.

"Does that hurt?" asked Browne.

"It burns like a hot poker," said Owen, grimacing.

"There is only one way this is going to get better and that's for you to stay off your feet. Mr. Jones will be delivering a tea to you three times a day, which should help. I am going to have the carpenters raise up the foot of your berth to help with the swelling. Go and get off your feet." Owen limped out of the kitchen, thoroughly miserable.

Pulverin was the next patient. Jones brought him in and asked him to take off his shirt.

"How are you felling, Captain?" asked Browne.

"Very well, but I want this patch taken off my back," said Pulverin.

"Have you had any fever, or shortness of breath?"

"No, I am fine," said Pulverin, irritated.

Browne moved behind Pulverin and placed his ear on his back. "Take a deep breath. Good. Again."

Browne opened a small leather case and pulled out a needle and thread, along with a pair of scissors. "This time, I want you to take a deep breath and hold it." Pulverin took the breath and Browne lifted up the leather patch. The tissue was pink and healthy, but the hole was still open. Browne let the patch down to cover the hole. "All right, breathe normally. Mr. Jones, I will need some help."

"Oh God, Sir! By 'elp', do you mean you need my finger again, Sir?"

"I am afraid so, Mr. Jones, but this time it will only take a second. And you don't have to put your finger *in* the hole, just on top of it. It is really very small."

"Really, Sir, I don't think I am up to the task." Pulverin began swearing in French and that seemed to turn the tide. Browne committed as many of the swear words to memory as he could.

"All right, Sir, let's get it over with," said Jones, walking up to Browne. "Can I keep me eyes closed, Sir?" Browne looked at Jones and raised an eyebrow.

"Captain, I need you to take another deep breath and hold it tight," said Browne, who then snipped the three stitches holding the patch in place. "Put your finger here and hold tight." Reluctantly, Jones placed his finger over the hole and closed his eyes. "You can breathe again." Browne threaded the curved sail needle.

"Captain, this is going to hurt like a son of a bitch. I have to put a needle into your skin and I need you to hold absolutely still. Can you do that?" asked Browne in French.

"Oui."

"Here goes!" Browne jabbed the needle into Pulverin's skin, under one side of Jones' finger and then up through the skin on the other side. Pulverin winced, but managed to hold still.

Browne pulled off the needle and did a triple wrap on the first throw. He pulled in the ends of the thread until the knot was just touching Jones' finger. "Captain, take a deep breath and hold tight. Jones, on the count of three, slide your finger out. One, two, three!" Jones jerked his finger out and Browne cinched down on the knot. There was only a slight hiss of air. He did the next throw and then it was over. "Breathe normally, Captain. We will need to pull the thread out in about five days."

"Merci beau coup," said Pulverin, putting on his shirt.

CHAPTER 54

O ne of the carpenters had whittled out a beautiful bow for
Conteh, who was absolutely delighted when Morgan gave
it to him on the ride over to the channel. The string had been
fashioned out of hemp fibers wrapped in cow intestine. Arrow
shafts were made of heart-wood mahogany that had been
turned on *Marquesa*'s ship's lathe. The quiver was a section of
bamboo with a wide hemp strap attached. Ship's carpenters had
made a target out of balsa wood and attached it to the bow of
the *Marquesa*.

Conteh began firing at the target about ten feet away and
then moved backward as his aim improved. After the first hour,
Conteh was hitting the three inch circle the majority of the time,
at twenty feet. Then he began to fire more rapidly and worked to
still retain accuracy. At the two-hour mark, the crewmen were
cheering him on and placing bets on the up-coming contest. It
was exactly what Morgan had hoped for; a diversion to take the
tension out of the men. Best of all, they were already halfway to
their destination and the sun had just peaked overhead.

Morgan was pleased that the fleet was running ahead
of schedule. He had changed "Plan B" again and more time
would be required. He came out on deck and passed the word
for Mr. Moss. Morgan walked over to the starboard beam of

the *Marquesa* and stood next to Collier and Balfor, who were watching Conteh and timing his shots.

"Gathering intelligence, Gentlemen?" said Morgan.

"Of course," said Balfor. "Are your plans moving along?"

"Absolutely. I solved the final problem five minutes ago," said Morgan, watching Conteh absently. Dan walked up and joined the group. "I think this is probably the most exciting thing I have ever done," said Morgan, searching his memory.

"Probably *the* most dangerous, as well," said Dan, flashing a smile. "Good afternoon, Captains, Commander." The men appreciated the humor and welcomed him.

"How is your back," asked Collier.

"It was painless at the twenty-four hour mark. But the skin is very dry and cracks open, so Browne gave me a cream to put on it. It's getting better." The deck began to shake as Moss walked up to the group. He was wearing his leather apron, as usual.

"Captain Morgan, I was told 'ta report to ya, Sir."

"Good afternoon, Mr. Moss. I was wondering if you could set that *other* project aside for a while and take on a new one?"

"It would be a pleasure, Sir. What is it you need?" said Moss eagerly.

"Mr. Moss, can you construct an artificial rail for the big launch? What I am trying to achieve is the illusion that the launch is riding higher in the water. Or lower, for that matter, when the apron is removed. The illusion will have to be repeated more than twenty times, so make it sturdy. Can you do it Mr. Moss?"

"Ya know ah can, Sir. But there is one problem. The paint will take a solid day ta dry, that is if ya want the apron to match the hull."

"We will figure out a way around it Mr. Moss. But we are in a bit of a rush. There is one, actually *two* more things we need. I need you to make two different sized cannons out of wood and a collapsible carriage that will fit in the bottom of the launch and *raise* the cannons high enough to be easily seen from the fort. Can you do it, Mr. Moss?"

"Ya know the answer to that, as well, Sir. But paint only dries so fast. Ah can't change the laws ah nature, Sir."

"Do the best you can, Mr. Moss. If you would like, we can have the deck cleared so that you can get a little sun on your creations," said Morgan.

"Much obliged, Sir." Said Moss, walking away, having already decided on materials he would use.

"Mr. Moss," said Morgan, with Moss freezing in his tracks. "Thank you."

"You are welcome, Sir," said Moss with a radiant smile on his face.

In the space of an hour the first cannon was brought up on deck to dry in the sun. Moss had left the underside of the cannon unpainted so that the men could carry it without soiling their hands. The gun had been constructed out of a palm log that Moss had set aside for use as a jury-rigged mast, if the need arose.

The second cannon arrived a few minutes later. It was a larger diameter than the first one and a good foot longer. Even ten feet away they both looked real. Carpenters were running back and forth to the launch, taking measurements for the carriage. There was a palpable excitement building on the *Marquesa*. Even Owen hobbled out on deck during the final fittings of the eight-inch wide apron, much to the chagrin of Browne, who insisted he at least sit in a chair with his leg propped up. The fort was coming into view when Moss walked up on deck with what appeared to be two rulers of some sort. The crowd applauded as Moss stepped into the launch and then bowed.

Moss began to assemble the "rulers" to the very aft side of the aprons. It was at that point that Morgan finally figured out what Moss was up to. Morgan could see that Moss had cut grooves into the dark hardwood rulers at eight inch intervals.

White candle wax had been poured into the grooves, which did not require a day to dry. From a quarter mile away, it would be easier for an observer to train his eye on an easily readable scale that the vague shadows between black shiplap planks.

"Fochin' genius," muttered Morgan.

"What? What is he doing?" asked Sara.

"You'll see in about thirty seconds," said Morgan.

Moss had foregone the paint altogether for the aprons. He had selected a blonde hardwood that had been oiled. The eight-inch apron sat atop the launch's rail, held in place with short dowels. The apron did not match the black paint on the side of the launch, but it didn't matter.

Moss and one of the carpenters lifted the apron up together and lowered it eight inches, so that it was now on the side of the rail, rather than on top. Small holes had been drilled through the side of the apron and then it was placed over the small wooden posts extending from the side of the rail. At the end of each post, a small hole had been drilled, through which a wedge was inserted, thus fastening the apron securely. The only remaining detail was the apron for the transom.

Morgan began clapping and the others joined in, not quite sure what it all meant. Morgan glanced back at Owen and winked. Owen smiled and waved back from his chair.

CHAPTER 55

The boats were hooked securely fifty yards off the Southern edge of Fort Island, directly in front of a thicket of mangroves. The Captains had been thoroughly briefed in Morgan's cabin and then they returned to their own boats. Then the process began.

Marquesa's launch was lowered into the water on her starboard side, which was out of view of the fort until the tide changed in about an hour. Ten men were crammed into the launch with the apron in the "down" position. The oarsmen pulled hard for the shore and ran the launch aground in the sand, just in front of the mangroves. The sheer density of the mangroves made it impossible for the fort to see the Buccaneers, who were filing back into the launch after a brief stretch, one by one and lying down this time. The apron was raised and the launch was pushed back into the water. All of the Buccaneers were concealed by the gunwales, except the oarsmen, on the return trip to *Marquesa's* starboard side. The oarsmen had to be replaced with fresh recruits because of the difficulty they had had with the current on the way back. The concealed Buccaneers climbed up the side of the *Marquesa* and changed their clothing in small ways, so that they would not be recognized. Then they climbed back into the launch and lowered the apron, while the fresh oarsmen came aboard.

This process was repeated ten times, so that it would appear that eighty men had been deposited on Fort Island. This also gave the paint on the cannons a little more time to dry. Then it was their turn. The collapsible carriages were placed in the launch and the first cannon was ceremoniously raised upward toward a yardarm by eight men, with the assistance of a block and tackle. One man could have easily done the work, but the theatre was designed to impress the Dons.

All of the *Marquesa*'s gun ports were opened one at a time, revealing her sizable inventory of cannons. The cannons were pulled back out of view a few minutes before they were "hoisted" up the yardarms and placed in the launch. The smaller "palm" gun was used to simulate the guns on the bow of the *Marquesa*, so that just before it was hauled up on the block and tackle, one of the bow guns disappeared.

The men had figured out what Morgan was trying to accomplish and they started to enjoy the show. Sunset was an hour away and once the sun was down, the Buccaneers would no longer have to use the apron, or the fake cannon in the boats. They could simply keep up a steady stream of launches going to and from the island, with a bonfire burning on shore and dim lamps in the boats.

"I am impressed, Sailor Boy. Alonso is going to be shitting his housecoat," said Sara, on the bow of the *Marquesa*, as the sun was setting.

"That, my dear, is the whole idea. The tide has changed and we have about an hour to kill. Could I interest you in a delightful Cabernet and a very cramped bathtub?"

"I am yours for the taking, but I think you deserve something special tonight. I feel like the Cleopatra that Marc Antony described in his letters back to Rome."

"Your library is bigger than mine," said Morgan, perplexed.

"Cleopatra's Generals had defeated an invading army from Thebes. They came back to Nicopolis and there was a huge celebration in their honor. Cleopatra fellated each one of her

Generals before a crowd of ten-thousand people, who cheered her on."

"Do you happen to know if she has any openings in her navy?" Sara swatted him on the backside and then led him back to the aft cabin. Morgan glanced back at the glow on the horizon to confirm his earlier observation; the sky was not red, it was a steel gray. The last time he had seen a sunset that color was the night before a hurricane. Probably nothing to worry about, he thought, it isn't even hurricane season.

"That was amazing," said Morgan, cuddling up next to Sara on the Captain's bed. "Can I return the favor?"

"Absolutely, but not right now. I think we should write a good bye letter to Alonso. Maybe we could leave one of the wooden cannons on shore and nail the letter to it."

"Sounds intriguing. What did you have in mind?"

"Well, he is pretty well destroyed as a warrior *and* a leader, for that matter. The only thing that he has left is his faith." Sara stared out the window in silence. Morgan felt Sara's body begin to convulse. Morgan backed away, and Sara sat up, slapping her thigh. Morgan instinctively looked around for wine glasses and found none. Sara kept slapping her thigh.

"Oh, yes! This is going to be good," said Sara.

"Care to let me in on the secret?"

"Remember when I told you I frequently had to keep my mouth shut to stay out of trouble?" Morgan nodded his head. "Well one of those times was when word reached Cartagena that your ship had blown up. A story circulated that the patron saint of Cartagena, Nuestra Señora de la Popa, had come back wet the very night that your ship exploded. Let me put this in perspective for you. In the center of town is a six-thousand pound statue of Señora de la Popa and I suspect that I was the only person in Cartagena who did *not* believe that the statue literally traveled six-hundred miles, sank your ship and then returned 'wet'. By the way, who *did* sink your ship? Never mind, that can wait.

"The point is, these are the most ignorant, bigoted and insanely superstitious people I have ever come across. They routinely suspend, or deny the laws of physics, which God created to allow the world to function, and ascribe miracles to the most mundane events. How *does* a marble statue transport itself twelve-hundred miles in a nighttime? How *can* you explain retrograde motion of the planets without placing the sun at the center of the solar system? It simply does not matter to them. 'The earth *is* the center of the universe and if you disagree with this we will torture you to death.'" Morgan was smiling. He knew that he would miss her. "Here is what I have in mind. I send Alonso a letter describing what the Buccaneers saw the night your ship exploded. I tell him that I have personally heard the story from over one-hundred Buccaneers and they all agreed on the following points: Nuestra Señora de la Popa was seen *after* the explosion. She pulled the lifeless body of Captain Morgan out of the water and placed him on the hospital ship. All of the Buccaneers on the ship, believers and non-believers alike, bowed down to the Señora on their knees. The ship's surgeon pronounced Morgan dead and the Señora re-appeared, smiling. The Señora extended her arm and pointed her finger at Morgan. The Virgin appeared in the sky behind the Señora and a lightening bolt shot out of the Señora's finger and struck Morgan on the chest. Morgan rose up and the Buccaneers bowed down again and prayed to the Señora.

"Morgan planned a land assault on the fort tonight, but the night before, the Señora appeared again and entered the Governor's mansion and went into Morgan's bedroom. A bright light issued forth from the bedroom and then the room went black. Morgan came down from the bedroom and greeted his men. I spoke with each of the sixty men there and Morgan was reported to have a white light around his head. The thing is, *I* was in the bedroom with Morgan when the Lady came. She was the most beautiful woman I had ever seen, but only Morgan could understand her.

"I tell you these things because she must have appeared to you many times as well, because of your faith and purity of thought. Let us rejoice that the will of God has been made manifest." Sara picked up the quill and began writing furiously.

"It is extremely gratifying to be on your *good* side," said Morgan, shaking his head.

"I haven't told you the best part. Alonso's mother gave birth to a deformed child when Alonso was six. The child was whisked away to a nunnery, because of the stigma of sin on the family. The town's people were told it had been a stillbirth and there was an elaborate funeral, but Alonso saw the child briefly as it was carried away by the nuns. The parents named the 'stillborn' child Angelica. Four years later, the Alonso that I 'ran away with' was born. Some time in his sixteenth year, the younger Alonso was told by…God, I have forgotten exactly who it was, maybe a tutor. Anyway, Alonso found out that he had a sister who was deformed and raised by nuns and died at the age of nine. The thing was, Alonso, the younger, was angry at Alonso, the elder, for never telling him about Angelica. Are you with me, so far?"

"I am and let me hasten to add, you should have your own room in the 'Hall'!"

"You know the right things to say, Sailor Boy, but you are getting me wet. Let me finish this idea. At the end of the letter, I could add a post script…say a private message from the Señora, that goes like this: 'I have no idea what this means, but the Señora asked me to give you the message that Angelica has returned from heaven to help you during this trying time'. If this doesn't shake his faith, nothing ever will," said Sara, grabbing another sheet of parchment. "The Angelica icing substantiates the remainder of the cake."

"Go ahead and finish your letter. I'll give you one of the cannons, but the other one goes into my study. Maybe I should have a plaque made that says, 'This cannon has done more damage than any cannon in history.'"

"I would say that was a fair statement. I will have this done in ten minutes," said Sara without looking up.

Morgan went out on deck and saw a team of men raising the *Marquesa's* launch upward, using block and tackle.

"Ahoy there! Avast that order! The launch is going to make one more trip ashore," shouted Morgan. Collier heard the shouting and walked over to Morgan.

"Is there a problem, Captain?" asked Collier.

"No Commander. I just wanted to drop off a departing gift for Alonso. Would you be kind enough to have the large cannon placed in the launch? The launch will leave on my orders. I want the smaller cannon delivered to my house upon our return. You seem worried, Commander," said Morgan, staring into Collier's eyes in the dim light of the binnacle.

"There are a couple of issues we need to discuss. Is this a good time?"

"Sure. Fire away."

"Let me have the cannon loaded first," said Collier. "Lieutenant Thatcher! Over here!" Collier explained what was needed and Thatcher left and began assembling a team. Morgan was relieved that the Westerly trade wind was holding strong.

"What seems to be the problem?" asked Morgan.

"The Swimmers went out today when we dropped anchor. I had a conversation with Dan, who told me that the bottom of Velasquez's boat is fouled with worms. He said he ran his nails over the surface and the wood just broke off in chunks. I went on board and she is leaking like a sieve. I don't think she is going to make it back to Jamaica, Harry," said Collier. Toredo worms were the scourge of Caribbean ships. Everything below the water line was fair game for the worms that burrowed deep into the hulls of the wooden boats, eventually destroying them.

"Do you have a plan?"

"Dan checked all the other boats and they came up fine. What I would suggest is that we distribute the men and cargo to the other boats and then load her up with prisoners and send her back to Maracaibo," said Collier. Morgan was silent for a few moments, weighing options, as usual.

"Make it happen, Commander, but not until we are out at sea. What else is troubling you?"

"Did you see the sunset tonight, Harry?"

"I did. But, this is not hurricane season," said Morgan.

"Granted, but it worries me, nonetheless."

"Our only strategy is to get as far north as we can before she hits, if she ever does. This would not be a good time to become shipwrecked on the Darien coast. The breeze has freshened, so let's take advantage of it," said Morgan, who felt someone gently grab his arm.

"Here is the letter to Alonso," said Sara, handing the letter over to Morgan.

"Perfect timing," said Morgan, "They just finished putting the cannon into the launch. Commander, when the launch is back and secured, please flash the green light."

"Understood, Captain," said Collier. The green light told the other Captains to release their sea anchors and prepare to make way when the red light flashed. If everything went according to plan, the fleet would stay closely grouped, with the *Marquesa* in the lead. When the *Marquesa* was squarely in front of the fort, she would make sail and the other boats would follow suit. The fast current combined with the stiff breeze would make the window of vulnerably relatively short, but there were no guarantees in a plan such as this. The biggest assumption of all was that Alonso would fall for the bait and actually turn his guns around.

Morgan had put himself in Alonso's shoes on many occasions and, had Morgan been the one in the fort, he would have sent a team out of the fort to spy on and harass the invaders. Had Alonso sent such a team? Were his cannon pointed out into the bay? Were his men heating cannon balls in braziers, so that when they hit Morgan's ships they would burst the wood into flames?

One thing was certain. With only nine cannon on the seaside of the fort, at least some of the boats would make it through the gauntlet. The fallback plan was that if a boat went down, her men were to stay to the center of the channel and find whatever floatation they could. The lugger, far and away the best sailor in the fleet, would double back and pick up survivors.

Morgan began pacing *Marquesa's* deck as the bosun approached the shuttered green light. *Marquesa's* launch was lashed on deck. The Buccaneers launched the sea anchor, tied to *Marquesa's* bow and the bosun opened the shutters, signaling the rest of the fleet to do the same. Morgan could not stand still. His legs wanted to race as fast as his mind was going. What have I forgotten, he asked himself for the thousandth time. The sea anchor inflated and there was a shudder in the ship. *Marquesa's* anchor began to slip and Collier quietly ordered the men to haul it up. The bosun opened the shutters on the red light and flashed it three times.

"Would you like some company, Captain?" asked Dan, walking beside Morgan.

"Hello Dan," said Morgan, somehow feeling calmer. "Can you believe we are doing this? In the next five minutes we are either going to be alive, or dead." Dan laughed, his white teeth being the only well-defined part of his face in the dim light.

"I think that is true of *every* moment, but I take your meaning. Not many people get a chance to do this kind of thing and I wanted to say thank you for taking me to the edge so many times in the last few weeks," said Dan, laughing again. The *Marquesa* was spinning as she floated with the rapid current, the sea anchor performing beautifully, keeping *Marquesa* in the center of the channel, moving like a bat out of hell.

"It has been a great pleasure for me, as well, Dan. We are in range of the fort's guns now," said Morgan, looking forward and seeing four Buccaneers unlashing the foresails. It was a balmy night and Morgan was grateful for the breeze, as sweat beads formed on his forehead and his heart pounded in his chest.

"It looks like they took the bait," said Dan, laughing. "By the way, I don't think the outcome of this matters, one way or the other." The *Marquesa* inched closer to the center of the fort and then the jibs were hoisted and she lurched forward. A pistol shot rang out in the fort as a lookout spotted the sails. More canvas was hoisted aboard the *Marquesa* and the boats behind her. Spanish Marines began assembling on the fort's battlements and soon there were chips of wood flying, as the musket balls began to strike the *Marquesa*. Morgan and Dan moved behind the mizzenmast for protection and they were joined shortly by Sara, bearing a pipe and a lamp.

"What do you mean, 'The outcome doesn't matter'?" A musket ball struck the mizzenmast and there was a harmless shower of splinters.

"I mean that if you are lost in the exquisite beauty of the process, the outcome simply ceases to have any meaning," said Dan. There was a ping of glass shattering, followed an instant later by another ping. A ball had gone through the aft cabin's windows.

"Did you leave a lamp burning in the cabin?" asked Morgan, shooting the question at Sara with a tad bit of anger. Sara was put off by the question initially, but the Panamanian in her redirected the anger.

"My name eez Matilda and I have place 'ed many of lamp in la cabana for the revenge of mi esposa, who is sink your sheep," said Sara, bending over and slapping her thigh. Morgan forced her back into an erect posture. There was something about her head directly behind the lamp, bent over, that distressed him. Dan processed her dialog and thought it prudent to abstain from laughter, but within a matter of seconds, he was letting out suppressed nasal farts. There was a gong as another musket ball hit the binnacle. Morgan caught the infection next and burst out laughing, standing erect, or erectly standing, beside his friends, aboard the *Marquesa*, with enemy fire pelting his ship in the straights of Maracaibo.

"Captain, I believe you have become lost in the beauty of the process." Another ball hit the mizzen mast and their posture returned to perfection. "Sara, thank you for making this possible," said Dan, who began to laugh again.

The *Marquesa* was now out of range and her crew was given permission to have a share of rum. The last boat in the procession, the worm-infested sloop, Captained by Velasquez, was now directly in front of the fort. Screams and curses could be heard over the din of the cannon wheels on the limestone floor of the fort. The first cannon was finally stationed in the center rampart and it fired a poorly aimed ball that fell short of the sloop. A second cannon was fired and the ball landed in Velasquez's wake. The sloop raised the remainder of her sails and within seconds, the she was out of harm's way. That was the sum of Alonso's might that night.

"Commander!" shouted Morgan. "Give them a seven-gun salute before we are out of sight!" Almost immediately the guns began to fire in sequence, three seconds separating the explosions. "Dan, would you care to join us in my cabin for a glass of wine?" Dan cupped his hands behind his ears.

"Could you repeat that, Captain," said Dan, in a loud voice. He laughed and said, "I would be delighted, Captain." As the trio stepped inside the cabin, Collier had the Buccaneers drop *Marquesa*'s hook, just outside the channel. He waited there for Velasquez to catch up, so that he could give him the bad news. With all hands sober, Collier figured that he could have the cargo transferred from the damaged boat to the other boats in about an hour. Rather than employ a launch to transport the booty from one ship to another, Collier had the fleet anchor in a line and then Velasquez's boat could be side-tied to each boat, where one-fifth of the cargo could be transferred.

Two hours later, the last of the booty was transferred to the *Marquesa*. Moss' men had repaired the windows in *Marquesa*'s aft cabin and then it began to rain. Velasquez addressed the captives that had been placed aboard his boat. There was only a dim hurricane lamp, but he could see their faces.

"Ladies and gentlemen, you are being set free and you have this fine boat to transport you back to Maracaibo. Does anybody know how to sail?" Three men and a woman raised their hands. "Very good. I suggest you wait here for a few hours, until the tide turns and then head back through the channel and drop *all* of your anchors close to the fort, where it is wide. There is a big storm coming and I would encourage you to ride it out on the boat, because you have no launch. You will be protected in the channel. Go now and see if your Admiral has hung himself yet." Velasquez climbed aboard the *Marquesa* and waved good bye to the woman he had spent the last six weeks with. Her eyes teared up as she watched him untie the bowline and toss it over to them. Velasquez could see her sobbing and he bit his lower lip in an effort to hold back his own tears. He was unsuccessful.

The *Marquesa* sped away, pushed by the twenty-five knot storm-wind that was, mercifully, coming from the south. With the wind at her back, *Marquesa* shot through the water at twelve knots and it was a smooth ride, because the raindrops flattened out the sea. Collier pushed the boat to her limit, which was known as "hull speed." Once you achieved hull speed, you couldn't make the boat go any faster, no matter how much sail was hoisted. Collier did not have the luxury of daylight to prove his conjecture, but when he ordered the top course set, he could feel the *Marquesa* dig into the water stubbornly and not yield an additional inch. Far safer to douse the top course and let the Lady move along at her hull speed, with the least amount of sail possible.

The wind was beginning to shift quite a bit now, occasionally gusting off the port quarter at thirty knots. When the shifting wind did hit her sails as a broad reach, *Marquesa* took the added force gracefully and bobbed back immediately when the wind shifted back to aft. In these circumstances, a Captain might order additional ballast thrown overboard, in order to speed the boat up. The *Marquesa*, however, had the distinction of being one of the few ships in history that had her ballast made up entirely of gold and silver. Collier smiled at the thought.

Nearly two hours into the storm, a westerly pelted the *Marquesa* with rain and gusts up to seventy knots. Collier quenched all sail and dropped two anchors off the bow of the *Marquesa*, one off the stern. The bow was pointed into the wind and the ride was not too bad if you happened to be below decks. Commander Collier had not seen the other boats in the last two hours and there were still three hours until dawn. He hoped that they had hunkered down as well, because although all of the boats were still in the Gulf of Venezuela, which was massive by any standards, they still had a seventy knot wind pushing them to the east and trouble was a constant companion.

The hallucinations had been going on for over an hour and Collier decided to call it a night. It was eight bells, or four in the morning and he had to check the anchor lines before he went to bed. "Damn! Those look like fire flies," he said aloud, on his way to the bow of *Marquesa*. Nobody heard him in the gale-force wind. His oilskins had failed again and he was drenched to the bone, shivering in the eighty-degree wind. "They can't be fire flies! We are twenty miles from the closest land," he said laughing. He walked aft as the new watch came topside. For no particular reason, Collier had the urge to throw himself over the side. This demon had been with him for years, but this time there were portraits of smiling people in the picture frames inside his head, that had been nearly empty on the last go-round. The fireflies were out in numbers now and it didn't matter if his eyes were open, or closed.

"I am going below for sleep, Lieutenant," said Collier to Thatcher at the binnacle. Once below, his prayers were answered. There was a keg of rum outside the door to his berth. He tapped

CHAPTER 56

At sunrise, Thatcher began to assess the damage *Marquesa* had suffered during the blow. The westerly storm wind had let up an hour before. The upper yardarm of the main mast had simply disappeared and he examined the deck for impact damage, but could find none. He assumed that some of the sail ties had loosened on the yardarm and the sail had partially filled, tearing the yardarm free of the mast and the gale-force wind carrying it safely out to sea. Finding the *Marquesa* otherwise seaworthy, he ordered the Buccaneers to make sail.

Thatcher studied the chart on the table next to the helm and realized he had absolutely no idea where they were. He recalled that there had been a strong southerly wind about the time that he had gone below to his bunk, so he assumed that Collier would have taken advantage of the wind and headed north. He also assumed that Morgan would want to stop at Ruba and lay in supplies, so he instructed the helmsman to steer northeast, placing the *Marquesa* on a close reach.

Thatcher sent lookouts aloft to search for the rest of the fleet, while he trained his telescope on the horizon. Almost immediately, he spotted two ships to the south. He ordered the mainsails lowered on all three masts to slow the *Marquesa* down, so that the stragglers could catch up. The top gallants on the fore mast and the mizzenmast would make the *Marquesa* visible to the other boats. The lookouts spotted another boat to the south, leaving only one unaccounted for.

As the ship came to life, Buccaneers began casting lines over the side to troll for game fish. Hand made lures varied widely in both color and design, but the favorite design seemed to be a six-inch wooden fish, weighted with lead shot and painted orange ocher. Ideally, the lures would track just below the surface of the water. Some of the Buccaneers preferred cotton lines, but most used hemp, because of its superior strength.

Most of the Buccaneers tied their lines to three foot wooden sticks that stood vertically in a holder and would snap off when a strike occurred, alerting the angler that he needed to attend to his line. The first hit was a Spanish mackerel, caught with a small yellow ocher lure. Then the tuna began a feeding frenzy and within minutes, six good-sized fish were hauled aboard, while five others managed to snap their lines. It was a competition now, to see who could bring in the largest tuna. The more experienced anglers brought out their best lures and fine-tuned them on the aft deck with pliers and whetstones on the hook tips. Demijohns went from water to rum in the pre-breakfast morning.

One of the ship masters, old school *Oxford*, had a "tackle spool" that had been made in Belgium. Every man aboard, even the non-fishermen, coveted that item. In fact, many of the other "tackle spools" had been fashioned after its design, which consisted of a large ebony pulley enclosed in a net-like cast brass enclosure. There was a crank handle, but it was used to return the line to the pulley *after* the line had been pulled in by hand, with the fish safely landed. When a strike occurred, the ebony pulley was braked by two patches of leather, that pinched the pulley equally on both sides. There was a screw control on top of the device that adjusted how much tension was delivered, which significantly reduced the number of line-breaks. The entire unit was fastened to a large hemp line that was tied to the base of the mizzenmast.

Jones walked to the aft deck and surveyed the catch.

"Good morning, Sir," said one of the Buccaneers.

"Good mornin' gents," said Jones distractedly, trying to figure out how many of the fish he was going to need to feed the three-hundred men aboard the *Marquesa*.

"What's for breakfast, Sir?"

"Fish, I should think," said Jones, making the Buccaneers laugh. "Fish *cakes*, to be precise, since I still have a bit of flour left." Actually, he had over two-hundred pounds of flour that was crawling with weevils. "The sooner you men get those monsters filleted, the sooner we eat." There was the sound of a branch snapping, forcing one of the Buccaneers to jump to his feet and attend to his tackle spool, which was smoking by the time he reached it.

Jones went below to the midshipmen's births and located Browne, who was fast asleep in his bunk. Jones shook his shoulder, "Time to rise and shine, matey." Browne came around slowly. "If you still want the secret recipe for fish balls, this may be your last chance. Browne mumbled something and went back to sleep. Jones shook Browne's shoulder again. "I didn't catch that, Sir."

"I said get me a razor!" screamed Browne.

"'Ave you decided to put an end to it all, Sir?" Browne went back to sleep. Jones shook Browne's shoulder again. "What do you want the razor for, Sir?"

"To shave the hair off my tongue," said Browne, holding his head and laughing. "Can you make me one of those 'get out of hell' teas?"

"It would be an honor, Sir," said Jones, "but you should at least consider mercy-killing. If you decide to go that route, do I still get to keep your saw?" Browne began to laugh, but then stopped abruptly and held his head. He swept one hand like a broom and went into a fetal position. "Fifteen minutes ought to be about right," said Jones.

CHAPTER 57

"Two days and counting, Sailor Boy," said Sara, lying on her side, with her head resting on her up-turned hand, staring down at Morgan.

"Don't remind me," said Morgan with his eyes still closed. The *Marquesa* jumped forward as the sails were set, one by one.

"Was that a hurricane last night?" asked Sara.

"This is what? May fourteenth?" said Morgan, opening his eyes and immediately feeling a sting inside as Sara came in to focus. "Hurricane season begins in June, as a rule, but I suppose it could have been a small one. We'll have to look for feeder bands when we go on deck." Morgan smacked his lips and reached for the glass of water on the nightstand. "I take that back. There would have been feeder bands in the sky yesterday if it had been a hurricane. So let's just call it a bad storm." Tears began welling up in Sara's eyes.

"Do you know the thing I am going to miss most about you?" Morgan shook his head. "Your smell! I know it sounds crazy," said Sara, bending over the bed rail to pick up her blouse so she could wipe her nose, "but I have had trouble sleeping my entire life. The first night we were together, I slept a solid nine hours for the first time in over a decade. And it's been like that every night since, excluding hurricanes and card games."

"Is that why you were so angry the night I went out with Owen and Comstock?" asked Morgan, very curious about where this exchange was heading.

"Absolutely! After the second bottle of wine I dozed off for about an hour and that was it. For some strange reason, the smell of you next to me shuts off my brain. Can you blame me for wanting to spend every night I can with you?" said Sara, tears starting to flow again. "I have this theory about intimacy and truth. I think they only occur with death in the background."

"How do you mean 'death in the background'?" asked Morgan, puzzled.

"Well, take for instance 'death bed confessions,' or 'last rights.' People choose to spill their guts when there is no longer anything left to lose. In our particular case, there is going to be a forced separation in two or three days. The 'death' here is the end of our relationship. If I was planning on spending the rest of my life with you, I would never have told you about the 'sleep-smell' connection, or the fact that I have never come with a man before I met you." Morgan's mouth dropped open. "That's right, Sailor Boy."

"I don't get it! Why the secrecy?" asked Morgan, totally mystified.

"I don't know about you, but every relationship I have ever been in has been a competition, in one way, or another. If the other person knows your weaknesses, they will inevitably exploit them. Take a series of small hurts over the course of a marriage, most of which are unintentional, and there comes a breaking point when the partner decides to hurt back. In our case, you could simply go away for a week and turn me into a zombie." Sara stopped and gave Morgan a chance to digest what she had said. "You seem shocked by this!"

"It's just that you seem so pessimistic! What about love and loyalty?"

"They are totally conditional and can be revoked at any time, given the right circumstances," said Sara.

"You live in a very bleak world."

"Put yourself in my position, Harry. Where am I going to find solace? Who, besides you, could possibly understand what has happened here? This has been the most exciting adventure of my life! The best sex, the best wine and the best sleep. What is there in my future that is going to compare to this? *You* have to be feeling something similar," said Sara, staring him in the eyes.

"I won't deny it," he said, looking down. "It is strange. When we stormed the fort in Maracaibo and I ran for the slow match, I realized that I could die, but I didn't *feel* like I was going to die. Now, I *do* feel like I am going to die." Sara saw tears rolling down his cheeks and she pulled his head into her bare chest and held him.

"This really isn't fair," she said, sobbing. There was a knock on the cabin door and a voice announced that there was coffee, when they were ready. Morgan pulled out of the embrace a trifle embarrassed. He wordlessly slipped on his pants and brought in the tray from outside the door.

"Also the best coffee," he said, handing Sara a cup and saucer. She laughed and sat down at the table, opposite Morgan.

"I saw the whole thing with my own eyes, but I still can't believe you actually pulled it off," said Sara.

"I had a little help. By the way, I have decided to put you on the payroll as an officer. You should walk away with a couple of hundred pounds."

"That is very generous of you, Captain."

"You earned every penny of it. Dan and Ward probably owe their lives to you."

"I wouldn't go that far, but thank you for the thought. What happens when we get back to Port Royal?" asked Sara.

"First we divide up the booty. Then everybody goes their own way. By the end of the week, the whores and wine merchants will have all the money and the Buccaneers will be pestering me about going on another raid. I have an apartment in town that you are welcome to stay at until your boat comes in."

"Will you be there?" Sara was openly sobbing.

"It would be bad form. I haven't seen my wife in almost six months."

"Did you miss her?"

"I thought about her now and again. It never has been a particularly romantic marriage, but we do enjoy each other's company."

"How often do ships return to England?" asked Sara, blotting her eyes with her blouse. "It varies quite a bit, but you should be able to get a passage within a fortnight."

Sara stared out the transom windows and began chewing on one of her nails, thinking of the overcast skies of London. A shiver passed through her body. There was a loud rap on the cabin door.

"Who is it?" shouted Morgan.

"Collier."

"I will be on deck in five minutes, Commander." Morgan slipped a shirt over his head and grabbed a wide-brimmed hat. "Sara, you should get dressed and come on deck. This is going to be the Conteh versus Collier competition." Sara looked up at him, but didn't budge an inch. "C' mon, the fresh air will do you good."

"I will be up in a few minutes."

After Morgan left the room, Sara jumped into the bed and grabbed Morgan's pillow. She lay on her back and covered her face with the pillow, inhaling deeply through her nostrils. A few seconds later the sobbing began, tentative at first, then gale force; then tectonic. It was complete and utter devastation, and she knew it. Up to this point, her life had been a series of successful games that had kept her in powerful realms, where a suggestion, here, or there could get her virtually anything she wanted. Suddenly, the thing she wanted most was out of her reach and she took a bite on the pillow and clenched her jaws as tightly as she could. When she let out the scream, a hundred-thousand feathers acted together and kept her secret.

CHAPTER 58

"We can play this any way you want," said Morgan, speaking softly to Collier on the foredeck. "But the way it was originally conceived, the question was, can Conteh fire eight arrows in the time it takes you to fire and re-load, and fire again. Balfor's lady happened to mention, in an unprotected moment, that you were planning to load two balls in your first shot and then quickly re-load with "powder only", and fire again. Naturally, I have a plan to defeat you that involves a four-arrow packet, delivered twice. I am sure you can see that if we go to this height of deceit, the original question will go unanswered." Collier was going to be wealthy in the next two days and that made the original bet insignificant. Collier pointed his pistol in the air and fired, discharging the two balls in the barrel. The shot was unexpected and in less than a second, two-hundred men had their pistols drawn. An exasperated angler on the aft deck angrily lowered a bucket over the side for water to wash out his pants.

Moss appeared on deck carrying the two "four-arrow stacks" that he had built, but Morgan waved him off. Moss and Conteh returned a few minutes later carrying the target and a strange wooden contraption. One of the carpenters brought up a cloth measuring tape and chalked off a twenty-foot line on the deck. Bets were being placed and demijohns were tipping upward on a regular basis. Moss' men attached the target to the bow rail in front of an area that was already damaged during the raid.

Moss and Conteh focused their energies on the wooden device that nobody on deck could quite fathom. It consisted two parallel sheets of thin wood that formed a sort of hollow table that was tilted at a forty-five degree angle. The table was supported by four wooden legs, two of which were adjustable for height. The lowest side of the table was shoulder-height for Conteh. Moss began sliding arrows sideways into the hollow of the table. One by one they began sliding up the forty-five degree slope, until the eighth arrow was finally inserted. Jaws were dropping open as Moss completed the set-up. Small wooden lugs with one hole each had been attached to the lower portion of the bottom board. Moss inserted delicate shafts from small feathers into each of the lugs, which kept the arrows from falling out. Jones and Brown began to applaud and soon the entire ship was cheering Moss on. Sara came on deck smartly dressed in Buccaneer garb and stood beside Morgan.

The intensity of the betting increased sharply. Conteh was now favored two to one over Collier, who requested a table be brought up to him. Nobody could argue with the request. Collier had been busy. When the table arrived, he reached into the pouch on his waistband and retrieved two cylindrical objects and placed them on the table. The hushed crowd studied Collier and the new cylindrical variables that had been added to the soup. He took the powder horn off of his neck and made a small pile of powder on the table.

To manufacture the cylinders, Collier had whittled a piece of wood so that it would fit inside the barrel of his pistol with some room to spare. He located some very supple young banana leaves and placed them over the tip of the round-bottomed dowel he had whittled and wrapped them with fine thread. Three days in the heat behind Jones' stove was enough to dry them out and turn them the tan color that everybody was looking at now. The next step was filling them with powder and covering them with a felt patch, glued in place with balsam. He then glued a ball to the center of the felt and kept the cylinders dry until they were needed.

Collier picked up one of the cylinders and placed it in the barrel of his pistol, then rammed it home. A second later he took a pinch of powder and placed it in the primer pan of the pistol, then cocked the weapon.

"Ready!" shouted Collier, deadly serious, with a grin on his face. While Conteh was getting ready, Collier fished another cylinder out of his pouch and placed it on the table. One could never be too sure.

Conteh took his stance and reached for an arrow. It slipped out easily and he was gratified to see another one slide down and take its place. The betting on deck was changing by the second. It was now an even split. Conteh had beads of sweat on his forehead and he prayed to his Gods that this contest would soon be over. From experience, he knew that the shellac that coated the surface of the lower table that his arrows slid down on, would be sticky in the afternoon humidity. His body told him that the humidity was rising. His body also told him that he needed to pee. He became aware of his right foot tapping. At first, he thought that it was because he was nervous, but then he realized that his foot was tapping in time to an ancient Mende song that he had heard since the day he was born. He allowed himself to be transported back to a campground in Africa and a smile appeared on his face. The outcome of the contest no longer mattered.

"Kie ing gwo ma," said Conteh, which meant, "No rust on God."

"Sorry," said Collier, perplexed.

"Ready?" asked Collier. Red day, thought Conteh. Not in my world. Grey day would be closer to the truth, thought Conteh, but if the English thinks it is 'red', it does not violate my ethics to agree with him.

"Red day," said Conteh. Conteh felt somebody staring at him and he looked up. It was Velasquez. Conteh was immediately transported back to the Hall, where Velasquez had ordered him to kill the priest. The memory of his cutlass cutting through the priest's neck slapped Conteh in the face. The sweat beads appeared on his forehead again and began dripping into his eyes. He realized immediately that if the memories of that day continued to flash in his mind, he would never be able to fire his arrows with any speed, or accuracy. Conteh closed his eyes and imagined that he was a caterpillar hanging upside down from a branch. He began wrapping silk around his body and, in his vision, one section of the silk contained all of the memories from the Hall. It had been excreted from his body and now protected him. When he opened his eyes, Conteh saw Lieutenant Thatcher staring at him with a worried look on his face. Conteh smiled to let Thatcher know that he was all right. Thatcher nodded his head at Conteh.

"Red day?" asked Thatcher.

"Red day," said Collier. Conteh shook his head almost imperceptibly

"Red day," said Conteh.

"On the count of three, Gentlemen," shouted Thatcher. "One, two, three!" There was an explosion that startled Conteh and his first arrow missed the three inch circle by nearly a foot and lodged itself on the periphery of the target. While Collier struggled to reload, Conteh fired three more arrows in the blue three inch circle and the Buccaneers went crazy. Collier fumbled his second cartridge trying to insert it in the barrel and the banana-leaf base crumbled and spilled powder on to the deck. Collier forced himself to relax and inserted the third cartridge smoothly into the barrel of his pistol. By this time, Conteh had fired two more arrows into the blue circle. Conteh's seventh arrow didn't slide all the way down the shoot and it cost him an additional half-second to retrieve it. Moss saw this and began wringing his hands.

The crowd of three-hundred men watching the contest sighed when the arrow jammed and then began cheering Conteh when he finally released the arrow. Conteh had heard stories about tribes that killed the losers in certain competitions and as he reached for the eighth arrow, he realized that he had never asked Moss what would happen if he lost. His already rapid pulse shot up another thirty beats per minute.

"He is on the eighth arrow," said Balfor, who was standing next to Collier. Collier had just finished ramming the cartridge with the short ramrod. He cocked the hammer of his pistol and put a pinch of powder in the primer pan as he swept the pistol away from the table and aimed at the target. Shortly after Conteh released his last arrow, there was an explosion.

Sara had backed up from the group she had been standing with and placed her back on the main mast for stability. She held a twelve-power English telescope in her hands and while the optics were not the best, she had a clear view of the blue circle that practically filled her field of view at thirty feet. The difficult thing with any magnification over seven, or eight-power was holding it steady enough to see what you were looking at. It was possible, with an elbow tucked high in the abdomen on a held breath, to see clearly in the distance, if and only if, your back was supported by a stable structure. Sara struggled to remember who had taught her this trick, but it was all in vain; her recall powers did not encompass anything other than written text. She smiled.

When Sara's heart beat, the telescope would rise above the target, then go back to the center of the target in-between beats. It just so happened that, when Conteh's eighth arrow hit the target, Sara's heart was in-between beats and she saw the target quiver as Conteh's arrow hit near the center of the blue circle. She wanted to shout victory, but the blast wave from Collier's pistol finally hit her and she ended up with her telescope trained halfway up the fore mast, where she found some ribald verse and erotic carvings inscribed in the wood that she committed to memory.

There was some confusion on the fore deck as to who had won the competition. The two judges on the port deck insisted that the arrow had entered the target first, while the two judges on the starboard deck argued that the ball had entered before the arrow. The match was declared a draw by Lieutenant Thatcher, with resultant boos and jeers by the Buccaneers, who quickly turned their attention back to the anglers assembled on *Marquesa*'s stern.

CHAPTER 59

Who had seduced whom? She wondered.

Sara sat in a chair pulled up to the Captain's table in the aft cabin, heels perched on the edge of the chair, hugging her knees. Tears bounced off of the white shift that was stretched like a tent over her knees. Supremely confident a few days ago, Sara could now see nothing in her future except pain. The desire to eat had left her and it would likely not return for many weeks.

She began laughing as she thought of her girlfriends in London, in between tears. "Prince Phillip," had become a code word for the particular man that one of them was seeing, who happened to be well-endowed enough to "fill her up". Morgan had passed that test, but there was more. There were the ten-hour sleepy nights that made her awaken feeling better than she had ever felt before in her life. Add to that the fact that the pleasure center in her brain had been stimulated almost continuously during the last several months and it does not require much imagination to see that she had simply fallen in love. It had happened so gradually that it was only now, one day away from the coast of Jamaica, that she understood the enormity of what lay ahead of her.

From experience, Sara knew that she would be bored to tears if she had to stay in London for any length of time. She would have to return to update the King and spend time with family and friends, but after that, she would need to move on. The Caribbean appealed to her like no place she had ever been, but if she stayed in Jamaica, her heart would be torn out every time that she ran into Morgan. That left Barbados, where the English presence was even stronger than it was in Jamaica. Maybe she could find herself a Captain there. Certainly not an English Naval Captain, but maybe a merchant Captain. Sara realized that she wanted a steady mate for the first time in her life. But where was she going to find somebody as free spirited as she was?

There was an off chance that Morgan would leave his wife, but she was not about to suggest it. Maybe he would be feeling as badly as she did. Maybe he would want to keep her on as his mistress. What would I do if he asked?

CHAPTER 60

The Blue Mountains of Jamaica were visible just above the horizon as the *Marquesa* slid along the Caribbean Sea on a beam reach. The rest of the fleet lagged behind, except for the lugger, which was a good ten miles ahead of the *Marquesa*. Jenkins was at *Marquesa*'s helm with his shirt off, grabbing the wheel every minute, or so, to make a slight adjustment.

Morgan sat on the fore deck with his back against the mast. He had *Marquesa*'s log book in his lap, happy to be out of his cabin and away from Sara. The last two days had been unbearable for both of them. He found it difficult to concentrate on the tasks that had to be completed before landfall. He had not made a single entry in *Marquesa*'s logbook since the ship had been taken and he felt so much turmoil inside that he could not summon up the energy to do so now.

The hundred Buccaneers on deck sensed that Morgan was in some kind of distress and they steered clear of him. That is, everyone except Dan.

"Hello Captain," said Dan with a grin on his face. "Mind if I join you?"

"Pull up a deck, Bushman," said Morgan, glad for the company.

"You look like a man who is about to separate from the most beautiful and most intelligent woman in the world," said Dan, sitting down in front of Morgan cross-legged.

"Is it that obvious?" said Morgan, embarrassed.

"Only to someone who has been through it before. Right now, I would imagine that you feel as though you have a knife in your stomach. Correct me if I am wrong," said Dan, grinning.

"Dead wrong, I am afraid. It is a cutlass and someone is twisting it." Dan laughed and Morgan began to laugh with him.

"Can you think back to the last time you felt like this?" asked Dan. Instantly, Morgan had the answer.

"Yes."

"Go back to the next time. I can see that you have that one also. Do you think there might be a pattern here?" asked Dan. Morgan went back in time and found five more events.

"You have my attention. What does it mean?" asked Morgan.

"Do you remember our previous discussion about recovery time? The length of time it takes to get past a woman?" Morgan nodded. "You did not learn to feel this 'feeling' at thirty, or twenty, or at ten. It was a long time before then. Kamalesh took me on a tour of my own history, much like the tour I am taking you on. Within a week, or so, I had a memory flash before my eyes that was the most terrifying experience of my adult life. When I was about five, I was at a birthday party and I became engrossed with a duckling that I saw in the distance. I went out to try and catch it, hoping that my parents would let me keep it as a pet. The duckling led me on a merry chase into the woods and I became hopelessly lost. I screamed out, but no one could hear me. I knew that I had misbehaved and I was certain that my parents had left me there because of it. It seemed like eternity before I heard voices calling my name. I ran toward the voices, but I had tears in my eyes and I ran into several trees. My face was bloodied, but I kept going, knowing that if I didn't,

I was going to be left behind and I would die. Finally, there was a happy reunion and all was forgotten. That is until the ripe age of twenty-eight, when I went through the separation from my wife.

"The point is, my five year old is still alive and well, frozen in time, as it were, orchestrating my adult behavior. If he is unhappy, or frightened, I simply cannot function. My presumption is that there was a similar event in your history, perhaps more than one. Kamalesh warned me not to go back past the 'event'. He said that only an advanced Yogi could function in that realm."

For the first time in several days, Morgan no longer felt like he was about to die. He gazed at the Blue Mountains in the distance and the cutlass in his belly was withdrawn. Heaven and hell in every moment went through his brain and this time it worked. Dan saw Morgan smiling and he knew that his work was done for now. Dan stood up and walked away without uttering a word.

CHAPTER 61

As the harbor came into view that afternoon, 17 May, 1669, Collier ordered a seven gun salute. It was a mob scene on the docks, as black stevedores, who were paid by the load, rushed their carts through the throng of inebriated people. There was a topless keg full of rum standing on the dock beside the lugger and people would come by with a cup or a demijohn and scoop out what they wanted.

A hush went over the crowd as the first of the silver ingots were retrieved from the lugger's hold. Then there was applause. Velasquez had fifty armed men carve a clearing through the sea of people so that the stevedores could navigate to the warehouse unmolested. A fiddler began to play in the afternoon sun and was immediately joined by a guitar player and a drummer. The whores from the Spread Eagle and John Star's were mingling eagerly with the Buccaneers.

Veronica, the Spanish spy who had been duped by Morgan and Velasquez, stayed on the edge of the crowd making mental notes of everything she saw. At one point, Velasquez happened to catch her eye and he winked at her. She responded by slapping the biceps of the arm that supported her raised fist. Velasquez smiled back at Veronica, turned his back to her and bent over. When he looked back at her again, she was laughing.

The stevedores mopped their brows and moved over into the shade of the warehouse, as the lugger pulled away from the dock. *Marquesa* moved slowly across the harbor with only her mainsails flying. Collier eased her up to the dock, lowering her sails one at a time. Morgan went into his cabin to retrieve his papers and say good bye to Sara. He took a deep breath and tried to calm his nerves.

Sara was dressed in the same red peasant dress that she had worn the night he met her. Her hair was pulled back into a ponytail, tied with a silk scarf. She had dried her tears and looked radiantly beautiful.

"I am glad you decided to wear pants this time," said Sara, smiling.

Morgan smiled back and walked over to the desk. He got down on his knees and pressed the release for the hidden compartment. He withdrew the leather folders and stacked them on the desk. He pulled out one of the twelve-pound gold bars and stood up.

"I want you to have this as a going away present," he said, walking over to her. She looked up at him and tears began running down her cheeks. He put his arms around her and tried to comfort her, but she broke down and began sobbing. Whatever control Morgan had over his emotions at that moment vanished. Simply put, it was the saddest day of his life and he knew it. He tried to choke down his tears, but there seemed to be an endless supply of sadness that had been locked away for years, violently coming to the surface.

Morgan heard the gangway lowered on to the deck of his ship and soon there was the monotonous vibration of the stevedore's carts, crossing back and forth across the deck. There was a tentative knock at the cabin door.

"What is it," said Morgan, trying to keep his voice steady.

"The Governor is here to greet you, Captain," said Collier.

"Thank you, Commander I will be there shortly."

Morgan disengaged himself from Sara and went over to the liquor cabinet. He poured two glasses half full of brandy and walked back to Sara.

"We need to get control of ourselves. Cheers," he said, downing the glass. He picked up the gold bar and pushed it deeply into Sara's bag. "You go first. I'll be right behind you," he said, wiping the tears from his eyes.

Sara downed her glass and then just stood there, unable to move. Morgan picked up her bag and thrust it into her chest.

"Go," Morgan whispered.

Morgan opened the cabin door and pushed her out. He closed the door and went back to the desk to make sure the compartment was closed. He loaded the leather folders into a canvas bag and opened the door again. When he appeared on deck, the music stopped and the people on the dock began applauding. More than anything else in the world, Henry Morgan wanted to run back to his cabin and shut out the rest of the world, but he forced himself to walk forward.

"Three cheers for Captain Morgan," shouted one of the Buccaneers. As the cheers began, Morgan took a bow and smiled. There was not a single person there who could sense that Morgan felt like his intestines were being ripped out of his belly. He saw Governor Modyford standing beside his coach, chatting with Sara. He felt a pang of jealousy and it made him smile. Dan stood at the gangway, smiling as Morgan approached.

"Ward and I are going up to the north shore for a few days. Would you like me to pay you a visit when we get back?" asked Dan. Morgan's pain suddenly vanished.

"Absolutely. Just ask somebody where the 'pink mansion' is. That's where I'll be. Oh, shit," said Morgan looking at the dock. Rebecca, his former mistress, who had mysteriously vanished a week before the Maracaibo raid, stood there, with her massive chest spilling out the top of her blue dirndl dress. Morgan shook his head from side to side. "This is going to be an interesting day."

"I take it she was the one before Sara?" asked Dan, laughing.

"Yes. We were together almost two years and then she disappeared."

"Ouch!" said Dan. "What a great teacher!"

Morgan tilted his head and stared at Dan, trying to decide if he was serious. The rest of the people on the dock and the noise they created evaporated in an instant, as Morgan stared into Dan's smiling eyes.

"I guess I have never thought about it that way before," said Morgan, pondering the implications. On an impulse, Morgan asked, "When are you and Ward leaving?"

"Tomorrow, or the day after. Why do you ask?"

"If you would like some company, I have the horses to get us there and back. There is a piece of property I want to look at near Port Antonio," said Morgan.

"You have yourself a partner, Captain," said Dan, laughing.

"Can we make it *three* days from now? I need to spend some time with my wife."

"Fine by me," said Dan.

"I need to shove off. The Governor always has a party for the officers the night after the ships return from a raid. You will be getting an invitation tomorrow. See you there."

"So long, Captain."

Morgan edged his way in between stevedores and walked rapidly along the gangway, uncertain about how he should approach Rebecca, or even *if* he should approach her.

Sara could feel the brandy kicking in and it helped to steady her as she walked along the deck, competing for space with the stevedores. Governor Modyford stepped out of his carriage into the hot sun as Sara walked across the gangway. A head shorter than Morgan and a decade older, Modyford was the very embodiment of the wealthy planter class, quite dashing in his own way. He was there to greet her when she stepped on to the dock.

"Hello, I am John Modyford, the Governor of the Island. Let me help you with that bag."

Sara was in no mood for the Governor's attention, so she jerked back on her bag and began yelling in French. Modyford jumped back a step in mock horror and raised his hands in surrender. He addressed her in French, greatly amused.

"I am terribly sorry if I have offended you, Mademoiselle…" said Modyford, fishing for a name. Sara let him feel uncomfortable for a while before she answered. She was impressed by his command of French. She had read his file, which was a good foot higher than Morgan's, though not nearly as interesting.

"Sara Vaughn, Governor. It's nice to finally see your face after all these years."

"I am not sure I follow you," said Modyford, genuinely perplexed.

"I am the one who has been coding messages to you and de-coding the ones you sent back. I am an accomplished *angler*, you see." Sara referred to the special edition of "The Complete Angler" that King Charles II had distributed to all of his high-ranking diplomats. Naturally, Sara had the book memorized.

Looking off in the distance, Modyford raised his eyebrows and moved his index finger back and forth across his lips, while he appraised the situation. He began to smile and then glanced back at Sara and began laughing heartily, pointing at her with his finger, until Sara began to get defensive.

"What?" she said.

"I am sorry, but I have hated you for years," said Modyford, chuckling. "Every time that a mail boat enters the harbor I am filled with the worst dread imaginable, because I know that it is going to contain twenty, or thirty communiqués from the King that *I* will have to decode with that damn book. The mental image that I had of you was that you were a short, overweight, middle-aged man."

Sara was so amused by what the Governor said that she temporarily let go of her pain and began to laugh hysterically, slapping her thigh all the while.

"If you don't mind my asking, what sort of terms are you on with the King, presently?" asked Modyford.

"Excellent terms, to the best of my knowledge. Why do you ask?"

"The diplomatic channels were full of gossip a few months back…"

"They were *supposed* to be," she said, cutting him short.

"Oh, I see," said Modyford, weighing the new information. "In that case, I have a proposition for you that will benefit both of us," he said smiling.

Sara simply did not want to hear what he had to offer. She wanted to find a room somewhere and hole up until she could find passage back to England and there was simply nothing that could ever dissuade her. She took a deep breath and sighed as Modyford began to pitch his plan.

"Here is what I propose," he said with a devilish grin on his face. "I am backlogged at least two months on correspondence and a mail ship arrived yesterday." That got Sara's attention, because it meant that she could probably hitch a ride on the homeward passage. "I would like to hire you for whatever length of time you are available to de-code all of the correspondence that has accumulated on my desk over the last two months. Make that four months. You can name your price."

Nothing in the world could have interested Sara less than what the Governor proposed. She simply wanted to be alone and begin the healing process. It was obvious to Modyford that she was going to reject the offer, so he sweetened it.

"Naturally I will see to your lodging in a very respectable place, of your own choosing, of course. A daily stipend for food and other expenses would be thrown in for good measure."

Modyford studied Sara and could see plainly that she was simply not interested. "That wardrobe of yours is certainly unbecoming a King's mistress. We could definitely improve upon that as well."

Sara glanced over at the dock near the gangway and saw Morgan embracing a girl in a blue dress, who had a waist that was about the size of Sara's thigh. Bitch! thought Sara. "Very well Governor. I accept your offer. Please have one of your people find me a private room at the Golden Arrow."

"I am afraid that cannot be done. You see, that establishment is owned by the Buccaneer Captains. It is very exclusive." Sara knew that there were four vacant suites at the Golden Arrow, because the owners had been crushed, or torn into small pieces when *Oxford* had exploded.

"*Make* it happen, Governor. I am going to town to find a dressmaker," said Sara, stepping into the Governor's massive black carriage. The driver seemed perplexed and looked to Modyford for direction. The Governor smiled at Sara's audacity and nodded his head at the coachman, who then snapped the reins.

As the four horses pulled the carriage away, the Governor whispered, "This is going to be interesting."